SCHOOLS
IN
CENTRAL CITIES

SCHOOLS IN CENTRAL CITIES

Structure and Process

Kathryn M. Borman and Joel H. Spring

Longman
New York & London

Schools in Central Cities
Structure and Process

Longman Inc., 1560 Broadway, New York, N.Y. 10036
Associated companies, branches, and representatives
throughout the world.

Developmental Editors: Nicole Benevento and Lane Akers
Editorial and Design Supervisor: Russell Till
Interior Designer: Joan Matthews
Production Supervisor: Ferne Y. Kawahara
Composition: ComCom
Printing and Binding: Haddon Craftsmen

Library of Congress Cataloging in Publication Data

Borman, Kathryn M.
  Schools in central cities.

  Includes index.
  1. Education, Urban—United States. 2. United States
—Social conditions—1970-   . 3. United States—
Economic conditions—1971-   . 4. Politics and
education—United States. 5. Education, Urban—Ohio—
Cincinnati—Case studies.   I. Spring, Joel H.   II. Title.
LC5131.B67 1984   370.19'348'0973   83-23876
ISBN 0-582-28405-8

*To the People
and Institutions
of Central Cities*

Contents

Preface

The subject of schools in general, and particularly the issues surrounding public education in central city schools, has generated considerable recent interest and debate. During the first six months of 1983, five widely noted national reports focused attention on literacy, effective schools, merit pay for teachers, and a host of related issues. These reports immediately became the center of political debate as presidential hopefuls and candidates for other offices made education a top consideration in their campaigns.

This book presents an account of public schools in central cities in the United States today. Our intention is to provide a straightforward analysis of the forces and trends that shape teaching and learning in these schools and to equip readers with tools to analyze schools in their own cities.

The organization of the book reflects our desire to present a comprehensive picture of the context, structures, organization, and processes of central city schools. The first three chapters provide discussions of the social, economic, and fiscal climates of central city schools as well as an analysis of the structures of power and lines of authority in school system governance. The next four chapters move the reader into the world of central city schools. These chapters present an analysis of teacher power, case studies of effective school principals, a discussion of the changing curriculum of the central city school, and an analysis of teaching and learning in central city elementary schools. The concluding chapter brings the volume full circle by considering the transition from school to work by the adolescent who is faced with change and transition throughout the teenage years.

The book is divided into eight chapters as summarized below.

Chapter 1.   The Decline of the Central City
This chapter examines demographic changes over the last 15 to 20 years. Social, economic, and fiscal trends during this period have conspired to create a relatively bleak prognosis for the well-being of central city residents including school-aged children and their parents. A changing industrial base and the subsequent loss and change in population structures have created fiscal problems of enormous magnitude for central city schools. These shifts have led to school closings and pupil transfers which have created hostilities among various groups at the neighborhood level. The picture remains bleak as federal policy continues to ignore the fierce competition among cities for jobs and people.

Chapter 2.   The Structure of Power in Central City School Systems
This chapter analyzes the struggle for political power in central city school systems. The most important factor in this struggle is the role of local civic elites who exercise either direct power through control of school boards or indirect control through informal networks. Control by local elites of city school systems was threatened in the 1960s and 1970s by the civil rights movement and school desegregation. By the 1980s, business and professional elites had reestablished control but with the inclusion of representatives from minority groups.

Chapter 3.   Administrating a Central City School System
The administrative bureaucracy of city school systems shapes and affects the policies established by boards of education and local elites. These administrative bureaucracies came under attack in the late 1960s and 1970s for being insulated from community pressures, isolated from the real world of the schools, and trapped by rule-oriented behavior. By the 1980s attempts were made to correct these problems through public accountability and administrative decentralization. But even with these changes, city school administrations still exhibit a desire to protect their public image, control public access to the schools, rely upon informal bureaucratic networks, and remain removed from the daily life of the schools.

Chapter 4.   The Principal as Middle Manager and Entrepreneur
In contrast to city school administrative structures, school structures offer greater flexibility and opportunity for entrepreneurial activity on the part of the building administrator. This chapter analyzes the role of the principal and presents two case studies of unusually effective city school principals in Cincinnati. Although hampered by ambiguities in defining their administrative role and plagued by myths of managerial and instructional leadership, these and other successful building adminstrators create increasingly good pupil performance,

smoothly functioning staff relations, pleasant school atmosphere, and harmonious community interaction with the school.

Chapter 5. Teacher Power: A Study of Labor

The decline in school budgets and the surplus of teachers in the 1970s caused teacher unions to shift their concerns from economic to noneconomic issues. Teacher unions are increasingly negotiating items for teacher participation in educational policy, curriculum, and textbook committees. These negotiated items, along with teacher building committees and participation in teacher evaluation, are increasing teacher power in central city school systems.

Chapter 6. The Changing Curriculum of
Central City School Systems

The curriculum of inner city schools is becoming more specialized and oriented toward job skills. This is the result of two trends. First, school desegregation plans in most cities included magnet schools with specialized curriculums designed to attract students of all races, Second, in the 1980s, the business community in many cities has become increasingly concerned with the work skills of school graduates. This has resulted in greater business involvement in designing an inner city school curriculum to meet the work needs of urban employers.

Chapter 7. Teaching and Learning in Elementary Schools

National trends in reading and mathematics achievement during recent years indicate an improvement in basic skills among central city elementary school children. This improvement can be linked to several factors including recent efforts to alter the structure of teaching and learning by creating more effective schools. Ethnographic and observational research in central city elementary school classrooms has forced us to begin to view the schooling process as mediating family background rather than as reproducing or transmitting social class-based cultures. Schools mediate both student personality, especially self-esteem, and student achievement, particularly literacy learning, in a manner quite different from the mediation of personality and achievement in the family.

Chapter 8. The Period of Adolescence and the Transition
from School

Because the period of adolescence is characterized by transitions and shifts in both individual development and social relations, adolescents occupy an unclear status in contemporary society. This chapter presents an analysis of the nature and effects of these changes and concludes by examining the school to work transition, and especially

difficult passage for the central city school dropout. There are indica-
tions that a supportive network of adults outside the family and school
are assuming increasing responsibility in easing this transition.

While the general planning of the volume was a joint effort, each
author was responsible for writing individual chapters. Sociologist Kathryn Borman wrote Chapters 1, 4, 7 and 8. Political historian Joel
Spring wrote Chapters 2, 3, 5 and 6.

We wish to acknowledge the help we received from staff members
of the Cincinnati Public School System. These people were generous in
their assistance to us in carrying out observations, interviews, and records research. We believe that their gracious cooperation is a symbol of
the growing desire to establish community-school linkages that is evident in central cities schools today.

SCHOOLS
IN
CENTRAL CITIES

1

The Decline of
the Central City

The decades bracketing 1900 gave rise not just to a decentralized metropolis but to an urban landscape in which core and periphery were increasingly differentiated by class and national origin.
R.D. NORTON, *"City Life-Cycles and American Urban Policy,"*
1979, p. 84.

Differentiation and an outward urge have replaced centralization and core orientation; differentiation and segregation substitute for the integrative role of the melting pot; social dynamics moved industrial location choices as well as those of residence.
BRIAN J.L. BERRY, *"Growth Centers in the American Urban*
System," 1973, p. 40

In the 1980s central city schools have been the cause of both hope and despair. Increased concentrations of poor and minority groups and the continued economic decline of central cities have placed a difficult burden on school systems. As the tax base of central city schools has eroded with the continued flight of industry and new knowledge-based technology from the city, the cost of providing the special educational services required by the remaining poor population has increased. City school systems find themselves fighting a continous battle to remain financially solvent under the pressure of increased costs and decreased incomes.

The hope for central city schools in the 1980s has been the renewed interest of the business community in the schools and reform movements which promise to revitalize inner city education. The business community has played an important and powerful role in the political

1

structure of city schools. During the segregation struggles of the 1970s the civic elites in most cities lost part of their historical control over central city school systems. This power was gradually restored in the 1980s as the business community became increasingly concerned with the quality of the high school graduates who were to be their future employees. The result of this renewed interest has been a closer linkage between the schools and business, the development of curriculums to meet the needs of the urban labor market and internal reforms designed to make central city school systems more efficient. While the involvement of business sparked the hope of a renaissance in central city schools there remained nagging questions about business control versus democratic control, and whether or not business should use the schools as training centers to meet their labor needs.

The hope of recent reform movements is that they will provide the tools necessary to educate an economically impoverished population. These reform movements got their start in research and political movements in the 1970s and entered the door of the city school in the 1980s. One reform movement, the push to establish more effective schools, promises to increase the basic skills through a renewed emphasis upon the instructional role of the principal, creation of better school climate, attention to student time on task and careful monitoring of educational progress. Another reform movement promises to make city schools more accountable for teaching basic skills by requiring the constant measuring and reporting to the public of student progress. One problem resulting from this constant measuring and public reporting has been the rise of the politics of testing and the assumption that increasingly better student performance on standardized tests is a direct indicator of increasingly effective teaching.

Whether or not these reform movements and increased business involvement in the schools will result in equality of educational opportunity and equality of occupational opportunity is still widely debated. New research in the sociology of education suggests that there is no easy correspondence between the work of educational institutions, and educational and job-related outcomes. In the 1960s and 1970s educational researchers hoped to find the means by which the school could provide equality of opportunity. While this research was being conducted, other scholars were claiming that family background and not the school determined educational outcomes. Today, educational sociologists paint a more complex picture wherein the school mediates family background, and educational outcomes are affected by a combination of school actions, family background and student actions in the context of educational environments. Resistance and mediation are now key terms for discussing the effect of schooling on educational and subsequent labor market outcomes.

Just as the issue of educational outcomes is considered in more complex terms, so is the actual functioning of central city school systems. The civic elite might hope that they can make the school system accomplish certain ends, but there is a major difference between making educational policy and implementing that policy in a complex organization. Standing between the policymakers and the student is an intricate structure composed of administrators in the central offices of the city school system, building administrators and teachers. All of these groups change and modify educational policies to meet their particular interests and educational goals. Administrators in the central offices tend to be overly protective of their power and are often accused of being out of contact with the real world of the schools. In many city school systems there is an often expressed feeling of division between those downtown and those in the "trenches." Teachers working through their unions have increased their power to modify and change educational policies. Indeed, one of the major changes in education in the 1980s has been the larger role of teachers in formulating and administrating educational policy.

Several reform movements have attempted to modify central city school systems to make them more responsive to the needs of the community and teachers. One reform effort has been directed toward decentralization of city school administration. This has resulted in the 1980s in the establishment of community advisory and budget committees for each school building. These committees allow more community input and decision-making at the local school level. In addition, teacher union contracts have been requiring the establishment of building committees designed to allow greater teacher participation in the administration of individual schools.

Both of these reform movements, along with effective school reforms, have made the principal a central figure in the hopes to renew central city education. Faced with a shortage of economic resources and increased community and teacher demands, principals have been forced to adopt a style that we call enterpreneurial. The central city principal must constantly negotiate and work for scarce resources from the school system and the community. Often, the quality of a central city school is dependent upon the ability of the building principal to negotiate her or his way through the educational establishment and find resources outside the systems. The principal must also play a major role in negotiating with the community through building advisory groups and with the concerns of teacher unions.

In the end, the most important issue is the effect of the central city school system on the individual student. At times one might wonder how a student survives in a system short of financial resources, entangled in union negotiations and hindered by administrative confusion. In fact, many do not survive. While test scores have been improving in central city schools, the percentage of school dropouts has increased. In addition, the transition from school to work appears to be increasingly more bleak as youth unemployment soars. Clearly understanding the relationship between schooling and entry into the labor market would be an important step in the continued renaissance of central city education.

The Central City and Its Demographic Context

The story of central city schools must begin with the demographic changes which have shaped the financial and social conditions of America's central cities.

Throughout the book, the term central city refers to a specific geographic and demographic concept. According to the Bureau of the Census, as of the most recent census (1980), the term applies to (1) any city with a population of a least 250,000 persons, (2) any city in which at least 100,000 persons are employed within the city limits, (3) any city of at least 25,000 persons where at least 40 percent of resident workers do not commute to work outside city limits and, in addition, hold at least 75 percent of jobs available within the city and, (4) any city with a population ranging between 15,000 and 25,000 that meets the two resident and job holding requirements mentioned in (3) and additionally has at least one-third the population of the metropolitan area's largest city.

In our view, the multiple referents for "central city" deprive the term of one of its important subjective meanings: the social and economic hub whose population and resources dominate its region. Indeed, prior to the 1980 census the term central city referred to the largest city in each metropolitan area. Throughout the volume "central city" is used to refer to the city whose name and institutions hold sway within a metropolitan area.

The United States is the world's most mobile nation. Each year, 40 million Americans change their places of residence. Often this results in the loss of school-aged children to the central city since families with children 18 years of age and younger are more likely to leave the central city than to enter it. For example, in Cincinnati, during a recent year (1979), the average size of an emigrating family was 3.6 persons whereas the average immigrating household contained 2.9.[1] Similarly, more than twice as many households with children left as entered the city during the course of the year. Because population (and what it represents in numbers, density, race, age, income, job skills, housing, and attitudes) is the school district's most important commodity, this chapter will examine recent trends in a number of indicators as they describe development in the nation's large cities.

To begin, it is essential to understand the nature of the geographic units and population indicators used in the discussion. Urban geographers face a major stumbling block in determining the most useful manner in which to view a large city. Most agree that the neighborhood is the basic unit. Indeed, the neighborhood is a useful concept with which to consider social need in urban places, particularly in connection with schooling since many cities' elementary schools are essentially "neighborhood schools," serving children who live within easy access to the building.

However, analysis at the neighborhood level obscures the fact that metropolitan regions are integrated economic units. That is, central cities and their surrounding suburban rings and outlying regions are tied together by a web of job-related dependencies. People may live in a community in the suburban ring but may commute regularly to work in the central city. In Cincinnati, 46 percent of workers in suburban households commute to the central city; "reverse commuting" involves 27 percent of city residents who pursue jobs in the outer fringe.[2]

Thus, it is important to consider the larger unit, composed of the central city and its suburban fringe communities, the Standard Metropolitan Statistical Area (SMSA). The SMSA unit was developed by the Bureau of the Budget (now the Office of Management and Budget) to define areas of daily interdependency using commuting as a criterion. While emphasizing the central city, our discussion will consider both components of the SMSA, the central city and suburban fringe communities. We will also occasionally speak of a relatively new unit, the Standard Consolidated Statistical Area (SCSA), a much larger geographical unit, as well as of the neighborhood, the basic unit of the city. It is important to make reference not only to the central city but also to the suburban ring and outlying regions which are frequently in competition with the city for its precious resources of population and jobs.

Major Trends and Their Implications

Trends help to define the needs of urban places by making reference to social, economic, and fiscal characteristics that have evolved in metropolitan settings over the last 10 to 15 years. Trends examined here focus upon a wide variety of urban characteristics, many of them cast in their metropolitan contexts. Social, economic, and fiscal traits correspond to problems faced by people, businesses, and local government, respectively.[3]

R.D. Norton argues that recent trends affecting urban places must
be seen in the context of three important factors:

1. decentralization
2. annexation
3. urban area growth[4]

Decentralization is the movement away from central city residences by
individuals. Annexation is the legal procedure allowing a city to extend
its borders, thus expanding its geographical territory. Finally, urban
area growth refers to the expansion of the SMSA in population growth.
The nature of these factors varies depending upon the state and region
in which a city is located and upon the historical moment. For example,
the major cities in the East and Midwest greedily annexed people and
property until the 1930s when state laws became more restrictive in
these regions. Because there is considerable regional variation in our
society, the discussion that follows highlights developments in cities
located in all areas of the United States: the East, Midwest, South, and
West.

Social Trends

Three major trends involve shifts in population that define important
social welfare dimensions of cities and SMSAs as a whole. The three
social dimensions are

1. shifting patterns of population density
2. changing rates of urban settlement by populations varying in
race, age, income, housing, crime, and social attitudes
3. altered patterns of migration

First, over the last two decades, there has been tremendous movement of populations away from the central city. Since 1970, the nation's
SMSAs (cities and suburbs combined) have been losing population to
non-SMSA territory. The most remote areas of New England, the South-
west, the Appalachian region, and other fringe areas have gained migrants at the expense of cities and suburbs alike (the SMSA). This shift
reverses a trend toward centralization that dates back to the early
nineteenth century and has resulted in the growth of population corridors linking two or more SMSAs. There are 13 of these corridors (SCSAs)
nationally. One of them is the Cincinnati-Hamilton-Dayton SCSA.

As recently as 1960, 42% of the nation's central cities began losing
population. The central city's loss was the suburban ring's gain *until*

1970 when *both* central city and suburban areas began to lose. Region- ally, population loss has been uneven. Though 83% of all central cities in the East lost population in the 1960s, only about 50% of central cities in the Midwest experienced population decline. However, during the 1970s, more than 90% of the central cities in *both* regions lost popula- tion. Although central city declines were much less prevalent in the South and West than in the East and Midwest, the number of central cities losing population more than doubled after 1970 even in the so- called sunbelt regions: whereas 20% of western and southern central cities lost population in the 1960s, 40% lost population in the 70s. With only a few exceptions, those central cities that did not lose population annexed additional acreage; between 1970 and 1975 they incorporated both land and population within redefined city limits. Among the entire group of 85 SMSAs nationally in 1975, only 11 central cities grew in population between 1970 and 1975 without annexing additional areas. All but one (Springfield, Massachusetts) were located in the South (St. Petersburg, Jacksonville, Miami, Tampa) or Far West (Spokane, Honolulu). Patterns of population migration, in sum, have placed the central city at a distinct disadvantage to suburban ring communities. As shown in Table 1.1, the central city has been losing its relative domi- nance in numbers of inhabitants for some time. Central city population as a proportion of the total SMSA population has been on the decline since the 1930s for most eastern and midwestern cities, suggesting that "an outward urge" has existed in our society for some time.

A second trend has been the increased concentration of older, poorer, and nonwhite populations in the central cities. As illustrated in Table 1.2, *all* large central cities gained black and other nonwhite population during the 1960s, but with few exceptions, these same cities lost white population. Cities that increased their numbers of white residents were, for the most part, located in the West and South. As an example, Houston's white population grew by 10% during the decade, an increase of 184,491 people. Cities in the Midwest whose white popu- lation expanded, notably Columbus, annexed acreage and population and also experienced continued economic expansion.

Not only did the racial composition of the central city change dur- ing the decade in question, but the age structure also became increas- ingly skewed in most cities, with fewer younger residents and greater numbers of people over 65 inhabiting the central urban areas. As illus- trated in Table 1.3, this tendency was particularly pronounced in the East and Midwest, although older, industrial cities everywhere (for example, San Francisco) were caught in the same bind. These age shifts reflect two general population trends: a decreasing death rate (and declining birth rate) resulting in a generally older population, and the previously mentioned patterns of migration from the central city to

TABLE 1.1
Population in Central Cities[a] and Suburbs
1900, 1930, 1960, 1970, 1975, 1976, 1980
(in thousands)

Region and SMSA	1900 CC	1900 S	1930 CC	1930 S	1960 CC	1960 S	1970 CC	1970 S	1975 CC	1975 S	1976 CC	1976 S	1980 CC	1980 S
EAST														
Washington, D.C.	279	133	489	219	763	1312	756	2104	715	2231	602	2253	638	2422
Baltimore	509	805	264	939	939	864	905	1164	852	1229	827	1317	786	1387
Boston	561	760	781	1387	697	1898	641	2112	637	2165	618	2114	562	2200
Buffalo	352	156	573	339	532	774	462	886	407	920	400	928	357	884
New York	3437	376	6930	1045	7781	2912	7894	3677	7482	3787	7423	3819	7071	2048
Philadelphia	1294	598	1951	1186	2002	2340	1948	2869	1816	2992	1797	3006	1688	3028
Pittsburgh	452	632	670	1353	604	1801	520	1881	459	1863	449	1854	423	1839
MIDWEST														
Chicago	1699	386	3376	1073	3550	2670	3366	3312	3099	3915	3074	3921	3005	4098
Detroit	286	141	1569	609	1670	2092	1511	2688	1335	2819	1819	2809	1203	3150
Minneapolis/St. Paul	203/163	94	464/272	146	483/313	185	432/316	1069	378/280	1171	372/272	1217	370/270	1472
Kansas City	164	182	400	301	475	617	507	746	473	799	458	804	448	878
St. Louis	575	283	822	596	750	1354	622	1740	524	1797	519	1815	453	1903
Cincinnati	326	291	451	393	502	765	452	932	413	968	410	966	385	1016
Cleveland	382	116	900	388	876	1033	750	1313	639	1328	626	1342	573	1325
Columbus	126	92	291	123	471	283	539	376	536	411	533	422	564	1093
Milwaukee	385	120	578	237	741	537	717	686	666	743	661	754	636	760

SOUTH

Jacksonville	28	11	130	26	201	254	528	—	562	—	532	540	196
Atlanta	90	108	270	192	487	529	496	893	436	1074	426	425	1604
New Orleans	287	33	459	68	627	279	593	452	560	534	581	557	629
Memphis	102	66	253	86	497	177	623	146	661	126	668	646	267
Nashville	81	42	154	69	170	292	448	93	423	139	431	455	394
Dallas	43	211	260	247	679	439	844	711	813	865	849	904	1685
Houston	45	76	292	165	938	480	1232	752	1326	945	1455	1595	1310
San Antonio	53	37	232	90	587	128	654	209	773	179	784	785	286

WEST

Phoenix	6	15	48	103	439	224	581	386	665	556	680	789	719
Los Angeles	102	65	1238	828	2479	3215	2812	3857	2727	3924	2744	2966	4149
San Diego	18	17	148	62	573	459	696	661	774	796	789	895	986
San Francisco	343	109	634	388	740	1540	716	2032	665	2144	663	679	2232
Denver	134	50	288	97	493	435	514	712	485	911	480	492	1051
Seattle	81	53	366	177	557	550	531	837	487	872	491	493	1059

[a] These are the 30 largest cities as of the 1970 census and as reported in U.S. Bureau of the Census, *U.S. Census of Population: 1970, Number of inhabitants* [Final report PCC1-A1], United States Summary, Table 28.

CC = Central cities

S = Suburbs

Source: U.S.A. Department of Housing and Urban Development, Office of Policy Development and Research, November 1980, *Changing Conditions in Large Metropolitan Areas*, HUD-PDR-637; also U.S. Bureau of the Census, U.S. Government Printing Office, 1982, *State and Metropolitan Area Data Book, 1982*.

TABLE 1.2
Population in Central City Areas, by Race

Region and SMSA	1960			1970			1980		
	White	Black	Other Nonwhite	White	Black	Other Nonwhite	White	Black	Spanish Origin[a]
EAST									
Washington, D.C.	344,876	441,257	6,867	209,550	537,871	9,834	171,768	448,906	17,679
Baltimore	610,350	325,833	2,817	480,021	420,244	5,431	345,113	431,151	7,638
Boston	628,694	63,427	4,879	524,338	104,483	7,692	393,937	126,229	36,068
New York	6,637,193	1,089,340	54,467	6,047,416	1,673,697	181,580	4,294,075	1,784,337	1,406,024
Philadelphia	1,467,466	528,528	6,006	1,278,281	654,729	15,588	983,084	638,878	63,570
Pittsburgh	502,528	100,868	604	412,439	105,060	2,600	316,694	101,813	3,196
MIDWEST									
Chicago	2,712,200	812,950	24,850	2,208,686	1,100,976	57,237	1,490,216	1,197,000	422,063
Detroit	1,182,360	482,630	5,010	838,827	660,481	12,091	413,730	758,939	28,970
Minneapolis/St. Paul	771,324	19,900	13,532	1,701,874	29,772	12,653	2,008,020	50,048	22,265
Kansas City	390,925	83,125	950	391,404	112,047	3,549	312,836	122,699	14,703
St. Louis	534,000	214,500	1,500	365,231	254,479	3,111	242,576	200,386	5,531
Cincinnati	392,564	108,432	1,004	325,347	124,890	2,262	251,144	130,467	2,988
Cleveland	622,836	250,536	2,628	458,049	287,594	5,256	307,264	251,264	17,772
Columbus	392,814	77,244	942	437,076	99,826	2,698	430,678	124,880	4,651
Milwaukee	675,051	62,244	3,705	605,148	105,399	6,453	466,620	146,940	26,111

SOUTH

Jacksonville	135,976	46,632	402	375,976	117,922	3,172	394,756	137,324	9,775
Atlanta	300,479	186,521	487	240,499	254,909	1,490	1,508,640	498,826	26,386
New Orleans	392,502	233,502	1,254	323,403	267,030	2,967	236,987	308,149	19,226
Memphis	312,613	183,890	497	379,088	242,541	1,870	333,789	307,702	5,225
Nashville	137,360	32,470	170	358,848	87,808	1,344	344,886	105,942	3,627
Dallas	547,953	129,010	2,037	626,544	210,255	7,599	555,270	265,594	111,083
Houston	720,384	214,802	2,814	904,875	316,829	11,095	978,353	440,346	281,331
San Antonio	543,562	41,677	1,761	597,847	49,711	6,541	617,998	57,700	421,954
WEST									
Phoenix	413,538	21,072	4,390	542,539	27,912	11,048			
Los Angeles	2,391,081	344,406	87,513	2,501,584	523,809	149,206	1,816,761	505,210	816,076
San Diego	528,306	34,380	10,314	619,366	52,949	24,384	666,863	77,700	130,613
San Francisco	874,530	158,301	74,955	724,955	220,826	131,418	395,081	86,414	83,373
Denver	457,997	30,073	4,930	457,994	46,828	9,262	368,068	59,252	92,348
Seattle	512,997	25,065	18,938	516,025	37,986	29,804	392,766	46,755	12,646

Sources: USA Department of Housing and Urban Development Office of Policy Development and Research, November 1980, *Changing Conditions in Large Metropolitan Areas*, HUD-PDR-637.

U.S. Bureau of the Census, August, 1982, *State and Metropolitan Area Data Book*, U.S. Government Printing Office.

aPersons of Spanish Origin may be of any race.

TABLE 1.3
Population by Age Groups in Central City Areas

Region and SMSA	Less than 18			More than 65			Working Age		
	1960	1970	1980	1960	1970	1980	1960	1970	1980
EAST									
Washington, D.C.	219,635	224,106	143,550	69,143	70,803	74,008	474,222	461,591	420,442
Baltimore	315,584	303,227	212,220	84,687	95,803	100,608	538,729	506,811	473,172
Boston	200,172	181,805	121,392	85,585	81,759	71,374	411,243	377,436	369,234
New York	2,164,527	2,234,819	1,767,750	813,827	947,878	945,585	4,802,646	4,712,103	4,348,665
Philadelphia	616,036	607,266	437,192	208,803	228,148	238,008	1,177,161	1,113,186	1,012,800
Pittsburgh	184,312	147,926	90,099	67,608	70,034	67,680	352,080	302,140	265,221
MIDWEST									
Chicago	1,104,118	1,081,398	853,420	346,575	355,287	342,570	2,099,307	1,930,204	1,802,000
Detroit	547,406	493,874	344,058	158,365	173,148	147,969	964,229	884,378	710,973
Minneapolis/St. Paul	241,867	213,780	138,970	102,040	106,397	100,450	452,093	424,323	400,580
Kansas City	146,884	163,996	118,720	55,172	59,551	55,104	272,944	283,453	274,176
St. Louis	231,803	197,634	118,233	92,184	91,240	79,728	426,013	333,326	256,039
Cincinnati	161,487	140,469	97,405	58,610	58,859	55,825	281,903	253,172	231,770
Cleveland	285,959	252,148	159,294	86,699	79,473	74,490	503,342	419,279	339,216
Columbus	157,128	176,569	151,152	41,008	45,549	49,632	272,864	317,482	363,216
Milwaukee	245,613	234,917	171,720	71,016	79,211	79,500	424,371	402,872	384,780

SOUTH

Jacksonville	68,041	185,836	151,740	18,334	35,900	51,840	114,625	307,064	336,420
Atlanta	161,422	159,535	124,950	38,700	45,224	32,300	286,878	292,141	267,750
New Orleans	218,868	201,670	160,416	54,086	63,072	65,169	354,046	328,658	105,830
Memphis	183,756	225,157	187,986	38,766	52,773	67,184	274,478	345,570	390,830
Nashville	54,257	146,842	114,205	17,517	39,494	50,050	98,226	261,664	290,745
Dallas	239,801	287,870	243,176	47,736	66,284	85,880	391,463	490,246	574,944
Houston	351,126	441,927	451,385	52,633	79,451	110,055	534,241	711,422	1,033,560
San Antonio	239,830	251,001	252,770	41,703	54,510	74,575	305,467	348,589	457,655

WEST

Phoenix	166,432	206,009	228,810	33,648	50,529	73,377	238,920	342,962	486,813
Los Angeles	850,751	937,086	747,432	297,320	333,759	314,396	1,674,929	1,903,755	1,904,172
San Diego	188,120	212,427	211,750	43,352	60,981	84,875	341,528	423,292	790,125
Denver	161,654	156,508	116,109	53,283	58,786	104,566	278,063	229,306	458,325
Seattle	180,217	152,697	110,700	72,057	76,082	61,992	304,726	355,621	319,308
San Francisco	288,232	258,799	86,768	139,595	147,346	75,922	679,173	671,055	330,302

Source: U.S.A. Department of Housing and Urban Development, Office of Policy Development and Research, November 1980, Changing Conditions in Large Metropolitan Areas, HUD-PDR-637; also U.S. Bureau of the Census, U.S. Government Printing Office, 1982, State and Metropolitan Area Data Book, 1982.

outer core communities, resulting in the loss of young people and young adults of working age. At the same time that individuals under 65 are leaving the central city, adults of retirement age are returning to the central city, leaving larger homes in the suburbs for smaller units, often rented apartment dwellings.

These overall patterns of change in the racial and age structures of cities have persisted into the 1970s resulting in parallel patterns of racial change in central city school enrollments, as shown in Table 1.4. Every city for which data are presented lost school enrollment in at least one of the three racial categories during this period but loss was particularly marked among white students. From 1970 to 1977, 84% of the students withdrawing from schools in Cincinnati were white, a figure that is representative of all cities losing students.

Not only are central city residents older and less likely to be white than they were 20 years ago, but they are also less wealthy and have remained so or have become poorer than their suburban counterparts. The per capita annual income for both central city and suburban residents for 1960, 1970, and 1975 indicates that those cities whose core residents had higher per capita income on the average than their suburban ring counterparts, had, by 1975, lost their leading edge. As we mentioned earlier, an area's population resources can be expressed in several ways. Per capita income represents individual wealth, the resources available to spend in the local community, invest in local banks, buy homes, and the like and is thus an indicator of community well-being.

Another population indicator, housing, is particularly important as a barometer of social need in the city. Moreover, since property taxes form the foundation for the support of public schools in most places, housing is especially critical to a discussion of urban education. Central city poverty tends to be concentrated in specific neighborhoods, generally low income tracts of rental housing units. Moreover, as described in the following passage from *The 1980 President's National Urban Policy Report*, places inhabited by the central city's poor have particular householder characteristics:

> Central city poverty tends to be concentrated in specific neighborhoods. This is particularly true for minority and female headed households. This pattern of concentration of poverty appears to have increased during the 1970's. One indication of this comes from trends in the poverty rate for census tracts where over 20% of the residents were poor in 1970. From 1969 to 1976 the rate of poverty in these low income areas in large central cities increased from 31% to 39%, and the proportion of female-headed and minority households in such areas also grew.[5]

TABLE 1.4
Central City School Districts Enrollment, by Race
(in thousands)

Region and SMSA	1970				1977				Change in enrollment 1970–77			
	Total	Black	Hispanic	White	Total	Black	Hispanic	White	Total	Black	Hispanic	White
EAST												
Washington, D.C.	142	135	1	6	125	119	1	4	−17	−16	0	−2
Baltimore	192	129	<500	63	160	120	<500	39	−32	−9	—	−31
Boston	97	29	4	62	74	31	7	32	−23	2	3	−30
Buffalo	70	27	2	41	55	25	2	27	−15	−2	0	−14
New York	1,140	392	292	438	1,077	408	312	328	−63	16	20	−110
Philadelphia	280	169	9	102	261	163	14	82	−19	−6	5	−20
Pittsburgh	73	30	<500	43	59	27	<500	32	−14	−3	—	−11
MIDWEST												
Chicago	578	315	56	200	521	311	73	129	−57	−4	17	−71
Detroit	284	181	4	98	238	189	4	44	−46	8	0	−54
Minneapolis/ St. Paul	67/50	6/3	<500/2	58/44	52/38	8/4	1/2	32/18	−15/−12	2/1	−/0	−18/−12
Kansas City	71	35	2	33	51	31	2	18	−20	−4	0	−15
St. Louis	111	73	<500	38	85	61	<500	23	−26	−12	—	−15
Cincinnati	84	38	<500	46	66	35	<500	31	−18	−3	—	−15
Cleveland	154	89	3	62	120	70	3	46	−34	−19	0	−16
Columbus	109	29	<500	79	97	32	<500	65	−12	3	—	−14
Milwaukee	132	34	4	93	109	41	5	61	−23	7	7	−32

TABLE 1.4 (continued)

Region and SMSA	1970				1977				Change in enrollment 1970–77			
	Total	Black	Hispanic	White	Total	Black	Hispanic	White	Total	Black	Hispanic	White
SOUTH												
Jacksonville	122	36	<500	87	110	36	<500	72	−12	0	—	−15
Atlanta	106	73	<500	33	82	73	<500	9	24	0	—	−24
New Orleans	110	76	2	32	92	74	2	15	−18	−2	0	−17
Memphis	148	76	<500	71	121	86	<500	36	−27	10	—	−35
Nashville	95	24	<500	71	78	24	<500	54	−17	0	—	−17
Houston	241	86	35	119	210	93	46	71	−31	4	11	−48
San Antonio	77	12	47	18	65	10	45	10	−12	−2	−2	−8
WEST												
Phoenix	29	2	4	22	27	3	5	19	−2	1	1	−3
Los Angeles	643	155	140	323	602	147	194	220	−41	−8	54	−103
San Diego	129	16	14	97	120	17	17	79	−9	1	3	−19
San Francisco	91	26	12	33	68	20	10	19	−23	−6	−2	−14
Seattle	84	11	<500	67	62	11	2	42	−22	0	—	−5

Source: U.S.A. Department of Housing and Urban Development, Office of Policy Development and Research, November 1980, *Changing Conditions in Large Metropolitan Areas*, HUD-PDR-637.

16

The same report also contains the suggestion that areas of poverty in cities are spreading.

Despite the increase of poverty in urban places, housing conditions on the whole have improved in recent years both because of increased stocks of newly constructed housing and widespread correction of severe structural problems, notably plumbing in existing housing. Nonetheless, compared with their suburban fringe neighbors, central city residents are generally less satisfied with living conditions in their neighborhoods. Although 75% of central city residents saw their neighborhoods as good to excellent in 1977, an even greater number (87%) of suburban residents gave their neighborhoods similarly high marks.[6]

Table 1.5 provides data on the nature of central city housing in 1970. With few exceptions, the general pattern is for housing to be owner-occupied in cities located in the South and West while the generally older housing units in the East and Midwest are typically evenly split between owners and renters. Closely associated with housing is household income. Median household incomes for owners and renters tend to be disparate, with owners' incomes frequently twice as high as renters' in the same city. For example, in 1970 in Washington D.C., the average income for a home owner was $12,000 as compared with $6,900 for a home renter in the same city. Washington is a good example of this phenomonon since renters' incomes are usually about half that of owners'. When a city is principally composed of renters, incomes on an average are likely to be lower than in cities where housing is principally owner-occupied.

Thus far we have considered characteristics of urban populations according to race, age, and housing dimensions that are routinely assembled by the Census Bureau or other national accounting systems. But the social characteristics of a population include more.

Social attitudes, inherent in responses made to questions about national policy and current societal conditions, reflect value and belief systems, which either support or hinder changes in social institutions, including schools. For example, individuals surveyed from 1960 through 1978 expressed changing patterns of response to a question concerning the role of the federal government in guaranteeing jobs and a good standard of living. The question was as follows:

"In general, some people feel that the government in Washington should see to it that every person has a job and a good standard of living. Others think that the government should just let each person get ahead on his or her own. Have you been interested enough in this to favor one side over the other? (If yes) do you think that the government should (a) see to jobs (b) depends on the issue or situation (c) allow each person to get ahead on his own (d) don't know.'"[7] Over the 18-year period, the survey showed that increasingly fewer individuals thought the govern-

TABLE 1.5
Character of Central City Housing, 1970
(percent of total)

Region and SMSA	Owner Occupied	One-Unit Structure	Housing Built Before 1950	Units in Structure with 4 or More Floors
EAST				
Washington, D.C.	28.2	36.8	67.9	30.5
Baltimore	44.4	61.3	74.6	6.1
Boston	27.2	14.6	85.0	24.6
Buffalo	44.0	27.1	92.6	4.4
New York	23.6	11.9	74.2	60.0
Philadelphia	59.7	66.6	78.5	8.1
Pittsburgh	50.1	52.7	83.6	8.0
MIDWEST				
Chicago	34.9	23.5	78.0	16.3
Detroit	60.0	54.4	84.3	7.7
Minneapolis/St. Paul	49.4/56.3	46.1/52.7	77.8/71.5	7.0/4.1
Kansas City	58.1	60.9	63.4	0.7
St. Louis	40.5	34.3	84.8	8.7
Cincinnati	38.5	34.6	72.2	11.5
Cleveland	46.1	37.6	85.5	6.4
Columbus	51.0	57.5	51.7	1.6
Milwaukee	47.3	38.9	66.0	5.5
SOUTH				
Jacksonville	67.6	75.1	38.5	0.9
Atlanta	41.0	49.0	41.4	0.4
New Orleans	38.6	44.1	68.2	2.4
Memphis	56.6	68.7	53.9	1.8
Nashville	59.6	67.3	39.3	2.2
Dallas	52.6	62.0	35.0	1.0
Houston	52.6	67.2	35.2	1.2
San Antonio	62.3	76.9	46.2	0.8
WEST				
Phoenix	70.0	72.3	25.6	1.1
Los Angeles	40.8	51.7	58.7	4.4
San Diego	50.7	64.6	36.5	2.0
San Francisco	32.8	33.1	82.0	21.4
Denver	50.3	58.3	55.3	9.3
Seattle	54.2	60.0	66.4	12.5

Source: USA Department of Housing and Urban Development, Office of Policy Development and Research, November 1980, *Changing Conditions in Large Metropolitan Areas*, HUD-PDR-637.

ment should take an active role and increasingly more thought individuals on their own should be responsible, suggesting that there is a growing emphasis on the individual pursuit of jobs and the good life and a decreasing emphasis on the role of the federal government toward these goals. All in all, these patterns point to an increasing "conservatism" (an emphasis on the free agency of the individual) and a decreasing "liberalism" (an emphasis on supportive governmental policies and structures in advancing social welfare).

When we begin to take a closer look at changing social attitudes by examining racial (black/white) differences in response to a particular aspect of social welfare, namely the federal role in school integration, the picture becomes more complex. In a survey spanning the years between 1964 to 1978, increasingly smaller percentages of both blacks and whites believed that the federal government should ensure school integration; however, almost three times as many blacks (60.3%) as whites (23.5%) still advocated this position by 1978. Also, although smaller percentages of both racial groups favored governmental involvement in integration by 1978, far greater numbers of whites than blacks wished the federal government would stay out of school integration efforts altogether. With respect to the issue of federal involvement in school integration, the social attitudes of blacks have not been tempered by increasing conservatism.[8]

But perhaps the differences expressed by blacks and whites on this issue reflect differences in perceptions of the federal government's role and *not* differences in attitude toward integration. During approximately the same period, blacks and whites were asked their attitudes toward desegregation as an issue separate from its policy implications at the federal level. Responses to whether individuals favor integration or segregation show a pattern of racial cleavage in attitudes. By 1978, the two groups were indeed closer in the matter of who favors desegregation (33.9% for whites, 55.4% for blacks) than they were in 1974 (36.6% for whites, 62.4% for blacks) primarily because, by the more recent date,[9] larger proportions of blacks support "something in between." These results suggest that there are continuing racial differences in social attitudes surrounding the issue of desegregation.

As we noted earlier, racial cleavage is clear in the demography of the SMSA. Although increasing numbers of black families are moving to the suburbs, as recently as 1979, black families constituted only 19% of suburban residents nationally. When attitudes toward school integration are calculated by subtracting percentages who favor policies promoting integration from those who favor policies maintaining segregation, a Percentage Difference Index can be computed. In this equation, the larger the negative number, the stronger the support for segregation. Studies show that there are negative responses to a policy of busing to achieve school integration by respondents in each of three residential areas: central cities, suburbs, and nonurban areas. However, the most vehement opposition is expressed by suburban residents. These results emphasize that racial cleavage in attitudes toward issues surrounding integration are mirrored in the split between the central city and its outlying regions, particularly its suburban fringe.

In Cincinnati, where only 7 percent of residents in suburban areas of Hamilton County are black, householders who had recently moved from the central city were surveyed about their reasons for settling in the suburbs.[10] Respondents were asked to rank their reasons for the city-to-suburb shift from among a list of 28 factors grouped into four categories:

1. housing-related reasons
2. neighborhood-related reasons
3. work-related reasons
4. school-related reasons

By far the largest number of factors (10) were included under housing-related reasons, a design problem in the questionnaire that may have biased the choice patterns of those who were surveyed. The largest percentage (55.6%) selected housing-related reasons as a first and/or second choice. Of those 8% who *did* rank schools as a primary cause of the move, the major concern was "quality of education in the public schools." Of those who had moved citing the school issue, 72% were Protestant, 19% were Catholic, and 9% represented various other denominations.[11] These results suggest that families leave Cincinnati primarily because they wish to improve their housing situations and not because they wish to seek better schools; however, it is difficult to interpret these findings in light of the relatively large number of factors included as housing-related issues at the expense of the remaining three categories including schooling.

To summarize, the central city/suburban differences in the social indicators of population density, patterns of migration, and various population characteristics (race, age, income, housing) are also present in social attitudes, particularly racial differences in attitudes toward matters of desegregation and integration. Central city residents, perhaps with less to lose than their suburban counterparts, were more liberal in their response to social policy issues regarding integration. However, at least in Cincinnati, for householders who move from the increasingly black central city to the almost completely white suburban fringe, housing, not schooling is the central reason for relocating the family. People who leave the city settle in suburbs that tend to be racially and economically homogeneous, that is, white and middle class. The residential and social boundaries that individuals establish speak eloquently of the conscious maintenance of "differentiation and segregation" in the SMSA. Boundaries between suburbs and the central city and between neighborhoods within the central city are maintained to contain socially and economically similar groups and to exclude those who are racially or ethnically different and less affluent.

Economic Trends

To understand the major economic trend to be considered here, that is, the decline of manufacturing in the traditional industrial belt comprising cities in the East and Midwest, it is important to look briefly at the nation's industrial cycle. The nation's aging industrial heartland comprises a manufacturing belt stretching from Boston in New England and Baltimore in the Middle Atlantic region through Cleveland, Cincinnati, and Chicago in the Midwest to Kansas City and St. Louis. This industrial expanse was the earliest seedbed of manufacturing innovation. From the period of initial industrialization prior to World War I until the immediate post-World War II era, these older SMSAs enjoyed economic hegemony and a diversified industrial base although they all depended on a specific technology:

> A single industry served as the technological wellspring for the development of industry after industry, from firearms and sewing machines to bicycles and automobiles. This fundamental source was the machine-tools industry. In a time when technology had minimal links with the world of science, the machine-tools industry served as a repository of practical problem-solving lore. In other words, the industry's development was a prerequisite to the development of the American system—the system that began with the use of interchangeable parts for the production of rifles in the 1830s and led eventually to Ford's 1913 assembly line.[12]

Ohio was the particular beneficiary of the machine-tools industry. In 1914, "one in five of the industry's 570 firms were located (in the state) while all the rest could be found elsewhere in the belt."[13] Cincinnati was especially active with approximately 200 firms thriving during the years immediately before World War I.

Areas peripheral to the industrial belt, in contrast, were dependent for the most part on single-resource processing industries such as leather or tobacco products. These enterprises developed at a slower rate and paid lower wages than those offered by machine shops in the belt. Thus, the Eastern and Midwestern states enjoyed a higher standard of living during this period than states in the other regions.[14]

However, following World War II and particularly during the mid to late 1960s, industrial growth in the West and South accelerated and at length surpassed industrial expansion in the belt. Norton points out that between 1963 and 1972, "the core lagged behind the nation's rate of increase to the extent of fully a million manufacturing jobs. Then, during the 1970s the link between the belt and the seedbed function (in industrial expansion) all but disappeared."[15]

These dramatic changes in the location of manufacturing expansion are rooted in changing sources of technological innovation, the rise of so-called "science-based" industries, particularly electronics and chemicals. Regional resource deposits and climatic amenities drew industrial expansion away from the East and Midwest. The clearest example illustrating this shift is Texas, the nation's leading gainer in manufacturing employment in the decade after 1967. Norton elaborates:

> By virtue of its sunshine and oil—and federal contracts, aerospace industry and scientists they have helped attract since 1940—the state has come to specialize not only in petrochemicals but also in electronics. . . . Texas has therefore become something of a seedbed in its own right. As such it has spawned a series of innovations that have had an international impact during the 1970s.[16]

And what of the heartland? Although it is not entirely lacking in expansion in both the manufacturing and service sectors, it lags behind the nation in manufacturing growth, as reflected in employment figures presented in Table 1.6. To make its losses even more painful, population has not decreased at the same pace as the shutdown in manufacturing, resulting in severe unemployment problems which particularly plague the central city. Although New England has recently seen a resurgence of manufacturing growth, particularly in the high tech computing areas, Newark, Cleveland, Detroit, and other cities in the belt have suffered high percentages of unemployment. In 1982, unemployment rates as high as 18% in Michigan and slightly lower in New Jersey and Ohio testified to the effects of technological change. In human terms, these figures represent increasing poverty among families who happen to live in cities left behind in the wake of industrial change.

Although the general patterns of social and economic trends we have described have implications for urban schools along a number of dimensions, the immediate impact of these trends for public schools rests in the meaning they have for the fiscal support systems that maintain public schooling. As is clear in what has gone before, certain regions, notably the South and West, currently enjoy relatively greater economic expansion than others (the East and Midwest). In all regions, the suburban ring remains divided from the central city both socially

TABLE 1.6
Manufacturing Employment in Central City and Suburban Areas (in thousands)

Region and SMSA	1963			1975			1976			1976 as a % of 1963	
	SMSA	CC	OCC	SMSA	CC	OCC	SMSA	CC	OCC	CC	OCC
EAST											
Washington, D.C.	50	22	28	63	20	43	62	18	44	81.8	157.1
Baltimore	191	104	87	167	81	86	165	76	89	73.1	102.3
Boston	293	83	210	257	52	205	256	52	204	62.7	97.1
Buffalo	163	57	106	152	48	104	139	51	88	89.5	83.0
New York	1147	927	220	836	608	226	809	594	215	64.1	97.7
Philadelphia	536	285	271	451	168	283	437	196	241	74.0	89.0
Pittsburgh	272	82	190	256	54	202	241	55	186	67.0	97.9
MIDWEST											
Chicago	861	509	352	858	386	472	861	382	479	75.0	136.1
Detroit	494	201	293	482	149	312	515	159	356	79.1	121.5
Minneapolis/St. Paul	164	110	54	207	128	79	204	109	95	99.1	175.9
Kansas City	111	62	49	114	51	63	117	52	65	83.9	132.7
St. Louis	260	129	131	235	92	143	240	91	149	70.5	113.7
Cincinnati	154	77	77	162	68	94	157	71	86	92.2	111.7
Cleveland	280	169	111	271	127	144	266	121	145	71.6	130.6
Columbus	80	66	14	78	56	22	NA	55	NA	83.3	NA
Milwaukee	194	119	75	204	100	104	201	97	104	81.5	138.7

TABLE 1.6 (continued)

Region and SMSA	1963			1975			1976			1976 as a % of 1963	
	SMSA	CC	OCC	SMSA	CC	OCC	SMSA	CC	OCC	CC	OCC
SOUTH											
Jacksonville	21	16	5	23	23	NA	22	22	NA	137.5	NA
Atlanta	96	52	44	109	43	66	NA	46	NA	88.5	NA
New Orleans	49	31	18	48	25	23	51	28	23	90.3	127.8
Memphis	47	43	4	59	52	7	61	52	NA	120.9	NA
Nashville	47	34	13	55	43	12	61	48	13	141.2	100.0
Dallas	110	86	24	158	111	47	NA	121	NA	140.7	NA
Houston	109	77	32	181	125	56	187	128	59	166.2	184.4
San Antonio	24	21	3	31	28	3	36	29	7	138.1	233.3
WEST											
Los Angeles	746	313	433	750	303	457	760	302	448	96.5	96.5
San Diego	60	49	11	71	46	35	75	50	25	153.1	227.3
Denver	70	38	32	98	48	50	98	43	55	113.2	171.9
Seattle	122	74	48	124	65*	59	120	57	NA	77.0	NA
San Francisco	196	92	104	173	64	109	179	64	115	69.6	89.4

NA = Not Available

*Based on the 1972 ratios.

Source: U.S.A. Department of Housing and Urban Development, Office of Policy Development and Research, November 1980, *Changing Conditions in Large Metropolitan Areas*, HUD-PDR-637.

and economically. In sum, central cities in the East and Midwest are particularly vulnerable socially and economically. This fact highlights the fiscal distress apparent in these cities' school systems, as we will show next.

Fiscal Trends

Given the shifts in population and manufacturing previously described, it is not surprising that aging central cities in the East and Midwest have been particularly hard hit with fiscal problems. Before turning to a discussion of the educational plight of these regions, we will briefly review the structure of local school fiscal operations.

A substantial proportion (48%) of educational costs are borne by the local community as a part of its fiscal burden. Remaining educational expenses are assumed by both the state (44%) and the federal government (8%). Educational services at the municipal system level are most frequently provided by a governmental structure separate from city hall but similar to a city office or department. There are some exceptions such as Chicago, Nashville, and San Francisco which have coterminal city and county school systems (see Table 1.7).

City (or county) revenues derive from several sources: real property taxes, sales taxes, income taxes and user charges. By far the largest source of local government funds is real estate taxes. For cities larger than 50,000, one fourth of all municipal revenues raised in 1977 were from this source.[17] Sales taxes are levied on most retail items and on some selective items such as cigarettes and liquor. Local income taxes provide an important source of revenue in cities in the 14 states that allow taxation by cities. Finally, user charges attached to such services as water, sewage, and metered parking generated 16 percent of total revenues in 1977 for cities larger than 50,000.[18]

In recent years, suburban areas have been able to supply newer, generally more pleasant facilities attractive to teachers and students for fewer per capita tax dollars than central cities. During the late 1960s "local taxes consumed 6.1 percent of personal income in central cities and only 3.4 percent in the suburbs."[19] Central cities burdened with ailing physical plants and increasingly dependent upon a population declining in numbers and average income, were generally forced to squeeze taxpayers even more strenuously to receive the necessary dollars to maintain services. Property taxes, which form the base income for most central city school districts, are especially vulnerable to the population shifts and manufacturing declines we have previously mentioned. As can be seen in Tables 1.1 and 1.7, cities in the East and Midwest that have been losing population are showing negative rates

TABLE 1.7
Adjusted Property Tax Base
Average Annual Rates of Growth
Central City

Region and City	1960–70	1960–75	1975–78
EAST			
Washington, D.C.	4.8	2.4	8.6
Baltimore	1.0	0.2	NA
Boston	0.9	2.0	−0.7
Buffalo	−0.4	0.1	−0.8
New York	3.8	2.8	−0.7
Philadelphia	1.6	3.3	0.9
Pittsburgh	1.0	2.2	−1.3
MIDWEST			
Chicago	1.9	−1.0	2.4*
Detroit	0.5	2.1	−5.0
Minneapolis/St. Paul	−0.4/1.0	3.2/−1.7	2.6/4.4
Kansas City	3.6	2.2	NA
St. Louis	0.3	−1.5	−1.8
Cincinnati	0.7	1.1	0.1
Cleveland	0.4	−1.6	−6.6
Columbus	4.5	5.1	1.7
Milwaukee	3.0	3.7	−1.7
SOUTH			
Jacksonville	3.5	10.3	10.8
Atlanta	5.8	3.7	3.3
New Orleans	2.3	2.6	1.0
Memphis	4.4	7.8	4.6
Nashville	5.9	7.0	7.4*
Dallas	5.2	5.2	4.5
Houston	4.6	13.0	8.1
San Antonio	4.0	8.8	8.4
WEST			
Phoenix	6.2	10.0	6.5
Los Angeles	5.2	4.2	8.9
San Diego	5.5	13.1	12.2
San Francisco	2.8	4.5	6.9*
Denver	2.3	6.1	3.9
Seattle	4.7	3.3	8.7

*City and county are consolidated.
Sources: U.S.A. Department of Housing and Urban Development, Office of Policy Development and Research, November 1980, *Changing Conditions in Large Metropolitan Areas,* HUD-PDR-637.

of growth in their property tax bases, and thus are faced with shrinking rates of return. Even a slight shift in population, an increase or decrease as small as one percent, is associated with a dramatic rate of change in the real property tax base. Although real estate has been highly inflationary in recent years, escalating property prices have not compensated for population losses in many cities:

> In a sample of large central cities, 15 with sharp population losses experienced a median increase in real property values of 41 percent between 1971 and 1976; in contrast, five rapidly growing cities had a median gain of 115 percent, nearly three times as great.[20]

Not surprisingly, these 15 cities with rapidly declining population were located in the East and Midwest.

With shrinking sources of revenue, central city school systems are hard pressed to maintain even par with suburban schools in providing such amenities as large grassy playgrounds, innovative (and expensive) curricular materials, and so forth. The prognosis for central cities will continue to be bleak during the 1980s as systems adjust to the special needs of their school populations. As seen by the *The 1980 President's National Urban Policy Report:*

> The decline in the population between 5 and 18 years of age is expected to result in a 10 percent decline in public school enrollment during the 1980s. The sharpest decreases will occur in grades 8 through 12. Enrollment declines will be most dramatic in large, needy, central cities, where enrollment will drop more rapidly than the total population. At the same time, per pupil outlays will rise as more attention is given to children with special needs. As a result, expenditures for public elementary and secondary education will rise even in school districts registering enrollment losses. In fact, if the pattern of the 1970s is repeated, outlays for public schools will increase most rapidly in needy cities.[21]

Thus, many central city schools are burdened with fiscal constraints merely by virtue of their geographical and economic locations. In addition, militant, unionized teachers have stretched school budgets by their demands for increased wages and benefits. Moreover, a general malaise among all youth, but especially central city youth, has made the central city's educational mission problematic indeed.

A wide range of services are commonly offered by most central city and suburban municipalities. Education, sanitation, public transit, parks and recreation, police and fire services, health and hospitals, welfare, and libraries encompass most but not all these services. By far the most problematic according to the Department of Housing and Urban Development is education:

> In terms of the nation's future, urban public education is clearly the number one problem in the urban services area. The ratio of high school graduates to all 18-year-olds has fallen since 1969. Dropout rates have risen particularly among minorities . . . test scores are lower than ever in many urban schools. For many pupils, schools are merely custodians. Many schools accept truancy as a fact of life. School crime and vandalism are at alarming levels.[22]

The report concludes its gloomy assessment of urban education by referring to the problems of pupil enrollment decline that we have already discussed.

In sum, despite decreasing numbers of students in many central city schools, costs continue to rise primarily because of continued growth in school expenditures per pupil coupled with increasing teacher wages and fringe benefits. For cities unable to increase their tax base by annexation of additional taxable lands, the resolution of fiscal difficulties seems almost impossible. City systems in competition with surrounding suburbs with their attractive low per capita tax programs must juggle students and school facilities in a manner that will keep tax-paying residents in place. However, things are even more complex. In addition to the fiscal constraints on city school systems, there are also social and political constraints.

In recent years, federal legislation and local legal battles have forced central city schools to provide equal access to educational facilities for all students. This, more specifically, has meant accessibility to all system schools by minority groups, particularly black students. Since black residents are often least able to provide tax-paying support by virtue of past economic discrimination and current economic stagnation, the school system is heavily dependent upon more affluent (generally white) taxpayers.

As we will see in the following section of this chapter, central city school systems run the risk of alienating both groups: white taxpayers and black and other oppressed minorities. The usual gamble taken by system managers is to design and implement integration plans with "stabilizing consequences" in order to prevent outward migration on the one hand and inequitable allocation of black minority students in the system's schools on the other.

As a consequence of the city's defensive posture, central city school policy in the 1970s was constrained in its development. For many large city school districts, policy emerged as a set of coping strategies designed to

1. provide "quality amenities" (attractive public schools), "uncontaminated by the presence of undesirable groups"
2. ensure fiscal responsibility unthreatened by default
3. maintain social order unblemished by institutional chaos and disciplinary disruption

These measures were formulated to attract and hold "desirable" citizens, those who were economically productive and could pay the bills.[23]

In the 1980s, central cities are compelled to pursue these same political ends since cities are embedded in an aversive national political system. We agree with Paul Petersen who contends that "As long as the larger political system permits capital and labor to migrate freely from one subunit to another, as long as regional or national governments use neither regulatory powers nor tax incentives to direct economic investment, central cities must struggle as best they can to entice both industry and labor into their political jurisdiction."[24] In other words, in the face of enormous competition from other cities and from their own suburbs, cities must lure population to establish work places and residences within their borders.

As we have seen, central cities nationally occupy an embattled position for scarce resources as a result of the social, economic, and fiscal trends previously discussed. School systems, caught in the web, must thus accomodate to the needs and demands, pushes and strains of cooperating and competing populations.

Once established in cities, individuals, as we have seen, do not necessarily remain strictly committed to an initial residential neighborhood. Brian Berry asserts that people change residences "in response to critical events associated with passage through different stages of the life cycle or with occupational career trajectories and also in response to the prospective presence of black families in the neighborhoods."[25] However, if residents are established in an ecological niche in the city, they often become fiercely protective of their institutions, particularly the local elementary or secondary school serving neighborhood children.

In examining the intersection of central city school policy decisions and neighborhood life, two case studies are presented here that focus upon neighborhood schools and residents of communities located in two economically struggling midwestern cities, Chicago and Cincinnati. Although initial events in Gage Park, a Chicago neighborhood, preceded incidents in Lower Price Hill, Riverside-Sedamsville, and the West End in Cincinnati by 10 years, developments in the two sets of communities took a remarkably similar course.

In both cases, city school systems, through board actions, became the adversaries of low income white community residents and, especially in Gage Park, of the local school administration. And, although a loose alliance initially formed among two low income white communities and a low income black community in Cincinnati, this coalition soon fell apart. The same pattern developed in Gage Park. Residents in the separate communities quickly perceived that their local neighborhood's best interest could not be served by a loose federation. Neighborhood self-interest dictated a separatist strategy of fighting the board alone to gain benefits for local schools and children. Thus, it can be argued that both black and white communities in struggles for scarce school resources will routinely enlist legal assistance, mass action at the neighborhood level (for example, a school boycott), media coverage, and the support of local business, religious, and local school administrative leaders to protect their educational institutions. Moreover, in contrast to white renters, white residents who are homeowners in low income neighborhoods will react with characteristically racist maneuvers to oppose desegregation. In sum, school boards face open hostility from white residents when attempts are made to desegregate schools in systems with expanding black populations and decreasing white populations.

Gage Park

The city of Chicago grew to eminence as a commercial center in the 1840s, seizing from Cincinnati, the deposed Queen City of the West, leadership in the role of western economic expansion in the late nineteenth century. Growth was rapid and with the arrival of blacks from the South and immigrants from eastern Europe, Chicago's population became a cultural mosaic.

From 1890 to 1920, movement of Chicago's segregated black population was inhibited by

> . . . violence, activities of neighborhood organizations such as, the Hyde Park Improvement Protective Club which "induced" real estate agents to develop dual listings to confine blacks to designated Negro districts and even proposed that the city enact a Residential Segregation Ordinance; and the general acquiescence of or active support of the majority of the white community.[26]

During the 40-year period that followed, the black population of Chicago remained ghettoized to such an extent that "only 3 percent of the city's white population, but 93 percent of the nonwhite population lived in areas 50 percent or more black in 1960, thus emphasizing the sharpness of separation of blacks and whites in the city."[27] During the 1960s, the ghetto expanded outward into surrounding neighborhoods to the west and north of the city's center (see Figure 1.1).

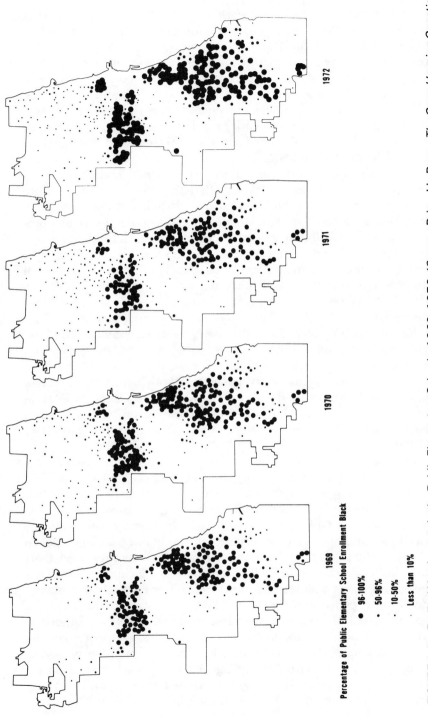

Percentage of Public Elementary School Enrollment Black

- ● 96-100%
- ∙ 50-96%
- · 10-50%
- Less than 10%

FIGURE 1.1   Radical Headcounts in the Public Elementary Schools, 1969–1972. (*Source:* Brian J.L. Berry, *The Open Housing Question: Race and Housing in Chicago, 1966–1976,* Cambridge, Ballinger, 1979, Figure 4.2, p. 145.)

1969   1970   1971   1972

Brian Berry's study of Gage Park, a white ethnic neighborhood in Chicago, reveals that schools function as important sources of neighborhood identity and pride. When a neighborhood school is integrated as a result of school policy decisions, local residents are likely to feel personally threatened. Many will feel they have no choice but to move away. This was the case in Gage Park in the late 1960s and early 1970s. In 1973, Gage Park had virtually no black residents. However, its geographical position gave Gage Park's residents cause for concern since other white ethnic neighborhood enclaves to the east and south of Gage Park had begun to "go black."

The unsettled conditions resulted in panicked home selling, as schools in neighborhoods such as Gage Park that were virtually all white became integrated. In 1965, the Chicago school board made the decision to desegregate Gage Park High School as a consequence of a program change in Lindblom, a nearby secondary school. Lindblom's curriculum was changed from a comprehensive set of course offerings to a technical program, leaving Gage Park School as the area's only school with a general program, and necessitating the redistribution of students. Several feeder schools that had formerly been streamed to Lindblom became part of Gage Park High School's catchment area.

For residents of Gage Park, the changing social composition of the high school that followed was a harbinger of other neighborhood changes and thus was perceived as a threat. Black parents, for their part, had endured exclusionary policies in both housing and school matters and, therefore, had a vested interest in the successful integration of Gage Park High School. Disorder began in 1967, only two years after the plan had been in operation, when blacks constituted less than half the student body.

In October of that year, blacks boycotted Gage Park High School to protest racially motivated violence occurring on school buses. The worst year of disruption occurred two years later in 1969. Not only had black enrollment increased significantly but, perhaps more importantly, racial turmoil in the society at large had accelerated. Chicago area Black Panther leader Fred Hampton was gunned down by police in his apartment during this period. Black students increased their complaints of police brutality which included the macing of a school bus transporting black children at some distance from the school building. Indeed, both police and school administrative staff, particularly the school principal, Mr. Hahn, were characteristically aloof and authoritarian in their response to students. The school's position, supported by the Gage Park community, was to deal in a harshly punitive way with "disruptive" students. Ironically, Gage Park High School had poorly served many white neighborhood youth before integration. These youth, alienated from the school program, a highly differentiated tracking system, had dropped out in large numbers before 1965. Many of them instigated the racial incidents that occurred following integration.[28]

By 1972, the lines separating black and white parents were drawn. Each group had its own concerned parents' organization and each organization made a formal presentation of its demands to the school principal and to the central administration. Initially, it had appeared as if both black and white parents might jointly serve on an advisory council to aid the principal. In fact, a Biracial Parents Committee was formed in 1969 at the time of initial unrest in the school. However, from the start, the principal had not acted in good faith. The group of black parents serving on the committee had been recruited by Principal Hahn but "were from the beginning suspicious of him because he had surreptitiouly taped their initial interview."[29] In drafting white membership for the committee, Hahn overlooked three large white neighborhoods with school memberships outside Gage Park, selecting representatives from the Gage Park Civic Association, a group dominated by right-wing interests. During this period, the Association sponsored a film produced by the John Birch Society, "Anarchy-USA," mounted a secretive "mobile parent radio patrol" whose existence was unknown even to the Association's executive board, and from 1960 led the attempt to change Gage Park High School's attendance boundaries to exclude blacks.[30]

Given this climate of distrust and fear, it is not surprising that by 1971 the Biracial Parents Committee was moribund, its membership splintered into several racially homogeneous organizations. As early as 1969, black parents had consolidated their efforts as the Concerned Black Parents of Gage Park (to the consternation of Gage Park residents who saw the group's very name as a threat). In November of that year, the Concerned Black Parents forwarded a nine-point document to the Chicago school board. The list of demands included:

> . . . fair treatment for both black and white students, special police, the removal of principal Hahn, a full day of school (black students had been bused home early many times when violence occurred), and investigation of white hate groups' activities in the Gage Park area.[31]

Meanwhile, white parents, acting officially through the PTA but also in league with the Gage Park Civic Association and other rightist organizations, drafted a plan to shift the school's eastern boundary to exclude most of Gage Park High School's current black enrollment. The rationale in this request to the board centered upon overcrowded conditions at Gage Park High School and underutilized space at nearby Englewood High School, then operating at 73% capacity. Black parents and other affected groups opposed the plan arguing that overcrowded schools in black neighborhoods had been alleviated by the use of temporary classroom units installed on school grounds and that Englewood, an unsound edifice constructed in the late nineteenth century, should be shut down altogether.

The school board, for its part, recoiled from the PTA proposal citing both legal constraints and lack of widespread support from affected areas outside the Gage Park community itself. According to Berry, two particular issues guided the board's decision. "The first was the fear, expressed by Julian B. Drayton, the Area B superintendent, that changing the boundaries in order to remove 660 students (519 of whom were black, 113 white and 28 Chicano) from Gage Park High School would violate the Armstrong Act, which prohibits moving school boundaries so as to encourage racial segregation." The second consideration that influenced the board of education was the disfavor with which the plan was greeted outside the Gage Park community.[32] Indeed, there was considerable resistance from both black and white community groups outside the immediate Gage Park neighborhood. The white ethnic communities that resisted the plan had not been consulted by the narrow constituency represented by the PTA and thus refused to throw their political backing behind the plan.

However, the PTA, led by Irene Shrader, continued its demands for boundary changes and in the fall of 1972 organized a boycott of the school. White students and members of local organizations, particularly the Gage Park Civic Association, participated in the 111 day boycott. This action was enormously effective in terms of both the participation of large numbers of students and residents over the three month period and the widespread coverage of the action by the media. Nonetheless, the boycott proved a pyrrhic victory for the Gage Park community forces. Large numbers of students either transferred or dropped out, blunting the community's case for overcrowded conditions at Gage Park High School. Even more tellingly, although almost no black families had actually moved into the neighborhood, large numbers of young white families with children began to depart. By 1972, the number of white students had decreased from 2,249 in 1965 to 761. In 1972, black students constituted 50% of the enrollment. Increasingly, white families sent their children to parochial schools and to public and private schools outside the neighborhood or simply moved from the community.

Berry's analysis of the Gage Park situation hinges upon his interpretation of the overall pattern of racial change that has characterized Chicago's white, low income ethnic neighborhoods. Chicago's black residents moved to west and central neighborhoods from areas of concentration in the east and south central portions of the city. The path that black mobility took was through neighborhoods with a mix of rental units and moderately priced housing. These tended to be communities inhabited by middle income whites whose resources allowed them the option to buy housing in other parts of the city or suburbs. In other words, black residential mobility was *not* typically through neighborhoods inhabited by low income whites. Thus, Gage Park as a residential area lacked appeal to upwardly mobile black families seeking housing. Neighborhoods such as Gage Park tended to become integrated by default, after panicked homeowners, fearing a plummeting real estate market in the face of "inevitable" integration, sold their homes and moved on.

As we have seen, white recalcitrance and resistance is hardly rational. Instead, it appears to be based on attitudes and values that are deeply embedded in the national character. Berry sees the black "threat" to white neighborhoods as a continuation of the "American dilemma" identified by Gunnar Myrdal in 1944. In race relations, the American on the one hand observes the "American creed," a strongly nationalistic blend of patriotism and Protestantism, but at the same time "thinks, talks and acts" on the basis of "personal local interests, economic, social and sexual jealousies, considerations of community prestige and conformity, group prejudice against particular persons or types of people, and all sorts of miscellaneous wants, impulses, and habits."[33] Thus, although racial change in the neighborhood was hardly likely, given patterns of black residential mobility, Gage Park whites, seeing black children in *their* high school, assumed "the worst."

Lower Price Hill, Riverside-Sedamsville and the West End

Whereas most Chicago neighborhoods are geographically contiguous, facilitating the easy flow of shifting residential populations, many of Cincinnati's central city neighborhoods are separated from each other by dramatic natural boundaries: the twisting Ohio River, the industrialized Mill Creek Valley, or steep, thinly populated hillsides. Although there have been patterns of successive residential inhabitance by racial and ethnic groups in many central city neighborhoods, others, some close to Cincinnati's downtown business area, have remained relatively stable over the course of the city's long history.

In Cincinnati, a substantial proportion (35%) of public school children throughout the system are from urban Appalachian backgrounds and are white. Most of these children's parents are blue collar workers without high school diplomas whose parents had migrated from eastern Kentucky coal fields, farms, and other rural areas in the Appalachian

region during the boom period of rural to urban migration and industrial expansion in the 1950s and 1960s. According to Gary Fowler,
"approximately 14,000 (22%) of the nearly 65,000 immigrants to the
Cincinnati area from 1955 to 1960 came from southern Appalachia;
another 10,500 came between 1965 and 1970. The majority (of these
migrants) . . . were from adjacent areas in southern Ohio and eastern
Kentucky."[34] Migrants to the city relied upon networks of established
kin to provide entry to the workplace, usually factory jobs requiring no
initial experience or training. For those who arrived fairly early in the
period, jobs were readily available. However, more recently, unskilled
work in manufacturing has been severely cut back, resulting in periodic
or chronic unemployment for those workers who for one reason or
another have been unable to upgrade their skills. Thus, although many
migrants advanced rapidly, others, newly arrived in the city, injured on
the job or overwhelmed by heavy financial burdens, were left behind.
These are the individuals and their families who remain segregated in
residential areas characterized by "extensive public demolition, especially for highway construction, public housing development, and industrial expansion."[35]

Two predominantly urban Applachian neighborhoods in Cincinnati
have been particularly vocal in their demands for change in school
structures: Lower Price Hill and Riverside-Sedamsville, contiguous
neighborhoods to the west of Cincinnati's downtown business district
(see Figure 1.2). The two neighborhoods are situated on a plateau between the steep rise of Price Hill to the south and west and the industrialized Mill Creek Valley to the north and east. According to Fowler, "In
1970, three of Cincinnati's five neighborhoods with the lowest socioeconomic status—Lower Price Hill, North Fairmount, and Camp Washington—were Appalachian sections of the Mill Creek Valley."[36] Although urban Appalachians constitute more than 75% of the residents
in both communities, there are clear distinctions between the two set-
tlements. The single most important difference is in patterns of residential settlement.

Lower Price Hill has functioned as a port of entry neighborhood for
over 100 years. A large settlement house in the center of the neighborhood provides residents with a variety of social services. Until recently,
it was staffed by the Verona Brotherhood and has served successive
waves of German, Italian, and, most recently, Appalachian newcomers.
Renters outnumber homeowners four to one and the average family
income (in 1980) was $10,504 (as compared with the city-wide average
of $20,262).

In contrast, 48% of Riverside-Sedamsville residents own their own
homes, and their average family income is $14,893. Riverside-Sedams-
ville residents, like Gage Park homeowners, see themselves as heavily

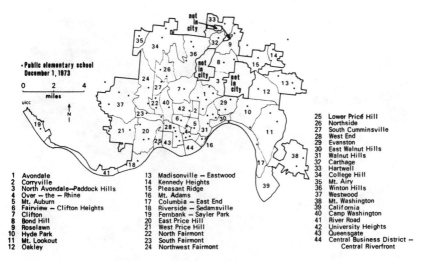

FIGURE 1.2   Residential Distribution in Neighborhoods of Cincinnati. (*Source: Gary L. Fowler, "Residential Distribution of Urban Appalachians," in The Invisible Minority: Urban Appalachians,* eds. William W. Philliber and Clyde B. McCoy, Lexington: University Press of Kentucky, 1981, Figure 4.1, p. 85.)

invested in their community. Many in fact moved from Lower Price Hill where they had been renters to their present community where it was possible to afford a first home. During events that followed the school board's decision in February of 1979 to close the neighborhood elementary school in Riverside-Sedamsville and reroute secondary school students from both communities to predominatly black schools, economic differences between the two neighborhoods eventually underscored ideological cleavages and severely weakened joint community opposition to board policy.

The board's action in 1979 was taken as a response to the system's two most pressing problems: a desegregation suit brought against the school by the NAACP in 1972, and the continuing prospect of declining enrollments necessitating school closings and placement of affected students in schools outside their neighborhoods. The situation confronting the Cincinnati schools in 1979 was similar to that facing Chicago some 10 years earlier, but was heightened by the legal action taken by the NAACP and a declining white schoolaged population (see Figures 1.3 and 1.4).

On February 12, the board announced plans to close eight schools and enact several boundary changes effective the following school year. Some shifts proposed by the board affected relatively affluent communities on the east side as well as the low income white com-

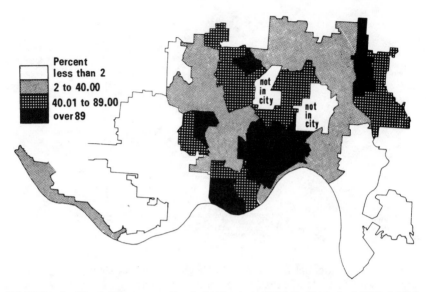

FIGURE 1.3   Black Elementary Pupils in Cincinnati Public Schools, 1973–1974. (*Source:* Gary L. Fowler, "Residential Distribution of Urban Appalachians," in *The Invisible Minority: Urban Appalachians,* eds. William W. Philliber and Clyde B. McCoy, Lexington: University Press of Kentucky, 1981, Figure 4.1, p. 85.)

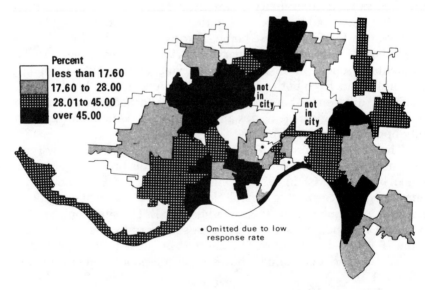

FIGURE 1.4   Appalachian Elementary Pupils in Cincinnati Public Schools 1973–1974. (*Source:* Gary L. Fowler, "Residential Distribution of Urban Appalachians," in *The Invisible Minority: Urban Appalachians,* eds. William W. Philliber and Clyde B. McCoy, Lexington: University Press of Kentucky, 1981, Figure 4.3, p. 88.)

munities of Lower Price Hill and Riverside-Sedamsville and a low income black neighborhood, the West End. In addition to closing the
Riverside-Sedamsville neighborhood school and reassigning students
to Oyler Elementary School in Lower Price Hill, the board recommended the reassignment of secondary students from both communities to predominatly black junior and senior high schools. The board
argued that the crowded conditions in predominatly white West High
and its feeder schools necessitated the reassignment of these students
to Porter Junior High and Taft High School, both located in the West
End.

Urban Appalachian parents from Riverside-Sedamsville and Lower
Price Hill began a series of militant demonstrations at the biweekly
public school board meetings, making news headlines during the remainder of the school year. An initial statement from the communities
took the form of a position paper drafted by an advocacy group, the
Urban Appalachian Council, an organization with links to local liberal
civic associations and institutions. The primary objection to the board's
action expressed in the Council's statement took the form of a sophisticated argument against desegregation plans which "maintain the pattern of racial and socioeconomic segregation" present in the system.
Accusing the board of proposing boundary changes which served only
a "legal purpose in generating some temporary statistics to assist the
school board in its legal battle with the NAACP," the Council proposed
its own rationale for "genuine integration." A metropolitan-wide solution would "probably be necessary" to ensure effective school desegregation. In addition, the Council outlined its three major educational
goals: quality education, specifically, a more flexible curriculum with a
substantial increase in the numbers of "culturally sensitive" classroom
teachers; cultural affirmation for all groups; and community involvement, particularly in curriculum planning, to judge "which methods
and texts really speak to the needs of students." An effective overall
integration strategy demanded "relative equality; in numbers and status of groups involved in the plan, socioeconomic mix, upgrading of
educational program, and a good human relations program for staff,
parents, and students."[37]

A more strongly worded document was issued by the West End ad
hoc committee, a group representing black parents with children attending Porter and Taft. Acknowledging their reticence at joining the
demonstrations and protests of the Appalachian communities, the committee expressed the hope that "Appalachians will not measure the
West End's concerns by the number of demonstrations that is participated in," since the West End had long been engaged on its own in
"the big question of educating all of the West End children." Reviewing
past school board practices and current administrative policy with a

pointed reference to the school system's superintendent, the committee summarized the efforts of West End parents over the past decade:

> West End has fought the racist educational system at every level for many, many years. The West End has consistently fought to improve the quality of education for each and every child in the West End. We have fought the racist tracking system that labels, permanently, children as EMR pupils. We have fought the high suspension practices that push our children out of the schools. We have fought insensitivity of educators and social workers who used their positions to enforce negative decisions upon our children. We have fought the belief held by the city's most prominent educator that "some children are not educable." The fight around the February 12 boundaries is but one more affront to our dignity as full American citizens by the Cincinnati power structure. Blacks and Appalachians are marginal people to this society. They are needed to clean up, wash up and do the dirty work for the society.[38]

Although the West End continued to acknowledge social class bias in the board's action and from time to time weakly objected to the planned boundary changes, the West End's major efforts vis à vis the school board were clearly focused on improving existing programs and services at Porter and Taft.

In fact, a major campaign of the West End's community council during the spring of 1979 was a "Back to Taft" movement designed to lure neighborhood youth to their community schools from other (predominantly white) secondary schools outside the West End. In the words of Sidney Cooper, field representative for the West End Neighborhood Services, "The West End community council is opposed to the boundary change. But since the Board of Education is going to impose their designs on the community, what can we do? We all know the real problem is that (under open enrollment) . . . all our kids are being bussed out." In the same interview with news reporter Barbara Zigli, another prominent West End leader objected to the boundary change but tempered his remarks with qualifications. The Reverend Melvin Jones implied that if the board was "willing to negotiate or improve educational programs and spend more money to fix up the schools in the West End," he would withdraw his opposition.[39] Clearly, at least as reflected in the statements of its leaders, the vested interests of the West End guided its response to the situation.

By the end of March, the Board of Education began to implement plans leading to the full enforcement of boundary changes, school closings, and pupil reassignment in the fall. Letters were sent to parents notifying them of their children's reassignment, and students from the urban Appalachian neighborhoods were scheduled to visit Porter and Taft in April and May to reduce their anxiety over the transfer issue. Meantime, Appalachian parents spoke more and more to the media of boycotts, lawsuits, and wholesale withdrawal from the schools although increasing strains and inconsistencies were apparent among their ranks.

Angry community council meetings continued to be covered by the media late in March. At one especially bitter Lower Price Hill assembly on March 19, the flustered council president, Barbara Desborough, was booed several times for suggesting a compromise plan whereby students would remain at Oyler, the local elementary school, through the ninth grade and move to Taft High School in their tenth grade year.

"No compromise, no compromise," bellowed Ola Raisor. "We'll mob the school board first. Let's see how they like getting beat up. They can put me in the Workhouse, but they can't keep me forever. When I get out, I'll move to Kentucky."[40]

However, despite the obvious opposition of some outspoken residents, community leaders in Lower Price Hill continued to press for compromise.

The press for compromise in Lower Price Hill was never apparent in the stance taken throughout the late spring by Riverside-Sedamsville. In a position paper released in late March and signed by Dan Gilday, president of the Riverside Civic and Welfare Club, and Mae Suttman, president of the Sedamsville community council, opposition to the boundary shift was expressed in the light of safety issues and the devaluation of property in the Riverside-Sedamsville community. City crime statistics were used to portray the West End as unsafe while the board's action was "going to drive the heart of the community, the young families, out of our neighborhood and further west in order to attend (predominantly white) . . . West High."[41]

Future joint community action was permanently eroded by the decision in early April to hire attorney William Flax to represent Riverside-Sedamsville in its confrontation with the board. Flax, a former area coordinator for the John Birch Society, was retained by a group of Riverside-Sedamsville community parents who vowed to raise $10,000 for anticipated legal expenses through door to door solicitations. In commenting on the case, Flax openly expressed his personal opposition to all forms of racial integration and described Porter and Taft as clearly inferior schools to which children were to be sent "against their wishes."[42] Not only was a wedge driven between the two Appalachian communities, but with the hiring of Flax, a gulf opened between the two communities and the black West End.

By the end of the school year, neither community had made much headway in its fight, now in the form of separate skirmishes, with the board. Lower Price Hill residents continued to attend school board meetings in a block, although their numbers had fallen from more than 200 at the height of the struggle in February and early March to about 20 in early May. Although two-thirds of the students at Oyler Elementary School boycotted classes on May 14, the boycott itself was a divisive issue in the community. Some leaders saw the boycott as manipulative and particularly distasteful since a major argument of the community had been that children were being used as pawns by an uncaring board. And, although many children did not attend welcoming programs at Porter and Taft, a few did attend and their reactions, all favorable, were widely published by the media.

Conclusion

The previous case studies have examined school board decisions in two midwestern cities. The Midwest and the East have been especially beleaguered by social, economic, and fiscal strains, creating a particularly harsh climate for residents and school officials alike. However, cities in other regions are having similar difficulties as industries, jobs, and population fulfill their "outward urge."

In order to determine the particular nature of the schooling context in your municipality, an analysis of recent events surrounding both industrial expansion (or shrinkage) and related population changes can be made. Appropriate questions here are:

- What is the size of the central city nearest to your residence?
- How does the central city's population compare with the population size of its surrounding suburbs?
- How has that relationship changed over the past several decades?

The same set of questions can be raised with respect to both the age and race structures of the central city and its surrounding suburban ring. Other community characteristics vital to an understanding of the social milieu concern the social characteristics of school district enrollments, the per capita income of central city and suburban residents, and the nature of central city housing, particularly information on homeownership. Tables 1.1 through 1.5 in this chapter should be consulted by those who reside in the 30 cities for which statistics have been assembled. However, a call or visit to local municipal offices, particularly city planning departments, will yield valuable information on the character of residential populations in your town.

A worthwhile exercise to determine social attitudes held by a given group will take you directly into the community. We suggest that you begin your "survey" by talking to local small business people in your own neighborhood to determine attitudes toward the government's role in social welfare. A good place to begin is with a merchant with whom you regularly trade. The question regarding the federal role in social policy discussed previously under Social Trends might be a good place to start. We do not suggest that you begin by interviewing individuals in neighborhoods where you do not feel comfortable, although we would suggest that perhaps the best way to become at ease in one's surroundings is by discovering what the prevailing values are.

In investigating the nature of the economic well being of your community, you may wish to start by referring again to Table 1.6, showing the profile of manufacturing employment in 30 major cities. Are you in a city and/or region that has enjoyed relatively good economic growth in recent years? Or has your area suffered decline? Closely related to economic functioning, as we have seen, is the annual rate of growth in the property tax base illustrated in Table 1.7. The well being of your community's municipal services rests heavily upon these figures.

Finally, you may wish to chronicle recent events in your neighborhood's schools by consulting newspaper coverage of related events in recent years. Some cities, such as Minneapolis, have been far more tranquil than others in their adaption to school desegregation, school closing, and pupil transfer operations. The ease with which such transitions are made is governed by population, economy and fiscal policy, and actions taken by the local school board.

By acquiring a sense of your city's population and school policy in recent years, you will be prepared to understand the nature of the activity occurring within your community's elementary and secondary schools. The remaining chapters of this volume move us into schools to view the processes and outcomes of administrating, teaching, and learning in these settings.

NOTES

1. "Mobility and Migration Patterns in the City of Cincinnati" (Cincinnati City Planning Department, 1979), p. 31. According to the *1980 President's Rational Urban Policy Report*, p. 12–9, household size is decreasing nationally and although households in 1990 will continue to be predominantly husband-wife families, the number of persons in all households nationally is expected to be no greater than 3.1 persons and is likely to drop as low as 2.4.
2. Ibid., p. 15.

3. *Changing Conditions in Large Metropolitan Areas* (Washington, D.C: U.S. Department of Housing and Urban Development, Office of Policy Development and Research, November 1980), p. 3.
4. R.D. Norton, *City Life Cycles and American Urban Policy* (New York: Academic Press, 1979), p. 84.
5. *The 1980 President's National Urban Policy Report* (Washington D.C., U.S. Department of Housing and Urban Development, August 1980), p. 4–5.
6. Ibid., p. 5–2.
7. Warren E. Miller, Arthur H. Miller, and Edward J. Schneider, *American National Election Studies Data Sourcebook, 1952–1978* (Cambridge: Harvard University Press, 1980) p. 172.
8. Philip E. Converse, Jean D. Dotson, Wendy J. Hoag, and William H. McGee, III, *American Social Attitude Data Sourcebook, 1947–1978* (Cambridge: Harvard University Press, 1980), p. 172.
9. Ibid., p. 61.
10. "Mobility and Migration Patterns in the City of Cincinnati," pp. 10–16.
11. Ibid., p. 16.
12. Norton, *City Life Cycles and American Urban Policy*, p. 123.
13. Ibid., p. 122.
14. Ibid., p. 128.
15. Ibid., pp. 129–130.
16. *The 1980 President's National Urban Policy Report*, p. 6–2.
17. Ibid., p. 6–5.
18. Paul E. Peterson, *School Politics, Chicago Style* (Chicago: University of Chicago Press, 1976), pp. 250–251.
19. *The 1980 President's National Urban Policy Report*, p. 6–2.
20. Ibid., p. 12–12.
21. Ibid., p. 6–18.
22. Paul E. Peterson, *School Politics, Chicago Style*, p. 25.
23. Ibid.
24. Brian J.L. Berry, *The Open Housing Question: Race and Housing in Chicago, 1966–1976* (Cambridge: Ballinger, 1979), p. 152.
25. Ibid., p.79.
26. Ibid., p. 5.
27. Ibid., pp. 200–01.
28. Ibid., p. 203.
29. Ibid., p. 208.
30. Ibid., p. 204.
31. Ibid., p. 205.
32. Ibid., p. 205.
33. Gunnar Myrdal, *An American Dilemma* (New York: Macmillan, 1944), p. iii as quoted in Berry, *The Open Housing Question*, p. 15.
34. Gary L. Fowler, "The Residental Distribution of Urban Appalachians," in William W. Philliber and Clyde B. McCoy, eds. *The Invisible Minority; Urban Appalachians* (Lexington: University Press of Kentucky, 1981), p. 84.
35. Ibid., p. 88.
36. Ibid.

37. "Position Paper on Cincinnati School Board Actions of February 12, 1979," Urban Appalachian Council, March 21, 1979.
38. "The West End and the School Board's Boundary Changes," West End Ad Hoc Committee, March 12, 1979.
39. *Cincinnati Enquirer,* March 31, 1979.
40. *Cincinnati Post,* March 20, 1979.
41. "Position Paper on Cincinnati School Board Action of February 12, 1979," presented by Dan Gilday, President of Riverside Civic and Welfare Club in behalf of Riverside Community and Sedamsville Community.
42. *Cincinnati Enquirer,* April 17, 1979.

The Structure of Power
in Central City School Systems

The political system is the means by which public policy regarding education is developed and translated into educational goals. The general topic of political power in education is extremely complex because it involves several layers of government, from the local through the state to the federal government, and professional and private interest groups. The concern in this chapter will be with the distribution of power among elite civic groups, school board members, minority groups, special interest groups, and the general voting population.

The policies that are generated by these local urban power structures are not easily translated into specific educational practice. Standing between the educational decision-makers and the child in the classroom is a hierarchical educational organization which includes a superintendent, a large central office staff, principals, and teachers. The policies of the decision-makers are shifted, molded, and changed as they pass through this complex organizational structure. This chapter will discuss the political world of these decision-makers, but the reader should understand that this is only the beginning of the story and that later chapters will discuss how the different parts of central city school systems affect educational policy.

Political power is best understood in terms of actions regarding specific issues. The two most important issues facing central city educational systems since the 1970s have been school finance and school desegregation. In a general sense, one can say that school desegregation was the dominant issue of the 1970s and that school finance is the dominant issue of the 1980s. However, there are certainly many other issues that occupy the decision-makers' time: teachers, administrators, school closings, discipline, competency-based education, and community interest groups.

A study of local struggles over school desegregation is one of the best means of understanding power in central city educational systems because the struggles pitted the power of traditional decision-makers against minority populations which had been excluded from power. The results of this struggle have not been a total revolution in the distribution of political power but greater opportunities for the participation of minority groups.

The Evolution of Urban Political Structures

One of the important things to understand about the development of central city educational systems is how the organization of school board elections can allow for the control of school boards by local civic elites. Civic elites are those people who exercise a great deal of power over the development of public policy at a local level without, in most cases, holding offices in government. They usually work through informal networks and civic organizations like a local Chamber of Commerce or service club. Civic elites do not view themselves as a conspiratorial group working behind the scenes for their own self-interest, but they view themselves as enlightened leaders working for the good of the entire community. One study of the occupations of civic leaders found that over 50% were bankers, industrialists, and heads of local businesses. The others included heads of local utilities, newspaper people, civic association executives, clergy, university administrators, and professionals (lawyers, doctors, etc.). Only 5% of this civic leadership was identified as liberals representing labor and civil rights organizations.[1]

What made the power of civic elites over central city educational systems possible were reforms in the early part of the twentieth century which made school board elections nonpartisan and at-large. The key phrase used over and over again during this reform movement was, "Keep the schools out of politics." Keeping the schools out of politics made it difficult for the average citizen to participate in school board politics. Making school board elections nonpartisan meant the exclusion of political parties from school board elections. Making school board elections at-large meant that school board candidates would have to campaign throughout the entire school system rather than in a particular district.[2]

Prior to the above reforms, it was much easier for the average citizen to gain a position on central city school boards because campaigns only had to be conducted within a relatively small geographical area. In addition, school board members could then represent specific groups within the particular district from which they were elected. This method of school board elections was attacked by reform groups in the early part of the twentieth century because it made the public school susceptible to political corruption and patronage. In addition, it was argued that only the best people should serve on school boards because the average citizen did not have a clear understanding of educational issues. Making elections nonpartisan was to eliminate the corruption of party politics from school board elections. Holding elections at-large was designed to assure that school board members represented the general interest of the entire urban population rather than the interests of a particular constituency. It also meant that a school board candidate needed more money and organizational backing to campaign at-large throughout the entire urban area.

What replaced the role of political parties in the wake of these changes were civic organizations which nominated, financed, and campaigned for school board candidates. In some cities these organizations sought broad community participation in the nomination process; in others, the nomination process was tightly controlled by a civic elite. In general, the results were that central city school board members tended to be drawn primarily from the upper social and economic class of the community. "Getting the schools out of politics" meant, in the final analysis, that a place on a central city school board was out of reach of the average citizen.

What became clear after the institution of these reforms was that politics was not eliminated from the schools. One of the important things pointed out in the literature of political science is that nonpartisan elections are really partisan in their results. Willis Hawley argues, in one of the most complete studies of the issue, *Nonpartisan Elections and the Case for Party Politics,*[3] that nonpartisan elections create a partisan bias in favor of Republicans. In Hawley's words, "What is referred to here as the Republican benefit thesis rests in part on the notion that Republicans enjoy a 'natural party organization' outside formal party structures." What this means is that Republicans receive greater support from business and professional groups and that it is easy for these organizations to slip into the role of a political party.

Hawley tested the Republican bias thesis by analyzing elections in 88 cities employing nonpartisan ballots in local elections. He concluded from this analysis that nonpartisan elections did enhance the chances of Republicans being elected. But this situation was not true in every case. The most important factors in differentiating between cities experiencing a partisan bias to nonpartisan elections was size and social class. In terms of city size, Hawley found that cities over 50,000 had a definite partisanship resulting from nonpartisan elections. Hawley wrote with regard to social class and size, "The data presented thus far provide support for the general proposition that nonpartisanship facilitates the election of Republicans in large cities and in those with a relatively high proportion of persons who are unemployed, of low income, of low education, and in low-status occupations."[4] In other words, nonpartisan elections in large urban areas with a concentration of poor people help to assure the power of a civic elite.

Hawley explains this phenomenon in terms of the role of informal business ties and civic organizations. Without the active involvement of political parties, these informal networks assume the dominant role. Hawley emphasizes that there is a positive association between high socioeconomic class and participation in community organizations. It is certainly difficult for a poor person to enter informal business networks or join the local Chamber of Commerce.

In terms of at-large elections, there has been some attempt in recent years to return to election by district. The most notable has been Dallas, Texas which in 1974 ended its method of electing a nine member board by at-large elections. The new method of elections was mandated by the Texas Legislature in 1973 and it divided the school system into nine districts of approximately 89,500 each. The change to election by district did have a significant effect on the social composition of the board of education by allowing for clear representation of minority groups. Since 1974, the Dallas School Board has been composed of six Anglos, two blacks, and one Mexican-American.

One of the past consequences of at-large and nonpartisan elections, was the exclusion of minority members from membership on central city boards of education. Without access to the informal networks of the community elite and having to campaign at large, minority groups found it very difficult to gain representation on central city boards of education. One of the major results of this was segregation in central city school systems.

Because of a lack of power and representation on central city boards of education, minority groups had to find other means for putting political pressure on central city school systems. After the 1954 Supreme Court decision, *Brown* v. *Board of Education of Topeka*, one means of applying pressure on local school systems to end discrimination against and segregation of minority groups was through the federal court system. Another method after the passage of the 1964 Civil Rights Act was to threaten local school districts with a cutoff of funds if discriminatory actions did not end. The 1964 Civil Rights Act required that no institution receiving federal money could discriminate on the basis of race or religion.

What the use of the courts and the federal government by minority groups meant was that local access to political power was not available and that other means outside local power structures had to be used. Since central city school districts had become tightly controlled by civic elites, which tended to exclude minority representation, other levels of government had to be used to gain minority rights. During the 1960s and 1970s the major political upheavals in central city school systems were the result of the intervention of the federal government through court-ordered desegregation and through regulations and guidelines requiring affirmative action to end discrimination. In addition, local minority groups engaged in protest meetings and community organizing as a means of bringing pressure to bear on local school systems.

It is therefore possible to view the fight over school desegregation as a fight for greater representation and control of central city school systems by minority groups. It is not unreasonable to argue that if minority groups had had greater power and representation in central city school systems, there would have been less discrimination and segregation. Consequently, an examination of the issue of desegregation of central city schools can provide insights into urban school politics because of the revealing nature of a political clash between those with power and those trying to gain power.

Central City School Politics and Desegregation

Any discussion over the last two decades of urban school politics must make a distinction between court-ordered desegregation and local efforts to desegregate. Court-ordered desegregation introduced an agency from outside the local school system which monitors and approves desegregation plans. Very often the courts appoint masters to control desegregation plans, masters who, consequently, exercise direct authority over the school system. On the other hand, local efforts to desegregate resulted in a political struggle between local power structures, civil rights groups, and antidesegregation forces. It is in the context of this interplay of political groups that one can gain insight into the workings of central city school politics.

The classic study of local struggles over desegregation is *Political Strategies in Northern School Desegregation* which was the product of a survey study of 91 cities ranging in size from 50,000 to large cities over 250,000. The primary goal of the study was to look at the major political actors in relationship to the characteristics of the cities and the political structure of their educational systems. The study looked specifically at the civil rights movement, the school board, the superintendent, civic leaders, and white protest in relationship to the development of desegregation plans.[5]

The major finding of the study was that civic leaders were the most important political actors in determining school desegregation plans. In the words of the authors, ". . . school desegregation is a political decision made by the elites rather than the masses."[6] Now it should be understood that this particular study does not take a negative view with regard to control by civic elites. It describes the elite as "progressive, concerned citizens" and as "capable leaders." The authors even go so far as to suggest, "In a secular society they the civic elite are the equivalent of a priesthood."[7]

The study found that elites function differently, depending on the characteristics of the particular city. For instance, cities that are large, ethnic, and slow growing tend to have more liberal elites. Liberal in this particular case means a willingness to advocate changing the social structure to solve social and economic problems. Conservative, on the other hand, means a desire to maintain existing social arrangements and adapt the individual to them. Conservative elites tend to be found in smaller, faster-growing cities with a relatively small ethnic population.

Just as the conservatism or liberalism of a civic elite is related to characteristics of the urban environment, so are the general responses to demands for desegregation. Civic elites are more responsive to demands for school desegregation when they are large, have a large blue collar ethnic population, a relatively low level of education, and are not in the West. Now these findings have several important meanings. Obviously, they suggest that the political style of a city is a reflection of size, location, and characteristics of its population. For instance, large cities of the Northeast with a major ethnic population would tend to be more liberal than small cities of the West.

The comparison of city characteristics in terms of actions regarding school desegregation also suggests that blue collar ethnic populations tend to be more liberal than other parts of the population. What is important about this finding is that for many years the blue collar ethnic has been painted as being the most violent resistor to school desegregation. It is suggested that blue collar ethnics, when compared with other members of the white population, tend to be more liberal with regard to race relations. More recent studies tend to confirm this conclusion. In a volume published in 1980, Andrew Greely of the Center for the Study of American Pluralism writes, "Indeed, the Irish Catholics are second only to the Jews in their support of racial integration, and Irish, German, and Italian Catholics are more likely to support racial integration than Anglo-Saxon Protestants living in the North."[8]

In terms of the attitudes of specific groups toward school desegregation, Greely reports responses by ethnic group of the percentage who would be willing to send their children to a mostly black school. The two groups with the highest percentage of positive responses are Hispanics (68%) and Irish Catholics (61%). The next groups in terms of positive responses are Scandinavians (55%), Slavic Catholics (55%), Irish Protestants (54%), and German Catholics (54%). The groups with the lowest positive responses are British Protestants (50%), German Protestants (51%), other Protestants (52%), Italian Catholics (47%), and Jews (50%). Although Italian Catholics and Jews have lower positive responses to the question of whether they would want to send their children to a mostly black school, on a Pro-Integration Scale, Jews rank the highest in terms of supporting integration, whereas Italian Catholics rank about sixth but above the score for Anglo-Saxon.[9] What the difference in these findings suggests is that whereas some groups might support desegregation they might not be willing to send their children to schools with majority black populations.

The more favorable response of civic elites to demands for school desegregation in cities with a high ethnic population could be a result of a combination of ethnic participation in the civic elite or that the civic elite tends to be responsive to ethnic politics when it is an important political factor. The confusing element in this explanation is the finding in *Political Strategies in Northern School Desegregation* that civic leadership is most supportive of civil rights demands if it is strong and sympathetic to the cause of school desegregation. The paradox in this finding is that the stronger the control by the local urban civic elite the less sympathy there is toward demands for school desegregation. Thus, a strong civic leadership is needed for positive actions for school desegregation, but the stronger the civic leadership the less likely they are to favor resonse to demands for desegregation.

The above findings do provide a set of data that can lead to certain tentative generalizations about the characteristics of central city school politics. First, of course, is recognition of the importance of the civic elite's role in controlling central city school policies. Secondly, the liberalism or conservatism is related to the nature of the particular civic elite and the characteristics of the particular city. One could generalize from the above findings that cities in the West with a strong civic leadership, small ethnic population, and high educational level would be more conservative in terms of educational policies than a large city in the Northeast with a weak civic elite, large ethnic population, and low level of education. Now the reader should be cautioned that all generalizations have exceptions but that a generalization plays a useful role when one needs some measure or means of comparison when examining a local situation. In addition, the reader should be reminded that liberal and conservative are being used to describe attitudes about social change.

The methods used by civic elites to influence educational policy involve the exercise of direct power over the election or appointment of school board members and the establishment of informal relationships with the school administration. As we will see later in the case study of Cincinnati, the use of both methods by a strong civic leadership can lead to its domination of educational policy. But, as we shall see in terms of Cincinnati, control of the school board by a civic elite is not the key factor in explaining positive school board action with regard to school desegregation.

The study, *Political Strategies in Northern School Desegregation*, found that the best predictor of the degree of action by central city school boards was not their conservativism nor their liberalism, but the degree of conflict. To understand the importance of the role of conflict, one must consider the general literature on school board politics. One of the guiding goals of the reform movement in the early part of the twentieth century was the reduction of conflict between school board members and between school board members and the school superintendent. The creation of harmony was considered the best means of preparing for the development of enlightened educational policies. For civic elites, a reduction of the degree of conflict on school boards often meant that they were securely in control. School administrators preferred harmony on the school board because conflict often meant that the school administration had to play politics with different factions. A school superintendent's job is often in jeopardy if school board members begin to fight among themselves. Therefore, the politics of consensus is desired by both civic elites and school administrators.

The lack of conflict in both school board elections and activities is one of the important findings of Zeigler and Jennings in their study, *Governing American Schools: Political Interaction in Local School Districts*.[10] They found that in most school board elections conflict over educational issues does not play an important role, and when conflict does occur it is often over how a school board member acts rather than the substance of educational policy. This politics of consensus continues when individuals are finally elected to the board. There tends to be a general consensus with regard to policy between school board members and between board members and the superintendent. The one major exception to this situation is when there are school board members who are from lower social and economic classes. This creates a conflict between the style and goals of the civic elite and the styles and goals of those outside that elite.

The fight over school desegregation has caused the major disruption of the consensus style of school board politics. The civil rights movement led to a demand for minority representation on school boards and for school boards to take action on a very divisive issue. The greatest conflict on school boards over desegregation occurred in those cities with the highest number of black elected officials and where elections are most affected by organized citizens groups which nominate and campaign for candidates.

The importance of the role of conflict in determining school board actions with regard to school desegregation is probably directly related to the threat the civil rights movement posed for established civic elites. It is possible that civic elites felt they could only maintain their power by acting on school desegregation. This would explain why strong civic leadership and school board conflict are both related to action regarding school integration. Although a school board might be controlled by a liberal civic leadership, it, is not driven to action until the leadership of that elite is threatened. One would assume that the action emerging from those sets of circumstances would be an integration plan which corresponded to values of the civic elite. As we shall see, this is exactly what happened in the case of Cincinnati.

The School Superintendent

The importance of the discussion of political responses to demands for school desegregation is what it highlights regarding the nature of central city school politics. As a period when established power structures were brought under attack, political actions and relationships became more obvious. One of the political actors forced to struggle for survival in a sea of controversy was the central city school superintendent. Like the modern central city school board, the modern central city school superintendent was a product of the reforms of the early part of the twentieth century.

When the school desegregation issues began to hit the central city school systems in the late 1960s and 1970s, central city school superintendents had pretty much established their role as powerful chief executives. Part of the reform movement in the early part of the twentieth century involved the professionalization of school administrators. As professionalization took place, the role of school superintendent began to be modeled after that of the business person. Adopting techniques from business management, the central city school superintendent began to function like the leader of a large corporation who was running a series of educational factories. The values associated with this role for the superintendent were very much in agreement with the values of the civic elite. As superintendents adopted this corporate model of school management, school boards began to make a clearer distinction between policy and administration. Within this framework, school boards were to make policy and superintendents were to administer that policy. One often-stated rule was that school boards were not to interfere with the superintendent's administration of the school system. The result was that the role and importance of the central city school superintendent increased greatly through the twentieth century.

During periods of relative calm in the central city school system, superintendents adopted the style of consensus politics. Their power was often firmly linked to support from the local civic leadership. Superintendents tended to join and attend the same civic organizations patronized by the civic elite. School desegregation threatened this whole system of relationships. The management of the schools was attacked because of the existence of segregation, consequently the superintendent often came under fire. Minority demands for representation and power often threatened the superintendent's base of power with the civic elite. Caught between the power struggle of the civil rights movement and the civic elite, many superintendents found themselves without jobs.

Superintendents were often forced to take an active leadership role when the school system was caught between an active and unified civil rights campaign and a civic elite which was conservative. The superintendent was forced to act as a mediator between the two opposing forces. These conditions were heightened if there were a number of black elected officials in the community. In some communities the superintendent took an aggressive role in trying to handle the desegregation issue; in other communities the superintendent was forced to act because of political pressures. The more aggressive superintendents also tended to be the most political in terms of having established wide contacts throughout the community.[11]

The important thing to understand about the political role of superintendents in this context is that they must often walk a very narrow tight rope between the pressures of competing political forces. At stake in this juggling act is not only the welfare of the school system but also the superintendent's job. Offending the civic elite could bring an immediate call from the school board to find a new superintendent. Offending community groups could lead to demonstrations and demands for removing the superintendent from office. The role of central city school superintendent is certainly one of the most demanding in our society, requiring professional knowledge about the management of educational systems and the political sophistication to survive among contending political forces. One can understand why a superintendent might prefer consensus politics and control by a strong civic leadership to avoid the politics of conflict.

Superintendents, school boards, and the whole public educational system became more politicized because of the desegregation movement of the 1970s. As Willie and Greenblatt write in their study of 10 school systems under court-ordered school desegregation, "It is only recently that educators have admitted that public school systems are subject to the same political pressures as other public institutions. With urban areas containing many diverse groups within their population, it has become inevitable that these groups will vie for control of the public school system."[12]

The issue of school desegregation moved school politics from the pattern of consensus politics dominated by the power of civic elites to a new era when civic elites must now more openly compete with other groups for control of school systems. As Willie and Greenblatt state, "Desegregation has made subdominant groups more aware of the effect they may have on educational change. . . . These groups have enabled parents who once conceived of themselves as powerless to use their collective influence to rectify situations that are unsatisfactory to them."[13] This has not meant the end of the power of civic elites over central city school systems but it has forced them to work in a broader political arena. As we shall see in the case study of Cincinnati, the civic elite were able to weather the storm of desegregation but they were forced to act in new ways.

A Case Study: Central City School Politics in Cincinnati

Cincinnati school politics followed the pattern of domination by a civic elite until a major political battle over school desegregation in the early 1970s forced a realignment of elite control. During periods of strong control by civic elites in Cincinnati, school superintendents were given a good deal of independent power in the management of the school system and they experienced a good deal of job security. Just the opposite conditions occurred during periods of conflict over school desegregation. Following the conflict over school desegregation, the local civic elite tended to exert greater control over the superintendent. The decade of the 1980s opened with the civic elite still in control of the board but with minority representation and a less independent superintendent. It is this alignment of forces that began the management of financial decline of the school system in the early 1980s.

The emergence of elite control in the early part of the twentieth century was primarily the work of a local physician, John Withrow. He had a major responsibility for the passage of the small school board bill by the Ohio legislature in 1913 which reduced the size of school boards and created at-large and nonpartisan elections. After passage of the legislation, Withrow worked to create an organization to replace the traditional role of political parties in school board elections. The first hint of the attempt to create this type of organization can be found in a letter Withrow wrote in 1913 to Frank Dyer, a former superintendent of the Cincinnati schools, and in 1913, superintendent of the Boston schools. Dyer was to return to Cincinnati after his retirement from the Boston schools to serve as a school board member from 1920 to 1931 with the support of the organization eventually created by Withrow. After the passage of the small school board bill in 1913, Withrow wrote to Dyer, "The small school board bill has passed and I am hoping to be set free from further cares and worries in connection with public education. I can't however, help being anxious about getting the proper board under the new laws." What he wanted from Dyer was advice about the creation of an organization that would assure a "proper board." Withrow continued the letter, "Therefore I write you to send me the method of formation of the Boston school council or association, or whatever they call that organization that they have there, as I am told, entirely apart from the legally elected board. I am wanting here to start a federated education council . . . to make nominations for the school board and express opinions on the fitness of all nominations made from any other source."[14]

It is clear from Withrow's letter that he viewed this form of organization as a method of circumventing the nonpartisan parts of the 1913 small school board bill. Withrow stated in his letter to Dyer, "Now that the new law forbids any political party, by primary or convention, from naming candidates for the Board of Education, these candidates are to be nominated by petition only. What I want to know is, is there a similar or substantially similar committee or council or federation in Boston?" There is no record of Dyer's response to Withrow's letter. What Withrow did in Cincinnati in 1913 was to form a Citizen's Council on Public Education composed of representatives of the leading civic organizations in the community. The Citizen's Council on Public Education used a nominating committee to select school board candidates and a campaign committee to assure their election. In 1921, the nominating and campaign committees were merged and absorbed the original organization under the banner of the Citizens School Committee.

Robert Curry, the former acting superintendent of the Cincinnati Public Schools, whose career in the Cincinnati system spanned a half century, from 1925 to 1975, wrote in the 1970s, "Until the late 1960s, the board members, with few exceptions, had been nominated by the Citizens School Committee and had not been opposed by other candidates." Later, reminiscing about his years in the schools, Curry wrote, "The committee, a group organized by Dr. Withrow many years earlier, had the sole function of nominating members to run for the Board of Education. Their nomination was tantamount to election. Indeed, there was no campaigning in the usual sense of the word." As an example, Curry cited the case in the 1960s when Harry Hopkins, "a nominee of the Citizen's School Committee, was elected to the board, he was in Europe as a representative of his company during most of November."

Harry Hopkins, like many of the nominees of the Citizens School Committee, was an established member of the business community as vice-president of the Tool Steel Gear & Pinion Company.[15]

Except for the 1937 election, and internal strife within the Citizens School Committee between 1941 and 1945 over support of an independent candidate, nothing seriously threatened the Committee's control of the school board between 1921 and the period of conflict over school desegregation in the late 1960s and early 1970s. The long tenure of many of the board's presidents reflects the stability of the Committee's domination of the board. John Withrow was president for the 10-year period between 1914 and 1924. Between 1924 and 1939 there were four different presidents before the 19-year reign of Dr. Fred Heinold, from 1940 until his death in 1959. And in the 1960s there were only two different presidents with one of them being the previously mentioned Harry Hopkins who managed to be elected while working in Europe.

During the early stages of the civil rights movement in the 1950s and early 1960s, the civic elite maintained a tight control over the school board. The unofficial head of the business community during this period was Neil McElroy, the president of Proctor & Gamble, one of the leading international corporations headquartered in Cincinnati. During the 1950s, McElroy served as Secretary of Defense under President Eisenhower and as chairman of the White House Conference on Education. Roger Crafts, an active member of the Citizens School Committee in the 1950s and president of the organization in the late 1960s stated, in reference to the period, "Those were the Neil McElroy days." As Crafts describes the period, business leaders would gather informally with Neil McElroy to decide educational and other civic issues. Crafts stated, "They would go to lunch and discuss a particular program. If they would decide what to support, Neil McElroy would just point his finger at Zimmer from the Gas & Electric Company, Lazarus from Federated Department Stores—right around the table saying your share is $6,000, your share is $5,000 . . ."[16]

While Neil McElroy was unofficial leader of the business community, an insurance executive, Ewart Simpkinson, functioned as official head of the Citizens School Committee. It was his energy and hard work that kept the organization running smoothly. The most important function of the Citizens School Committee was the nomination and campaigning for school board candidates. Simpkinson assured that the seven members of the nominating committee of the Citizens School Committee were representative of the elite of the Cincinnati business community. Simpkinson described his philosophy in a letter to Ralph Lazarus, a member and later chairman of the board of directors of Federated Department Stores, a national retail corporation with headquarters in Cincinnati. Federated had 20 divisions including Bloomingdale's, Abraham and Straus, Bullock's, and I. Magnin. Simpkinson wrote Lazarus, "It is important for us to have top quality membership because our job is to select and persuade high-grade citizens for this responsible work in our city." His conception of high-grade citizens included primarily businessmen and executives from firms like Proctor & Gamble, the Kroger Company, Federated Department Stores, and heads of local banks and utilities.[17]

The type of efforts made to control the membership of the Board of Education is most strikingly revealed in a letter Simpkinson wrote in 1959 to Kelly Siddall, vice-president of Proctor & Gamble, after the president of the board had unexpectedly died of a heart attack during a trip to Cleveland. "This is a tragedy, but it also gives us a golden opportunity to get someone on the Board of Education without a competitive election." Simpkinson emphasized that, "Whomever we advise the Board of Elections . . . that name is guaranteed election. This means that we can get the caliber of man who would be possibly unavailable if he had to run under a competitive public election." In a "PPS" at the bottom of the letter, Simpkinson wrote, "Someone from the Proctor & Gamble organization would be ideal if you could make the suggestion."[18]

Minorities on the Board

When the civil rights movement and the demand for school desegregation began to be felt in the 1950s, the civic elite realized that something needed to be done about minority representation on the Board of Education. The one thing that the leadership wanted to assure was that minority representation would be congruent with the values of the civic leaders. As one member of the Citizens School Committee wrote Simpkinson in 1959, "I think we will be faced with the decision of having to nominate someone from the minority community in this next election. . . ."[19] For this purpose, Simpkinson had appointed to the Nominating Committee a local black physician, Charles Dillard. In 1959, the Nominating Committee membership included Rueben Hays, chairman of the board of the First National Bank of Cincinnati; Walter Beckjord, chairman of the board of Cincinnati Gas and Electric Company; Kelly Siddall, administrative vice-president of Proctor & Gamble; Mary Schloss, the wife of the president of Kahn's Meat Company; Edward Wagner, president of Wagner's Sons Company; and Arthur M. O'Connell, vice-president of Thomas E. Wood Company.

No minority candidate was nominated by the Citizens School Committee in 1959, but a beginning was made in the search for the "right" black candidate. In 1961, another attempt was made to nominate a minority candidate. In a letter to Carlton Hill, the president of the Fifth-Third Union Trust Company, Simpkinson wrote, "The public does not yet realize that we are going through a fairly critical period of this phase of the Citizens School Committee activities. Having Dr. Dillard on the nominating committee two years ago was the first time a Negro candidate had ever been on this committee." Simpkinson explained the continuation of the search for a minority candidate. "Having the counsel and advice of Dr. Clarke this time made it possible to develop a good list of prospects from the Negro community and it was very significant that your committee was ready to endorse one of these candidates. . . ."[20]

Though no minority candidate was nominated in 1961, there was consideration given to using the strategy of appointment as opposed to election. Simpkinson outlined this strategy in another 1961 letter to the head of Fifth-Third Union Trust Company. Simpkinson explained to Carlton Hill, "If we should endorse a colored person, we can be reasonably sure that there might be a white candidate running independently and if he were a good one our candidate might well be defeated." The strategy suggested by Simpkinson was, "If a colored person were put on the Board of Education by appointment and then endorsed by us he would have a much better chance of being elected and he would feel more welcome and we might be able to get a more effective person."[21]

The method of appointment did not have to be used when finally, in 1964, the nominating committee selected its first black candidate, Calvin Conliffe, for the Board of Education. Conliffe was more representative of the corporate elite in the Citizens School Committee than of the local minority community. When Conliffe was elected in 1964, he was an engineer, inventor, and manager for the General Electric Company.

Conliffe's election to the board was the attempt by the civic leadership to deal with the issue of school desegregation by allowing token minority representation without making any major effort to develop a plan for integration of the students. In fact, the Board of Education, like most other central city school boards of the period, was fighting vigorously in the courts against a school desegregation suit brought against the system by the NAACP. The school board eventually won this suit in 1967, but there was little opportunity for cheering by the civic elite as the Citizens School Committee suffered a major defeat in the school board elections and entered a period that would lead to major changes in the political climate of the schools.

In 1967, a series of events occurred that would force the civic leadership in Cincinnati to seek wider involvement of the population in the control of the schools. The first event, which marked the beginning of financial problems that would plague the school system through the 1970s and 1980s, was the issuance of a special report on the financial crisis. The eventual outcome of this concern was the creation of a citizen's task force to investigate the causes of public discontent with the schools. The second event was the election defeat of two candidates of the Citizens School Committee by two candidates preaching fiscal conservatism and the need for increased discipline in the schools. These two non-Citizens School Committee members on the board were more conservative in political philosophy and racial attitudes than had been the candidates of the civic leadership.

Citizen's Task Force

Both the report of the citizen's task force and the defeat of the two candidates were to have profound effect on the organization of the Citizens School Committee. The citizen's task force was called Cincinnatians United for Good Schools and its leadership was drawn from the ranks of the civic elite with its chairman being John R. Bullock, a partner in the prestigious law firm of Taft, Stettinius, and Hollister; the secretary-treasurer was Clint Pace, manager of community affairs and shareholder relations for Proctor and Gamble. Bullock's leadership of the task force set the stage for Taft, Stettinius, and Hollister to assume a commanding role in school board affairs in the late 1970s and 1980s.

The Cincinnatians United for Good Schools hired Roald Campbell, at that time Dean of the Graduate School of Education at the University of Chicago and the Midwest Administration Center of the University of Chicago, to conduct a survey of the Cincinnati schools. In their report, delivered in 1968, they spoke directly to the issue of the limited representation of the Citizens School Committee. The report stated, "Traditionally, the Citizens School Committee, a nonpartisan organization which has existed since 1914, has been the principal sponsoring group for school board candidates." But in a recommendation that was obviously critical of the Citizens School Committee, the report argued, "If the Citizens School Committee be retained, its membership should be broadened to include representatives from many other segments and organizations of the city. The purpose of the Citizens School Committee should be to get wide participation in selecting broadly representative, able, and devoted citizens for school board membership." Besides calling for broader representation within the Citizens School Committee, the survey report recognized that the heart of the problem was the structure of school board elections and the report recommended that, "Cincinnati and other major city districts in Ohio may wish to join in seeking to amend the law to permit 9 to 11 board members, the majority elected at large and the remainder from subdivisions of the city."[22]

Although nothing concrete was done about changing Ohio law, there was a move to throw open the doors of the Citizens School Committee to greater community participation. The period of the 1960s was, of course, one in which black communities in most urban areas were making greater demands for participation in the decision-making processes. The Citizens School Committee had, as mentioned earlier in this chapter, controlled the entry of minority representation on the school board by carefully nominating a black candidate they felt reflected their values.

With demands from the black community and the recommendations of the school survey, the Citizens School Committee adopted a new constitution in 1969 which created an essentially new organization composed of individual members and delegates from 31 organizations that supposedly represented the major parts of the Cincinnati population. With this broader based representation, the Citizens School Committee was able to nominate four candidates who could capture all four of the positions available on the board in the 1969 election.

Ironically, the broader based representation that made it possible for the Citizens School Committee to win in 1969 eventually caused the civic elite to withdraw its support within four years. In addition, two of the candidates that won in 1969 would pave the way for the creation of a new organization that would win support of the civic elite and replace the dominant role of the Citizen's School Committee. One of these candidates was Charles Lindberg, a partner at Taft, Stettinius, and Hollister and representative of the civic leadership in the broader range of candidates in the 1969 election. It was during this period of the late 1960s and 1970s that Neil McElroy's leadership of the Cincinnati business community was beginning to slip because of an illness which ended in his death. Leadership, at least in terms of school board politics, would be taken over by Taft, Stettinius, and Hollister. The other candidate, Mary Schloss, would prove to be the link between the past and future control by the civic elite. She had served as recording secretary of the Citizens School Committee in the 1950s and had continued her active role in the organization until her nomination in 1969. After her election in 1969, she remained on the board into the 1980s. She was a lawyer and her husband was president of a major Cincinnati meat processing firm and vice-president of the Consolidated Foods Corporation of Chicago. The other two candidates were supposed to reflect the broader representation of the Citizens School Committee. One was a black minister and the other was a housewife.

The contradiction between attempts to be broadly representative of the community and assure that actions taken by the school board reflected the wishes of the civic elite began to become apparent in 1971 when Calvin Conliffe, the black engineer from General Electric who had been handpicked for the board in the 1960s, resigned. In his place, the board appointed Ron Temple, a black faculty member at the University of Cincinnati and a militant in terms of his strong advocacy of school desegregation. Temple's appointment initiated a period of major school board conflict and action regarding school desegregation.

If we cast these events in the framework of previously discussed patterns of central city school politics, we can see that this pattern was fairly typical, with a school board controlled by a civic elite that does little about school desegregation until conflict occurs on the board. And, as we shall see, the conservatism of the civic elite is not a factor in initiating action but it is a factor in the type of action taken. In addition, it is important to emphasize that the civic elite did not lose control because of the battle over school desegregation, but it did lose some of its power.

The appointment of Temple to the school board led to a division between those labeled as liberal and those labeled as conservative, with the liberals having the majority of power until 1974. The terms "liberal" and "conservative" in this particular case meant attitudes toward school desegregation, with liberals being in favor of immediate and complete desegregation and conservatives in favor of a more gradual approach.

What became the center of controversy was a report issued by a Citizen's Task Force on Racial Isolation in the Schools. The study was commissioned by the school board in 1972 and the report was delivered in early 1973. The majority report of the *Task Force on Racial Isolation in the Schools* called for immediate desegregation of the schools, both racially and socioeconomically. In addition, a minority report was submitted which created a shouting match at the Board meeting over whether or not it should be distributed with the majority report. The minority report was written by David Schiering, a lawyer at Taft, Stettinius, and Hollister, and school board member in the late 1970s and early 1980s (serving as president in 1983). It was Schiering's minority report that eventually became the basic plan for school desegregation in Cincinnati.

The report on *Racial Isolation in the Schools* heightened the already existing tension between the liberal and conservative factions on the Board and forced a reorganization of board politics. Board conservatives withdrew from the Citizens School Committee and formed a new organization called the Better Neighborhood Schools Committee with leadership coming from the law firm of Taft, Stettinius, and Hollister. What this meant was that the civic leadership had abandoned their traditional organization because of its growing liberal temperament resulting from broader representation. Under the banner of the Better

Neighborhood Schools Committee, conservatives were able to capture a majority of positions on the board in the 1973 election.

After the 1973 election, the lame duck majority on the board passed a resolution calling for the desegregation of the schools both racially and socioeconomically, beginning in 1974. When the new conservative board came to power in 1974, they rescinded that resolution and began to implement the basic ideas that had been contained in David Schiering's minority report on *Racial Isolation in the Schools.* This became the basic strategy for handling desegregation in Cincinnati and set the outline for school development for the next two decades.

Against the background of school politics around the country, Cincinnati followed several typical patterns. First, it was the civic leadership that did have the major responsibility for implementation of a school desegregation plan. Secondly, it only occurred after major conflict on the Board of Education. In addition, the situation forced the civic leadership to realign itself to assure domination of the board. It also meant that the form desegregation would take would follow the interests and values of the civic elite. In this context, the school desegregation plan for the Cincinnati schools followed the traditional desires of the civic elite for a differentiated and specialized educational system.

One of the traditional patterns of educational policy advocated by civic leadership was for specialized educational programs which tended to follow social class lines. After the rise to power of the Citizens School Committee in the 1920s, an increasing emphasis was placed on high schools specializing in the future social destinations of the students. Cincinnati established a classical high school, Walnut Hills, which was to provide preparation for college. As one superintendent expressed it in the 1920s, Walnut Hills was to be for the managers and inventors and the other schools were to be for the workers. In addition, Cincinnati instituted a series of specialized trade schools in the 1920s to provide trained workers for Cincinnati industry. Under the power of elite control, education was organized to serve the needs of particular social groups. Those needs, of course, were defined by an elite group which had an interest in preserving their own status and power through the educational system.

Alternative Schools

When the civic elite finally gave direction to school desegregation in 1974, they chose an approach that was least threatening to their interests in the educational system. This was a desegregation plan with a primary focus on magnet or alternative schools and voluntary integration. This was in contrast to the liberal approach of forced integration by race and socioeconomic class. The magnet school idea, which had been adopted by many other urban systems in the country, placed emphasis upon specialized schools that would attract students from around the city and would attempt to achieve a racial balance. The hope was that racial balance would be achieved through voluntary actions without disturbing the role of the schools in promoting social segregation.

Indeed, magnet schools became a focus of desegregation effort during the same period that increased attention was being given to vocational education. The combination of magnet schools and vocational education created a much more elaborately separated educational program. The push for expanded vocational education in Ohio had begun in 1969 when the governor of the state had made vocational education an important part of his plan for industrial development and decreasing unemployment. On a national level it was being argued that vocational education needed to be expanded to aid the disadvantaged and end problems of chronic unemployment. These arguments tended to contain a socioeconomic bias because there was often an assumption that it would be the children of the poor and lower middle class that would fill the ranks of expanded vocational programs. Cincinnati adopted its plan for vocational education in 1970 which called for the addition of vocational facilities to five high schools by 1976.

The social class orientation of the vocational additions to the high schools was made very specific by the superintendent of the Cincinnati schools in 1971 when, after reporting to the Board that the schools would receive the largest construction grant ever approved by the State Board of Education for building vocational facilities, he stated, "The proposition before all citizens who wish to break the poverty cycle is simple. If the poverty cycle is to be broken, employment will be a factor."[23] The new vocational facilities were built during the same period that alternative schools began to appear.

The first two alternative or magnet schools, the School for Creative and Performing Arts and the City-Wide Learning Academy, were established in 1973. In 1974, the board members adopted a number of resolutions affirming their support of alternative schools as the key to racial desegregation. In the following year, alternative programs were begun in Montessori education, fundamentals, reading, math and science, French/English and multi-age. These additional programs in 1975 pushed the alternative school programs down into the elementary grades which in many ways changed some basic features of elementary education. There had existed a tradition of secondary students attending particular schools for special programs but not the elementary age group. Desegregation had made educational specialization a possibility in the lower grades.

David Schiering stated in an interview in 1982 that the main concern of those labeled conservatives in the school desegregation fight was with "white flight" and what they considered would be the subsequent decline of the city. They believed that immediate desegregation with mandatory busing would spark an increased movement of middle-class whites to the suburbs, leaving the city as a haven for minority groups and the poor. One of the main goals of the alternative school program was to create special programs that would be so attractive that they would keep the middle class in the city and hopefully attract many to return to urban living.[24]

Given the above argument and concern about white flight, one could argue that one of the major goals of the conservative school desegregation plan was to satisfy the perceived needs and desires of the middle class. In contrast, immediate and forced desegregation would have had as its major area of concern the actual integration of minority and economic groups. By trying to balance middle class desires and the need to achieve racial integration, the conservative Board of Education neglected the issue of the integration of different economic groups. In fact, the school system seemed to accept the fact of continuing segregation according to social class with the expansion of vocational education assuring continued segregation of economic groups.

Whereas the early 1970s can be pictured as a triumph of civic leadership over opposing forces, the late 1970s and early 1980s can be pictured as a period of greater assertion of the role of the Board of Education and a decline in the relative power and position of the superintendent. During this period, the school system was rocked with a number of issues other than school desegregation. It was closed several times because of a financial crisis, energy shortage, and teacher strike. In addition, there was a great deal of controversy surrounding the issue of school closings. All of these issues, with the exception of the energy shortage, will be discussed in more detail in later chapters. The major concern at this point is how the management of these continued crises affected the shifts of power within the school system.

As discussed earlier in the chapter, central city school superintendents were often caught between the demands of the civil rights movement and the traditional power of the civic elite. This was the plight of Superintendent Donald Waldrip, who was hired by the liberal-dominated board in 1972 to lead the school desegregation effort. But he quickly discovered that his fortunes were tied to the political composition of the board. When the liberals were defeated in 1973, there was an attempt to assure Mr. Waldrip's place in the system by passage of a resolution extending his contract. This bitter battle was won; however, it was eventually undone by the conservative-dominated Board in 1976 when board members forced Waldrip to resign and accept a contract as a consultant to the school system.

What is significant about Waldrip's successor and present superintendent, James Jacobs, is that he is a member of the central office staff of the school system rather than a national educational leader brought into the school system. Except for acting superintendents, Cincinnati has had a long history of searching for national names to command the school system. This type of search gives a great deal of prestige and promise of power to the role of school superintendent. It fits the traditional model of educational management, with the Board of Education leaving primary administrative control in the hands of a strong leader.

Hiring from within the system creates a different set of expectations regarding the role of superintendent. Rather than being viewed as the great leader coming from outside, the insider is viewed as a competent manager who has already proven his or her worth to the leaders of the community. The outsider must establish relationships with community leaders but this is after assuming the role of superintendent. On the other hand, the insider has already established those relationships and is immediately burdened with political debts upon assuming office. Since there is an immediate assumption of political debts on the part of the insider, there is less freedom of action in relationship to the elite leadership of the community. One could argue from this perspective that hiring from within the system rather than bringing in the leader from outside the system weakens the role of the superintendent.

Weakening the role of the superintendent often means strengthening the role of the Board of Education or civic leadership. In fact, there is evidence for greater involvement of the civic leadership in the actual management of the schools. To a certain extent it might reflect an increased level of distrust of the civic leadership with educational administrators. Local civic leadership has become more involved in financial management as the school system has encountered one financial crisis after another.

In 1977, the business community in Cincinnati formed the Cincinnati Business Committee to assist the school system with a wide range of problems. In 1978, the Cincinnati Business Committee committed themselves to aid in the reorganization of the school system to provide greater efficiency in purchasing, food service maintenance, conservation, and finance. In 1979, the Cincinnati Business Committee developed an administrative reorganization plan for the school system, and in 1980, the school system carried out a whole list of recommendations from various task forces organized by the Cincinnati Business Committee. At the Board of Education meeting on January 14, 1980, the superintendent of schools listed the contributions of the business group in helping to make decisions which led to the reduction of the number of school administrators, the closing of school buildings, and reducing costs in transportation and energy.[25]

The Cincinnati Business Committee continued the strong link between Proctor & Gamble, one of Cincinnati's largest corporations, and the school system. Proctor & Gamble donated the time of one of its executives, Tom Collins, to serve as executive director of the Cincinnati Business Committee. In addition, the plan for the administrative reorganization of the school system was completed in 1979 under the leadership of one Lloyd Crawley of the Management Systems Department of Proctor & Gamble. In one sense Proctor & Gamble and the Cincinnati Business Committee have functioned as a shadow government working behind the scenes to make major policy decisions. The superintendent gave recognition to this role at a board meeting when he stated, "You should understand that none of these reports would be possible without the assistance of a man who has worked behind the scenes all year. . . . I speak of the executive director, Tom Collins."[26]

The administrative reorganization of the school system planned by the Cincinnati Business Committee with primary help from Proctor & Gamble reflected the distrust the business community had of the school administration. During the battle over school desegregation in the early 1970s, conservatives on the board were highly critical of the creation of area superintendents as part of the liberal plan to more closely link the schools to the community. It was condemned as an unnecessary expansion of administrative staff and an added burden to an already financially strained school system.

In fact, one of the problems faced by Cincinnati and most other school systems was the rapid expansion of administrative staffs during the 1970s. Cincinnati in 1970 had 3.38 administrators for every 1,000 pupils. This number had steadily increased until 1977 when there were 4.45 administrators for every 1,000 pupils. This represented an increase of more than one administrator for every 1,000 students. This increase was significant but it was less than other central city systems. For instance, the mean average for central city school systems in 1977 was 5.2 administrators for every 1,000 students. Cities with ratios higher than Cincinnati were New Orleans with 6.7, Indianapolis with 7.6, Tulsa with 7.4, and Oklahoma City with 8.8.[27] In 1980, following the recommendations of the Cincinnati Business Committee, 54 administrative positions were eliminated from the school system.[28]

With the increased involvement of the business community in the schools and a superintendent who was primarily dependent on local support for his power, the goals of the educational system became more conservative. For instance, in 1978 the school system adopted nine specific goals which included developing closer relationships between industry and the schools. In the words of the superintendent, "Our goal is to establish at least 10 corporate relationships from which our schools will benefit through the knowledge, understanding, and expertise of these businessmen and women. We also want to develop guidelines and procedures for the 'Adopt-a-School' program in which a business or organization will work closely with its 'adopted' school." This plan, which was eventually implemented, was developed by the Cincinnati Business Committee.[29]

Three of the other eight goals for that particular year were directed specifically at issues dealing with financial and administrative efficiency. Another goal was improving discipline and another was implementing federal mandates regarding special education. Only two of the remaining three goals dealt with instruction and the other goal dealt with racial integration of the schools. The two goals dealing directly with the educational program involved improving basic skills and developing a competency-based educational program.

There was nothing in these goals that reflected liberal concerns about equality of educational opportunity and equality of opportunity. Even the goal of improving racial balance was dependent upon the expansion of alternative schools. As mentioned before, alternative schools were the more conservative approach to school desegregation. This conservatism was reflected in a plan to establish an alternative military high school. The only thing that prevented the establishment of the military high school was the refusal of the Defense Department in 1979 to provide funding for the project. By 1982, alternative schools had expanded to include about 20 different programs located at approximately 40 different schools. The majority of alternative school programs were designed for talented students. In 1982, six elementary schools and five junior highs had college preparatory programs. In addition, there were alternative programs in math and science, French bilingual, German bilingual, Spanish bilingual, creative and performing arts, and international studies. The alternative programs for the noncollege bound included an Applied Arts Academy, an Academy of Physical Education and a City-Wide Learning Community.

Thus, the goal of improving racial balance, which extended into the 1980s, emphasized an alternative school program which could be argued was directed primarily at keeping the middle class in the school system. The two educational goals in 1978 of improving basic skills and establishing a competency-based education program eventually had to face the realities of financial problems and planned reductions. In June of 1979, the superintendent was forced to announce that it would be impossible to implement a competency-based program once it was established because of a lack of money.[30]

With the direct involvement of the business community in the schools, the goals and plans remained essentially the same. In 1980, the only differences between the goals that year and those for 1978 were the dropping of competency-based education and the inclusion of the development of a staff improvement program. By the 1980s, the majority of concern was being directed toward financial issues and the political problems surrounding the closing of schools. Lost in the financial discussions were the earlier demands of civil rights groups and liberals for integration by race and social class, and attempts to provide greater equality of opportunity and equality of educational opportunity. Restoration of control by the civic elite after the civil rights struggle of the early 1970s resulted in the implementation of primarily conservative educational policies and greater involvement of the business community in the administration of the schools.

Conclusion: How to Analyze the Political Structure of Central City Schooling

The triumph of conservative control in Cincinnati did not have exactly the same parallels in other cities. The reader will recall from the previous discussion that civic leadership in eastern ethnic urban centers tended to be more liberal than the civic leadership in an urban center like Cincinnati. But the story of political control in Cincinnati does provide a general framework for analyzing the political structure of central city school systems in the United States. Of major importance is the relationship of civic elites to formal and informal control of educational policy.

If an individual were embarking on the task of understanding the role of the civic elite within his or her own central city school system, then one of the first things that must be considered is the methods of election to the school board. Not all school systems have at-large elections. Some do have elections by district which makes it more difficult for the civic elite to exercise control of the election process. But in either the case of district or at-large elections the important thing to identify is the existence of organizations that nominate school board candidates and campaign for their election. If these organizations exist, then the individual analyzing the school system should examine who is represented on the nominating boards of those organizations. In some cases these organizations contain a broad representation of the community; in others they are tightly controlled by local civic leadership. In cities that have election by district, it is possible to find a variety of different community organizations working within particular districts. In some cities, like Chicago, where the mayor appoints school board members, the investigator should examine the process by which names are recommended to the mayor. These recommendations may come from an advisory group dominated by a particular community group.

After examining the pathways to the school board, the investigator should look closely at the social composition of the Board of Education. Several questions need to be asked regarding the representativeness of the Board of Education. The first is whether the board's membership reflects the social composition of the community. If, for instance, the board is primarily composed of leading business people and professionals, then one could suspect control of the board by a local elite. In making this type of analysis, one should keep in mind that even though minority groups are represented by minority members, these individuals might not be representative of their communities. For instance, a black board member who is also an insurance executive might not be considered representative of a local black community experiencing high levels of unemployment and poverty.

Social composition does not tell the whole story regarding representation. Of equal importance is the kind of representation exercised by board members. For instance, the arguments for control by civic elites were always based on the concept of trustee representation which means acting in terms of what one considers to be the best interests of the community. On the other hand, delegate representation tried to act according to the expressed desires of the community. One can analyze board decisions to determine whether the Board of Education is acting as a trustee or delegate representative.

Another important consideration in this context is the degree of power and control of the Board of Education in relationship to the school administration. One of the widely debated issues in educational literature is whether the board or the educational administration has the greatest degree of control. One way of attempting to judge this is in terms of the relationship between the superintendent and the Board of Education. For instance, does the superintendent control the flow of information from the school system to board members? How much does the Board of Education involve itself in the educational programs and operation of the school system? Of course, the Board of Education might not need to involve itself if the superintendent clearly represents their wishes in the administration of the system. One interesting way of approaching this issue is to consider the means used by the Board of Education to select a superintendent. If it is a tightly controlled process where the desires of the civic elite have the major influence, then one can assume the selection of a superintendent whose values and philosophy closely parallel those of the civic elite. In this case, the Board of Education might not have to exercise much control since the superintendent will control in accordance with their desires.

Analyzing the formal mechanisms of control should be balanced with a close look at the informal mechanisms of power For instance, are there community groups that have to be organized to work with the school system? In the case of Cincinnati it was shown how the development of the Cincinnati Business Committee became a means for the civic elite to exercise direct influence over the administration of the schools. In this situation, an organization that is not controlled by the public or responsible to the public can influence the whole direction of a school system. As with the Board of Education, the investigator should look closely at the social composition of these types of organizations.

Another means of indirect control in many urban areas has been local educational foundations which provide money for educational research and for studies of local school problems. Often these foundations become sources of ideas for dealing with local school issues. It is important to look closely at the controlling board of these foundations to gain some clues as to the types of plans and research they would be willing to support. One should understand that foundations do not give support to any type of project but only to those the particular foundation considers important. Those decisions are often a reflection of the values of those controlling the foundation.

After the investigator has analyzed these different aspects of control, there might begin to appear the outlines of an informal network of relationships. For instance, members of the organization having the greatest power over nomination of school board candidates might also belong to another community group which works directly with the school administration. Or the membership lists might be shared between the nominating group, community groups, and the local foundation. If there is no sharing of actual names between groups, then it might be possible that the members of all important groups mix informally in clubs or civic associations. Very often civic elites are held together by informal social contacts where membership in a particular club or civic association is the key to entering the elite. Many important decisions can be made at an informal lunch between the superintendent and civic leaders.

Another way of investigating informal networks is in terms of the role of employees in leading companies. Very often companies will assign employees to work on local community projects, including the schools. This is done to improve the local image of the company and to assure that community decisions do not adversely affect the company. Sometimes these company employees are the central links for binding together informal networks.

If the particular central city school system being investigated displays a great deal of conflict between representatives of different community groups then the same type of analysis discussed above should be applied. Minority populations often display the same types of informal networks as the civic elites and develop their own elite leadership. Any type of special interest group involved in school politics usually has some type of formal and informal organizational structure. If conflict occurs in school board elections then it is important to determine which populations in the city are voting for the representatives of which groups.

Any investigator of urban school politics should always keep in mind that a large organizational structure exists which stands between the decisions made by the board of education and the child in the classroom. As mentioned at the beginning of this chapter, there is a great deal of distance between the educational decision-makers and the student. This distance is filled with a hierarchical structure of a large central office staff, principals, and teachers. Decisions are changed as they pass through this complex organizational structure. Understanding the political world of educational decision-makers is only the first step in understanding the development and evolution of central city school policies.

Notes

1. David Kirby, T. Robert Harris, and Robert Crain, *Political Strategies in Northern School Desegregation* (Lexington, Mass.: Lexington Books, 1973), p. 116.
2. For a general discussion of these political changes see Joseph Cronin, *The Control of Urban Schools* (New York: Free Press, 1973), pp. 39–123; Joel Spring, *Education and the Rise of the Corporate State* (Boston: Beacon Press, 1972), pp. 85–80, 128–135; and David Tyack, *The One Best System* (Cambridge: Harvard University Press, 1974), pp. 126–67.
3. Willis D. Hawley, *Nonpartisan Elections and the Case for Party Politics* (New York: John Wiley & Sons, 1973), pp. 22–23.
4. Ibid., p. 84.
5. Kirby et al., *Political Strategies*, pp. 1–19.
6. Ibid., p. 84.
7. Ibid., p. 118.
8. Andrew Greeley, "School Desegregation and Ethnicity," in Walter Stephan and Joe Feagin, eds., *School Desegregation* (New York: Plenum Press, 1980), pp. 133–157.
9. Ibid., pp. 136–37.
10. Harmon Zeigler and M. Kent Jennings. *Governing American Schools: Political Interaction in Local School Districts* (North Scituate, Mass.: Duxbury, 1974).
11. Kirby et al., *Political Strategies*, pp. 89–105.
12. Charles V. Willie and Susan Greenblatt, *Community Politics and Educational Change* (New York: Longman, 1981), p. 339.
13. Ibid., p. 340.
14. Margaret Withrow Farny, *Sevenmile Harvest: The Life of John Withrow 1854–1931* (Caldwell, N.J.: Progress Publishing Company, 1942), p. 174.
15. Robert P. Curry, *Fifty Years in the Cincinnati Public Schools, 1925–1975* (Cincinnati Historical Society, undated), pp. 52–54.

16. Taped interview with Roger Crafts, December 21, 1981.
17. Ewart Simpkinson to Ralph Lazarus, July 15, 1954, Box 2, Cincinnati Historical Society Manuscript Collection (hereafter CSC MSS).
18. Ewart Simpkinson to Kelly Siddall, October 20, 1959, Box 3, CSC MSS.
19. Charles Judd to Ewart Simpkinson, October 9, 1959, Box 3, CSC MSS.
20. Ewart Simpkinson to Carlton Hill, undated, Box 3, CSC MSS.
21. Ewart Simpkinson to Carlton Hill, April 17, 1961, Box 3, CSC MSS.
22. The Midwest Administration Center, University of Chicago, *Report of Cincinnati School Survey*, August 1968, pp. 99–101.
23. *Cincinnati Board of Education Proceedings, 1971*, p. 72.
24. Interview with David Schiering, March 5, 1982.
25. *Cincinnati Board of Education Proceedings, 1978*, p. 169; *1980*, p. 28.
26. *Cincinnati Board of Education Proceedings, 1978*, p. 169.
27. *Cincinnati Board of Education Proceedings, 1977*, pp. 219–220.
28. *Cincinnati Board of Education Proceedings, 1980*, p. 28.
29. *Cincinnati Board of Education Proceedings, 1978*, pp. 383–85.
30. *Cincinnati Board of Education Proceedings, 1979*, pp. 229–30.

3

Administrating a Central City School System

Many of the major problems in the administration of central city school systems have been caused by public schools adopting an industrial bureaucratic model. This model has created conditions that have allowed critics to charge central city school bureaucracies with isolation from the real world of the classroom, insulation from community desires and needs, inability to innovate and change, and a primary desire for organizational survival.

The organizational behaviors produced by this industrial bureaucratic model can be understood in terms of the interaction of individuals within a particular administrative structure. The organizational structure does not determine behavior but it does provide a framework in which people pursue power, ideals, income, status, and institutional survival. A description of the formal structure of central city school administrations does not provide a complete picture of how the system actually functions. Interlaced with the formal structure is an informal organization created by the actions of individuals working in their own self-interests or what they perceive to be the interests of the students. Therefore, to understand the administration of a central city school system one must understand the nature and intention of the formal organization and how individuals interact within that structure.

Development of the modern, formal organizational structure of central city school systems paralleled the development of elite control of central city schools discussed in the previous chapter. As school board members became remote from public control, so did school administrations as they built large central bureaucracies. In fact, school administrators used as models the very business and industrial concerns headed by urban elites. School superintendents and other administrators portrayed themselves as heads of large organizations very similar to modern corporations and borrowed freely from the management techniques used in business and industry.[1]

The adoption of an industrial model to central city schooling can be explained from several perspectives. On the one hand, it was the language of modern business which was most understandable to urban elites. It is not difficult to imagine these urban leaders preferring school people who shared the same language and viewpoint with regard to management and organization. In other words, central city school administrators tended to conform to the expectations of central city leaders in terms of organizational style. On the other hand, organizing a bureaucratic structure modeled on business and industry centralized and protected the exercise of power from public control.

The formal characteristics of the organizational model adopted by the schools in the early part of the twentieth century included centralization of authority at the top of a hierarchy and rational planning. Rational planning was to indicate how people were to fit together in the organization and work for accomplishment of a particular goal. It was assumed in this model that rational decision-makers at the top of the hierarchy could develop plans encompassing the total organization and that these plans would include particular goals for each individual within the structure. Once the plans were developed, they could be issued and passed down through the hierarchy with each individual in the chain of command complying with the instructions related to their place in the bureaucracy. It was assumed that this rational and hierarchical model of organization would make it possible to engineer efficiency and design organizational plans with specific goals.

Ideally, the industrial bureaucratic model was to work like a machine with the superintendent and top administrative staff putting in a plan with specific goals and pushing a button causing the entire system to react and conform with the smooth efficiency of gears meshing and shafts turning. In the total picture of school control, the board of education was to decide on general policy and the superintendent was to develop the organizational plan to put that policy into effect. All members are to look upward in terms of authority, with teachers looking up to principals, principals looking up the chain of command to the central administration, and the central administration looking up to the superintendent.

The problem with this bureaucratic model is that there are some major differences between operating a factory and operating a public school system. The major influence the public has over the management of a factory is the purchase or nonpurchase of its products; and even in this case, decisions about improving sales are made by management in terms of what they decide the public wants. Where this organizational model breaks down in education is that public schools do not sell a product and therefore are not as open to the pressures of the marketplace as is business. As sociologist Brian Rowan explains, "Schools receive funding, not on the basis of how much learning they produce per dollar expended, but rather for following certification or curricular or other externally imposed requirements."[2] In using a business model, public school administration becomes more isolated from public control than business because influences from the marketplace are lacking.

The industrial model combined with elite control of school boards insulated central city school systems from public power. A description that best symbolizes this insulation has been given by political scientist Paul Peterson in his book *School Politics Chicago Style.* Peterson describes the Chicago School Board as holding its meetings in a room where members sit in a semicircle with their backs to the public audience. A single loudspeaker hangs from the ceiling making it difficult for the public to determine which board member is speaking. A row of administrators is symbolically seated between the public and the board. In Peterson's words, "The very layout of the board room accentuated the separation of the board from the outside world."[3]

Another problem with the industrial model when applied to public schools is that it assumes a tightly linked chain of command with each member accepting the authority of those above in the hierarchy. It is difficult to maintain this model in an organization where everyone claims to be a professional and with those at the bottom of the hierarchy being professionally trained teachers. As a hierarchy of well educated people, it is reasonable that each member in the chain will want to express some form of professional autonomy, not just accept commands from above.

In addition, it is often the case that members of an hierarchical structure are more concerned with their own survival within the organization then with the overall goals of a particular management directive. Organizational policy, therefore, is not something that flows smoothly through the system with each member acting according to plan. Individuals tend to define their own stake in the plan and attempt to shape or change it according to their own interests.

The combination of desire for professional autonomy and an instinct for individual survival have made it virtually impossible for central city school systems to function according to a strictly rational hierarchical model. Indeed, one of the major criticisms of central city school systems is the inability of the bureaucracy to achieve an objective because of the behavior of individual members. This is particularly true

Cincinnati Public Schools
Organization Chart

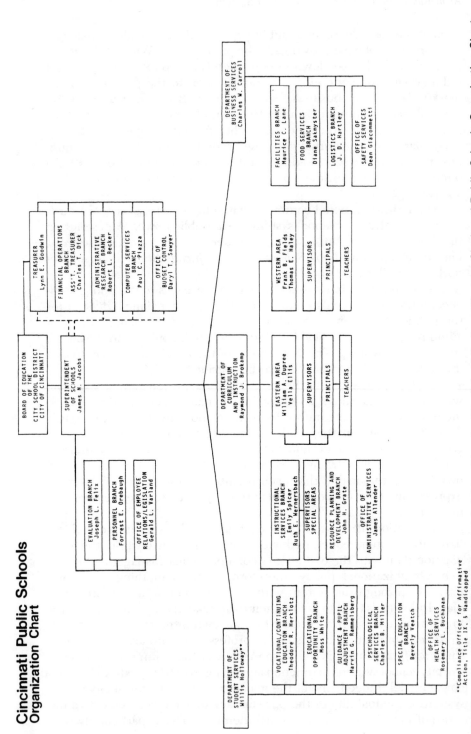

FIGURE 3.1 Example of the Central Administration of a City School System. (*Source:* Cincinnati Public Schools Organization Chart, Evaluation Branch, December 1982.)

of an objective involving any type of change or innovation that might threaten organizational positions and power.

The major criticism of the inability of central city schools to change and innovate, and their insulation from public control, occurred in the late 1960s and 1970s with the demands for school desegregation, improved programs for minority groups, and greater community participation. The difficulty outside groups had in achieving any of these goals led to a thorough analysis of central city school bureaucracies. In the late 1970s and early 1980s, this criticism has been tempered by a more complete understanding of how people function within organizations. The next section of this chapter will review the major analyses of central city school bureaucracies that emerged from school desegregation struggles and how they were refined in the context of understanding individual motivations. As these analyses reveal, one of the main problems of central city schools is the organizational model that dominates its behavior.

Bureaucratic Pathologies

The two most important works that focused on the problem of central city school bureaucracies in the climate of the late 1960s were Rogers' study of the administration of the New York school system, *110 Livingston Street,* and Gittell and Hollander's research on *Six Urban School Districts.* Rogers' study emphasized the inability of the bureaucracy to change and deal with current problems, and Gittell and Hollander stressed isolation from public control.

In *110 Livingston Street,* Rogers presents the New York school bureaucracy as having created a wasteland of new programs and failed attempts at school desegregation. The problem was not the lack of good intentions or programs, but the inability of the school administration to get anything to work. As examples, Rogers described programs like Demonstration Guidance, Higher Horizons, More Effective Schools, All Day Neighborhood Schools, College Bound, and African Studies as genuine attempts to improve the equality of minority education which failed because of administrative ineptitude. In Rogers' words, the plans were "especially impressive compared with what many other big city school systems have done. But they haven't produced any results, because the system itself doesn't work."[4]

The failure that Rogers found in the system was the result of the type of bureaucratic model used in public schooling. He contrasted the two polar opposite forms of bureaucratic models, authoritarian and professional, to highlight the problem inherent in public school administration. He argued that the New York public schools operated under the authoritarian model which, of course, is typical of industrial organizations. The characteristics of the authoritarian model, he wrote, are a high degree of centralization, authoritarian leadership, hierarchy, discipline enforced from the top down, specialization, and a high degree of politicalization of bureaucratic members. In contrast, the professional model, which he claimed was characteristic of universities, had flexible centralization, collegial rule, limited hierarchy, colleague discipline, limited specialization, and a high degree of professionalism oriented toward the intrinsic rewards of professional recognition and status.[5]

Rogers' complaint was not just with the model, but also with the bureaucratic pathology that had become part of the system. What he saw was a system that was insulated from community pressures and control, unable to change, a battlefield for warring divisions within the bureaucracy, and trapped in rules. One top level executive on the Mayor's Commission on Human Rights described the system to Rogers in these terms: "The Board of Education is like an old man with arteriosclerosis. They make a good statement and it sits there like a heart pumping, but there are no veins or the veins aren't working. They are hardened. The bureaucracy is so paralyzed."[6]

At the top of Rogers' list of bureaucratic pathologies was overcentralization with many levels of command and an upward orientation by subordinates. The centralization of services on matters like curriculum, staffing, budgeting, supplies, construction, and maintenance often led to decisions being made that had little relationship to the real needs of the schools. Decision-makers in the central bureaucracy were insulated by several layers from the real world of the public schools. This means that plans and programs originating from the central office often did not take account of the many variations and problems that can occur from school to school. Centralization of authority also makes it difficult to obtain services. As an example, Rogers cited teacher complaints "that they sometimes get supplies several months or a year late; if they want to receive them in time to coordinate them with their programs, they pay for them out of their own pockets."[7] In addition, there were the problems of ordering new books that were not on the official, and out of date, booklists. Even more serious was the problem of staffing schools in a centralized system. As an example, Rogers gave the lengthy story of the problems facing a junior high school principal trying to get teachers for a newly opened integrated school. At one point, to contact the administrator in the central offices responsible for staffing, the principal was forced to send a telegram. By the second month of classes there were still 13 unfilled positions in the school.[8]

Centralization, according to Rogers, makes it difficult for schools, teachers, principals, and others at the bottom of the chain of command to make the types of decisions required with changing circumstances and conditions. Those at the bottom must constantly look upward for approval, which not only delays decisions and actions, but also the decisions will be made by those far removed from the problem. However, centralization did not mean for Rogers the existence of a tightly knit structure; in fact, he considered another pathology of the system was the isolation of units within and their limited coordination and communication.

The two major problems arising from this pathology were the lack of coordination and the turf battles for power and expansion which took place between the various units of the bureaucracy. Within an authoritarian bureaucracy, Rogers argued, members look toward extrinsic rewards of power, status, and promotion as opposed to professionalism. This means different units within the bureaucratic structure are more concerned with extrinsic rewards than with service to the client. Principals and teachers in the system are often faced with a multitude of often contradictory statements coming from different parts of the bureaucracy, and the bureaucratic units are more concerned with their own prestige and advancement than with helping the schools. In terms of introducing educational reforms in the face of bureaucratic politics, Rogers wrote, "These loyalties, cliques, and internal power struggles were an essential element in headquarters politics. . . . Predictably, the divisions competed in trying to secure larger shares of the scarce resources of the system. 'What will this do to our unit?' was the usual question when reforms were discussed."[9]

In addition to overcentralization and bureaucratic politics, Rogers identified the pathology of "compulsive rule following and rule enforcing."[10] He found this a particularly frustrating problem when dealing with desegregation. Many bureaucrats would hide behind rules to avoid having to make desegregation decisions that might be offensive to other administrators. Blind obedience to rules not only slowed down the bureaucratic process but also was used as a means of organizational survival. Often rules were a means for inaction by a bureaucrat who might dislike a proposal or feared that the proposal threatened survival in the organization.

Despite the authoritarian industrial model adopted by the school bureaucracy, Rogers found a degree of informal decentralization resulting from the rebellion of field personnel against the central office staff. School personnel tended to divide themselves into headquarters people and field people with field people claiming they had to deal with the real problems of the day-to-day workings of the school while headquarters people were out of contact with the schools. Rogers quoted one field superintendent, "At the field superintendents' association meetings you'd see this distinct division between the district men and the headquarters men. The latter were regarded as being in an ivory tower by the men in the field. Anything coming out of headquarters . . . they regarded with a jaundiced eye."[11] This sense of separation and superiority by field superintendents and principals often led to open rebellion against central office directives. Other writers would come to see this rebellion as a healthy process that made it possible for the system to work. Rogers saw it as a pathology in the system that made it difficult to function and carry out proposals.

What frequently happened was that field superintendents and principals would reinterpret central office directives in terms of what they believed was their superior knowledge. This made it impossible, according to Rogers, for the system to implement many of its reform policies. As an example of what he called passive sabotage, he found district superintendents and principals not informing black and Puerto Rican parents about the transfer opportunities with Open Enrollment. Open Enrollment was a program designed to aid desegregation by allowing minority children to freely transfer out of schools with a high minority population. Rogers felt that the central office had spent a great deal of time in careful preparation of the plan. The blame for the failure of the plan he linked with rebellion and sabotage by local principals. On the one hand, principals of schools from which students would most likely transfer were afraid of the loss of student population and not only avoided informing parents, but when they did inform them, they tried to discourage transfers by talking about the difficulty of children going home for lunch. On the other hand, principals in receiving schools tried to discourage transfers into their schools by placing incoming students into "slow and/or segregated classes" and by imposing stricter disciplinary measures. These actions were more active forms of sabotage as compared with passively not informing parents of the plan.

When the field rebellion against the central office is combined with the internal battles between different units of the central office, there emerges a picture of a bureaucratic system that is both vertically and horizontally fragmented. The pathology of the system is in its inability to function as an authoritarian bureaucracy with a smoothly functioning hierarchical system where orders flow from the top to the bottom. In terms of horizontal fragmentation, the turf battles and struggles between bureaucratic units make it difficult for rational decision-making at the top of the bureaucratic structure. Vertical fragmentation resulting from field rebellion makes it difficult to implement a decision.

One of the major issues that emerged from Rogers' discussion of the New York school bureaucracy was whether or not the pathology was an inevitable consequence of the schools adopting an industrial and authoritarian model of bureaucracy. As we shall see in later discussions, the problems Rogers found in New York were not unique to that system. This would suggest that the problems are inherent in the model and not the result of particular circumstances and actors. From this perspective overcentralization, bureaucratic struggles, compulsive rule-following, and field rebellion are inevitable results when an industrial bureaucratic model, normally controlled by the forces of the marketplace, is applied to the public schools which lack those controls and influences. If one takes this position, then the only remedy is the application of a new bureaucratic model to central city school systems.

In terms of New York, Rogers wrote, "The present study leads me to the conclusion that the existing bureaucratic structure of the school system in New York City is no longer viable and must be scrapped." He did find some hope in plans for decentralization but that hope was qualified by a deeply pessimistic belief in the existing structure to ever meaningfully decentralize. He believed that the continued drift in American society was toward increased bureaucratic centralism. In his words, "I would conclude, then, that there may be no solution for the failures of big cities and urban education over the short run, and that conditions will probably get worse before they improve."[12]

Gittell and Hollander's study of *Six Urban School Districts* provided the same dismal picture of central city school systems unable to innovate and respond to the changing needs of urban populations because of school bureaucracies. In their study of Baltimore, Chicago, Detroit, New York, Philadelphia, and St. Louis they found administrations suffering from overcentralization, large bureaucracies, and insularity caused by internal promotions.[13] In their discussion of bureaucracy, they did not concentrate on the types of pathologies Rogers found in the New York schools. What they raised as the most important issue was bureaucratic destruction of democratic control.

They noted with irony that the public schools that had been heavily influenced by democratic theory had become "the most nonpublic of governmental services." From their persepctive, the public schools had taken decision-making from the teachers and parents and placed it in the hands of professionals insulated from public control in large bureaucratic structures. These professionals, they argued, had become convinced that they were the only ones qualified to make educational decisions. For the authors, "The concept of public accountability has been abandoned." In each of the cities they studied they found school people insisting upon the need to keep decision-making in the hands of professionals.[14]

Therefore, Gittell and Hollander added another element to the growing critique of the administration of central city school systems. Not only were schools insulated from the public by bureaucratic centralization but also by the ideology of professionalism which justified excluding the public from control of the schools. This ideology of professionalism they saw as primarily serving the interests of educators. They concluded that the result of a centralized bureaucracy and the ideology of professional control was "a static, internalized, isolated system which has been unable to respond to vastly changing needs and demands of large city populations."[15]

The picture of central city school administrations that emerged from these studies of the late 1960s presented little hope for improvement of the quality of urban education. Not only were they portrayed as pathological and rigid, but also as undemocratic and beyond public control. Central city schools did respond to the charge of not being accountable by defining accountability not in terms of public control but of accounting to the public through published test scores. As will be discussed later, this lead to the recent phenomenon of the "politics of testing." As for the inability of the central city school bureaucracy to innovate and meet the needs of urban populations, more recent studies have suggested some flexibility and dynamic change within the bureaucratic structure.

Control and Conformity in a Loosely Coupled Bureaucracy

McGivney and Haught, in "The Politics of Education: A View from the Perspective of the Central Office Staff," state that their findings "tend to confirm those of Gittell and Rogers," but they differ over the ability of the system to innovate and bring about change.[16] They did not arrive at the pessimistic conclusion that there was little hope for central city schools with the existing model of bureaucratic organization. In one sense, their study heralds a new period when researchers, rather than dismissing the system, attempt to find new hope through informal networks and the entrepreneurial skills of those enmeshed in the system.

The need to perceive itself in control of a situation, McGivney and Haught found, is the most important need of the central office staff. The desire to control a situation, they argue, has the greatest explanatory and predictive power with regard to the actions of the central office staff. The need to control covers a wide range of activities, from controlling racial disturbances and the hiring of personnel to the construction and repair of school buildings. In other words, if one wants to predict the behavior of the central office staff in any situation, it would be the desire to control a situation. The key to understanding the processes of control, they feel, is in the informal networks in the central office. The central office acts in this fashion, they argue, because of the conflict between concern with professionalism and concern with maintaining the school system as a public, open institution.

The ideology of professionalism, McGivney and Haught maintain, allows the central office staff "to view itself as having expertise in curricular, pedagogical, financial, and personnel areas."[17] With this belief in its expertise, the central office establishes norms and rules that define appropriate behavior for professionals. From the perspective of professionalism, it becomes unprofessional to publically criticize other professionals. McGiveny and Haught see this behavior in direct conflict with the school system as a public institution under public control. They refer to this openness of the school system as operating in a "fish bowl." The threat of public criticism in this situation is viewed as a threat to professionalism.

The researchers found a general negative attitude by central office staff people towards any type of public input into the school system that is not under the control of the central office staff. Though the central office does recognize the public nature of the school system, McGivney and Haught wrote, "they believe that most of the claimants for a voice in school policy such as citizen committees, parent groups, city hall, and others, are 'unrepresentative' of the public at large."[18] They found that the central office staff tend to view most outsiders wanting to make changes in the school system as troublemakers.

Therefore, the desire to control is a result of the desire to avoid any public criticism of members of the central office staff. While McGivney and Haught explain this phenomenon in terms of the ideology of professionalism, it is possible to use other types of arguments. For instance, one could argue that since the achievement of a school system is not measured by the sale of products, other types of measures must be used. Of importance to a public institution is its image and the degree of public criticism. Within this framework the issue is public image and not the ideology of professionalism. The desire to control could reflect a desire to maintain a good public image and protect the job security of the members of the central office staff.

In terms of control, McGivney and Haught give the general example of the efforts of the central office "to establish and maintain central control over communications to such agencies as city hall, the State Education Department, principals, and teachers, and other extra-school-system groups."[19] They also found other processes designed to assure control over the hiring of new personnel. One of the examples they give is the hiring process for a vacant position on the central office staff. The contractual agreement between the teachers' association and school district required posting the job at least 10 days before selection. What actually happened was that the position was filled seven days before the notice was posted by an "acting administrator" who in the words of the superintendent would be removed if some "whiz kid comes along." In other words, unless there was some dramatic event, the acting administrator would become the permanent administrator.

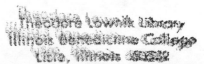

To accomplish the above example of controlling the hiring of an administrator, the central office staff had to rely on informal rather than formal procedures. One of the gatekeepers in this informal process volunteered to the researchers that "no promotion takes place in the central office except with the approval of Assistant Superintendent X and me." It is in the understanding of this informal process that one can, according to McGivney and Haught, understand the methods used by the central office to exert control.

The researchers, in the unidentified central city school system they studied, divided the central office into two major subgroups with each subgroup composed of minor subgroups. Each subgroup met informally each day with one subgroup being oriented toward the Board of Education and the other toward building principals and teachers. Minor subgroups in each of the two major subgroups also interacted each day in both formal and informal situations. In all cases, the proximity of offices facilitated daily interaction.

In matters of control and decision-making, the actions of minor subgroups were essential parts of the informal structure of power. The general pattern for decision-making, they found, is for a minor subgroup to research consensus about a particular policy proposal. The researchers found that proposals accepted by a minor subgroup "will be accepted by the major subgroup of which the minor subgroup is a part." They found that proposals that were considered by the major subgroup without first receiving acceptance by a minor subgroup were delayed until they received that acceptance; and McGivney and Haught argued, "Proposals submitted in major subgroups by isolates will be either rejected or delayed."[20]

After going through this informal network and once consensus is reached in one of the major subgroups, a proposal is submitted to an administrative council meeting for agreement by the whole central office. Again, a proposal introduced into administrative council without major subgroup approval is delayed until that action occurs. If consensus is reached in favor of a proposal by the central office staff, then it is sent to a school board study meeting for consideration. In the researchers' words, the central office staff "utilizes the board's study session to produce a predictable vote for or against a proposal at the official board meeting."[21]

The above description of the informal and formal process of decision-making places a great deal of power in the hands of those involved in the informal process in the central office. This power is enhanced by the central office staff's claims of expertise and access to information about the school system. The major threat to this control is proposals initiated from outside this policy-making process. The response of the central office to these situations is to make an "effort to control the initiations of outside groups by intercepting such proposals before they are submitted to the Board of Education or by attempts to impugn the credibility of outside groups. . . . "[22]

The amount of effort to control public input into the system, according to the researchers, depends upon the degree of public criticism. The central office will increase its control if negative reactions by the public to the school system increase. The attempt to control will also increase as challenges to the staff's role as professionals increase. In other words, public criticism of the school system will result in a greater effort by the central office staff to control public access to the decision-making process. An expansion of this argument made by McGivney and Haught could be that the more the public demands to control the school system, the more the bureaucracy makes an effort to assure its own control.

In fact, the researchers found that proposals submitted to the Board of Education by an outside group were sent back to the central office for review and consideration. The central office then considered them through the informal process of minor and major subgroups. This led the researchers to the conclusion that proposals submitted by outside groups will not be acted upon by the school board until they have been considered by the central office staff, and that any conflict over outside proposals will be resolved by the central office to the degree that they control the situation.

The desire to control for purposes of professionalism or protection of image does not preclude innovation. Innovation is allowed within the system as long as it passes through the informal networks which assure control by the central office staff. From this standpoint, McGivney and Haught concluded, the activities of the central office staff could not be completely explained by bureaucratic theory. What they found was that formal structure was interlaced with an informal network. They argued that "far from being impersonal in its application of rules and regulations, it [the central office staff] was extremely involved to the point of being creative in its treatment of both clients and colleagues." In addition, they found the central office staff willing to test and implement a variety of innovative programs in the local school system; but in "each case all the changes had to earn the blessing of the subgroups comprising the COS."[23]

The McGivney and Haught study does not question the basic argument that bureaucracies of central city school systems are isolated and insulated from public control by an authoritarian structure exhibiting certain pathological symptoms. What the study demonstrates is that a more thorough analysis is required to explain the actions of the members of the bureaucracy. In this case, the desire to protect professionalism or public image explains why the members of the bureaucracy seek to maintain control over all policies and actions affecting the schools.

From this point of view, one can explain the difficulty Rogers found in introducing reform into the New York public schools. The problem was not that the system was suffering from "arteriosclerosis" nor from a pathological inability to respond to any reform movement, but that the reform was introduced from outside the normal informal channels of bureaucratic control. It should be remembered that this occurred during a period when the schools were under heavy attack from community groups. According to McGivney and Haught, it is precisely during the periods of heavy criticism that the central office staff seeks to maximize its control. Within the context of this argument, the introduction of new programs by the Board of Education and outside groups during a period of public criticism would result in the members of the bureaucracy, the central office staff, attempting to maintain their control by delaying or stopping the proposed changes.

The McGivney and Haught study was an important step in adding greater depth to the understanding of how a central city school bureaucracy operates. Of fundamental importance to their approach was to raise the question of why the actors within the organization performed in certain ways? What they discovered was that people do not act by a set of rigid rules established by the bureaucratic structure; rather, the action of individual members of the bureaucracy can be explained as attempts to survive and operate within a particular organizational structure. Many of the things that Rogers described as pathological components of the New York school system can be explained within this framework.

For instance, consider the case of what Rogers called "compulsive rule-following and rule-enforcing." As mentioned earlier in the chapter, one of the problems in the adoption by the schools of an industrial bureaucratic model is the fact that school funding is not based on output or the purchase of a product by a consumer. Schools receive funding on the basis of meeting externally determined regulations at the local, state, and federal levels. This means that schools gain their resources primarily through conformity to regulations. The orientation of the members of the bureaucratic structure of schools is not toward responding to the needs and desires of the public or marketplace but toward meeting the requirements of external regulations. In the words of sociologist Brian Rowan, "As external agencies come to hold the purse strings and define the rules of the game, administrative time and attention turn to the demands of conforming to externally imposed regulations."[24]

Admittedly, the issue of sources of funding does not explain all the reasons for rigid conformity to rules, but it does explain certain other behaviors resulting from conformity. For example, one of the complaints by Rogers was the isolation of the bureaucratic structure from what was actually happening in the schools, and the split between those in the field and those in the central office. This separation sociologist Rowan would explain in terms of the orientation toward conformity to rules imposed by external agencies. Rowan writes, ". . . as administrators turn increasingly to the demands of conformity, they devote less time and energy to core instructional problems."[25] In addition, he argues that as external demands for conformity increase so does the administrative staff.

From the above perspective, bureaucratic growth and separation between the central office and the schools is primarily a result of response to outside regulation. This creates the rather ironic situation whereby attempts at greater control over the bureaucratic structure lead to what one might argue are negative effects in terms of directing administrative concerns toward problems of teaching. His study of schools in the Bay Area of San Francisco revealed that increases in administrative staffs were primarily caused by the need to conform to outside regulations. Or in Rowan's words, "As administrative time and attention are focused on documenting conformity, less attention is given to managing instructional technologies."[26]

Therefore, the consideration of the sources of funding helps to provide a partial explanation for compulsive rule-following and the breakdown between the central office and the field. It also helps to explain what has been referred to as the "loose coupling" of educational organizations. The term "loosely coupled" became popular in the 1970s to explain what Rogers and Gittell and Hollander had found in the 1960s to be the major problem: that the bureaucratic system did not work for making decisions at the top and having those decisions obeyed through a chain-of-command.

As the term "loose coupling" suggests, elements within an organization are not held together in tight linkages that allow for a smooth flow of commands but are tied together loosely allowing for decisions at different levels. One organizational theorist, Karl Weick, has provided the example of loose coupling in the relationship between a school counselor and a principal. Weick writes, "The image is that the principal and the counselor are somehow attached, but that each retains some identity and separateness and that their attachment may be circumscribed, infrequent, weak in its mutual affects, unimportant, and/or slow to respond."[27] Many of the criticisms of educational bureaucracies can be explained by loose coupling, such as lack of coordination, unresponsiveness, the slow spread of influence through the organization, and the split between authority and the technical core of an organization.

The problem with applying the term "loosely coupled" to the organization of central city school systems is that they were never intended to be loosely coupled. Historically, we know that an authoritarian industrial model of bureaucracy was adopted by the schools. To say that the present organizations of schools are loosely coupled is to obscure the fact that they were intended to be tightly linked organizations and that their failure to achieve that ideal has to do with the way people act once they are in that type of organization.

The approach taken by Rowan helps to explain why school bureaucracies have taken on the appearance of being loosely coupled organizations. Rowan argues that school bureaucracies need to be understood in terms of their institutional environment. This environment creates a structure which helps to determine the shape and actions of the organization. In the case of schools, state and federal legislation, regulatory agencies, and professional organizations create an environment that causes a split within the bureaucratic structure. Whereas the bureaucratic structure adopted by the schools was intended to be tightly linked, these linkages have been weakened by the requirement that the structure respond to outside forces and demands. In Rowan's words, "Local school district administrative staffs appear to be structured by the demands of their institutional environments, but as these demands increase, internal coordination and control over ongoing instructional technologies are decreased, and district administrative components become loosely tied to school-level personnel and activities."[28] For Rowan this suggests that as attempts at outside control increase, school systems will become increasingly loosely coupled.

Bureaucratic Self-Interest

In the studies of McGivney and Haught and Rowan, one can find an explanation of bureaucratic behavior in view of how individuals are forced to act for their own survival in an institutional structure. This approach helps to explain why central city school systems exhibit what Rogers called bureaucratic pathologies. But there is still another explanation of bureaucratic behavior which treats the system as an organic whole without reference to the internal politics and social dynamics of the system. Like the attempt to explain bureaucratic behavior in terms of how people survive in the system, this approach attempts to explain how bureaucracy works for the survival of the whole.

This approach is taken in Peterson's study, *School Politics Chicago Style*. In the framework used by Peterson, the organization is treated as a whole that takes on a life of its own with a common set of interests, operating routines, and values. These common linkages create an interdependent organization where the internal activities are not as important as the activities of the organization considered as a whole. Peterson describes the organization as seen in this framework "as an autonomous, self-guiding, enclosed system which, for all its size and complexity, is motivated by a parochial concern for its own persistence."[29]

From this point of view, central city school administrations will primarily be interested in policies that will benefit the organization as a whole. This means that the reaction of central city school administrations to any policy established by a Board of Education or outside group will be in terms of how it enhances or threatens the existence of the entire bureaucratic structure. Now this argument is similar to that of McGivney and Haught in that the members of the bureaucracy want to maintain control. In this case, the desire by individual actors for control can be viewed in terms of protecting the entire organization.

Peterson provides a list of the major policies of interest to central city school bureaucracies when considered as an organic whole.[30] It is important to remember that these policy concerns shape the actions of the members on other issues. The two interests that top the list are increased salaries and an increase in the number of jobs in the bureaucracy. Increasing the number of jobs allows for greater promotion opportunities for those already in the bureaucracy. The third interest on the list is also related to improving promotion opportunities by recruiting for high level positions only from the lower ranks of the organization.

The desire to promote from within helps to explain why central city school bureaucracies have tended to be insulated from the change that might occur by bringing new people into the top posts of the organization. Hiring from outside the bureaucratic structure threatens the promotion opportunities of those within the organization. This means that the organization as a whole will work against any policies designed to bring newcomers into positions that could block the career opportunities of those already in the system.

The final three items on Peterson's list are a desire to increase protection of the organization from outside pressures, increase the "prestige of the organization," and assure the longevity of the organization. All of these can, as mentioned before, be used to explain the desire of the administrative staff to maintain control. They also highlight the major concern school bureaucracies have with image and public relations.[31]

Peterson provides an example of this organizational self-protection in his description of the struggle surrounding political decentralization of the school system. He agrees with most writers on education on the use of the ideology of professionalism to protect control by the school bureaucracy. The arguments for decentralization emerged from a background of protests over racial segregation with the demand for greater citizen participation. Greater public participation was perceived by the school organization as a threat to its control. In an interview survey conducted by Peterson of 59 principals and district superintendents, only 15% favored moderated plans for community participation and the rest objected to any changes.[32]

The early plans for political decentralization reflected the desire of the bureaucracy to maintain control even over what was supposedly a democratic process of community involvement. Again, it should be remembered that the initiative for decentralization did not originate in the bureaucratic structure but from pressures outside the organization. The desire of the organization was to respond to those pressures with the least threat to its own power. It attempted to accomplish this by specifying in its plans the actual representation in education councils which were to be established in six districts. The plan called for the first 25% of the membership of the councils to be selected by the district superintendent with the remainder of the members to be selected by the first 25%. In addition, the plan specified four categories that were to be equally represented on the council including the professional staff of the schools, members of business and industry, youth and civic groups, and parents. As Peterson points out, this plan almost guaranteed that councils would not be representative of the social composition of the districts.

In addition to controlling the membership on the education councils, the plan greatly restricted their power by making the council advisory to the local district superintendent only on issues dealing with staffing ratios, extra programs, and recreation programs. These policies so greatly limited the power and representation of the education councils that they did not threaten control and were useless as vehicles for community input into the schools.[33]

Following this initial plan, the board proposed that communities be involved in the selection of principals and that the councils be given more independence from the district superintendent's office. Peterson argued that in this case the board had become so involved in the procedures that it was difficult for the organization to completely subvert the plans, but they were able to influence the plans to minimize the impact of community participation.

The organization continued to maintain control over the selection of principals by establishing a procedure in which the district superintendent could determine which community leaders were to be contacted for recommendations regarding the selection. Those recommendations were to be confined to a list of eligible candidates chosen by the organization. Community influence over building principals was increased through a more representative local council with a longer list of items that could be considered by the council.

This pattern of response to cries for decentralization and greater community power over the schools resulted in a school organization that has become fairly typical of central city school systems around the country. Major, direct community influence is confined to the local school advisory groups. This means that the giving up of some control is confined to the field and does not directly remove power and control from the central administration. As Peterson describes in Chicago, decentralization resulted in principals and district superintendents having advisory groups, but not the area superintendents above them nor the central administration.

Peterson comes to an important conclusion regarding the organizational response to decentralization. He argues, ". . . organizational resistance to sharing power with outsiders was increasingly successful the closer proposed changes approached real centers of power with the organization."[34] In this context, local school advisory groups can be viewed as the answer to public demand for greater participation without threatening the control of the central bureaucracy. In addition, it contributes to the split or loose coupling between those in the field and those downtown.

The demand for greater community participation in the schools was set against a background of racial disturbances. Local school advisory groups were just one response to these demands. The other was an increase in the number of minority members represented in the school administration. Peterson argues that for Chicago, the hiring of minority group members for administrative positions was "a relatively painless means of reducing school disruptions."[35] It was painless because it did not threaten the actual structure of authority though it did threaten the interests of existing members of the bureaucracy.

Peterson's study of Chicago school politics provides another way of understanding the workings of central city school bureaucracies. His conclusions are not that much different than those of other writers on the topic. By treating the bureaucracy as an organic whole, he is led to place more emphasis on the common set of interests shared by the members of the bureaucracy than on the internal differences. These common interests reflect primarily a concern with economic and professional self-interest. The things that are commonly supported are things that enhance the bureaucratic structure and improve the economic opportunities of those within the structure. Of primary importance in achieving these ends is the assurance that the organization maintains control.

The desire to maintain control as a means of protecting the organization helps to explain the other response to the demand for community participation, which was the accountability movement. The accountability movement, like the local school advisory committees, developed in response to racial disturbances that were linked to demands for greater community participation. One of the great criticisms of central city school bureaucracies in the late 1960s was that they were no longer accountable to the public.[36]

The response of school organizations to demands for accountability were predictable in terms of desires to maintain control. Accountability resulted in a major concern with the reporting of test scores by individual schools within a school district and by making principals accountable for improving the test scores of their individual schools. The translation of demands for community participation into accountability through test scores allowed the school organization to maintain control through its professional expertise in giving and reporting of standardized tests. In this case, the argument of professionalism was used to protect the authority of the organization.

The major work to give focus to the accountability movement was Lessinger's *Every Kid a Winner*. Lessinger dismissed direct community control of the schools as destructive for an organization that should be governed by professional expertise. He compared the situation with that of a hospital where the community does not vote on the procedures to be used by a surgeon before an operation. The decisions in this case, according to Lessinger, should be made by those with the proper training and knowledge. The patient on the other hand does have the right to complain but it is the experts who must decide the best means of answering these complaints.

Lessinger's argument fit nicely into the industrial bureaucratic model adopted by the schools because his argument supported a centralization of decision-making power. Of course, the major difference between industry and the schools is in their relationship to the marketplace. In this case, the organization has to respond to complaints as opposed to the purchase or nonpurchase of a product. The nature of the complaints are to be brought under control and given a specific content in the form of achievement test scores.

Lessinger, without specifically recognizing the fact, proposed the addition of another industrial model to the school bureaucracy. This was in the form of a national accounting firm which would evaluate school systems through standardized testing and report the results to the public. It was to function like a public accounting firm except that it would be staffed with "educational engineers" who were to use their expertise in testing and statistics to provide the data for public debate about the schools.

Although there has been a movement for national assessment of the schools, most of the testing for accountability has remained in the hands of local school officials. Some states have adopted state-wide competency examinations but these have not threatened the hierarchical model of control. In these situations, state education agencies can be viewed as being just one step higher in the authority structure. With either local testing or state testing, the control of both the content of public information and decisions about public complaints is left in the hands of professionals in the bureaucratic structure.

Therefore, the accountability movement avoided what Lessinger called the attempt to "throw process of governance to populist chaos in which every citizen claims expertise . . . on the grounds of having gone through school or of having a child there."[37] But in the process of maintaining the control within the central bureaucracy, it shifted the burden of improving test scores to individual schools. Like the establishment of local school advisory councils, the burden of the reform falls on the shoulders of the local school principal. The central core of the authority structure is to protect itself and the field is used to absorb the majority of the changes.

One result of accountability has been the politics of testing which centers around such issues as the types of tests to be used, the methods of reporting to the public, and the methods of improving test scores. The politics of test scores became so important by the early 1980s that test scores became a major issue in the mayoral campaign in New York City where tests had been used to determine whether students should be promoted from certain grades. For those students not promoted, special summer programs were created where the promotion tests were administered at the end of the program. A political uproar occurred because it was claimed that school officials manipulated the test scores to allow a large number of students to be promoted at the end of the summer. This made the system look good in two respects. First, the system showed it had standards by requiring the tests for promotion, and second, it looked good by providing a remedial program that seemed to work.[38]

The above example can be explained easily in terms of what has already been discussed about the behavior of central city school bureaucracies. One would assume that the organization would try to use test scores to enhance its public image, and the above example illustrates that point. Following the same line of reasoning, one would assume that a school system would try to choose a test that produced scores that made the system look good. The author of this chapter has witnessed a debate in a school system over the use of the Metropolitan Achievement Test versus the California Achievement Test. One of the central motivations for the adoption of one over the other was that one would show higher gains to report to the public.

In another example described in an ethnographic study of Chicago school principals by Morris, Crowson, Hurwitz, and Porter-Gehrie, it was found that when a building principal realized the importance of demonstrating improvements in test scores, she began to select average students as opposed to below average students. The result was greatly improved scores for the entire school. In this situation, the principal was primarily concerned with demonstrating success within the boundaries established by the central office. This reaction fits the previous discussion of the split between the field and the central office, and loose coupling. It also highlights the fact that individuals will tend to react to organizational structure in terms of their own survival and self-interest.[39]

Discretionary Insubordination

As suggested above, the idea of self-interest can be used to explain the actions of members of the bureaucracy as well as the actions of the bureaucracy considered as an organic whole. In fact, the ethnographic study of Chicago school principals finds the pursuit of self-interest and survival as the key element in making the system work. Morris et al. argue that principals must often disobey or ignore bureaucratic directives and procedures to make the system work. Unlike Rogers, who condemned this type of disobedience as a bureaucratic pathology, these authors consider it a managerial art that corrects the actions of a bureaucracy removed from the day-to-day workings of central city schools. Within this framework, discretionary insubordination by school administrators is essential for individual survival and the survival of the organization.

The Chicago study was conducted by closely following 12 principals through their daily school routines. The records of how principals actually operate in a school setting provide a rich source for understanding administrative behavior. It is from the context of this close observation of administrative behavior that the authors conclude that ignoring and disobeying rules make it possible for a central city school system to function.

Their basic argument follows the theory that as the size of an educational bureaucracy increases, it becomes increasingly impersonal and dependent on a rigid chain of command. It is assumed that for the system to work, all administrators will adhere to the command chain. "What is not so commonly understood in organization theory," according to the authors, "is the companion and somewhat contradictory idea that the need to *ignore* the chain of command also increases in urgency as the bureaucracy becomes larger."[40] From the viewpoint of the authors, ignoring and disobeying orders is necessary to dilute what they call the "dehumanizing effects" of impersonal, large scale organizations. The conclusion of this argument is that discretionary insubordination is not only necessary but also humanizes the system.

The authors argue that disobedience to the chain of command in central city school systems has become an art form that reflects a sensitivity to human needs. The artful insubordinate tries to maintain a low profile while using subtle techniques to disobey bureaucratic commands and rules. In the words of the authors, "The object is to disobey in such a way that the disobedient behavior produces the maximum effect locally, that is, within the school, but minimum impact on one's superiors."[41] This form of disobedience, the authors stress, is not a result of an individual irritation with a command or procedure, but out of concern for the welfare of an educational program, students, or school. The type of disobedience approved by this ethnographic research, and considered humane, is where an individual administrator decides that obedience to an order or rule will be damaging to the educational system.

The researchers categorized the various types of insubordination witnessed within the school system. The first type is where the actor is unwilling to make any major impact on the bureaucratic hierarchy. An example of this mild form of insubordination was of a principal who was ordered to reduce the number of his assistant principals from four to three. The one the principal wanted to get rid of had greater seniority in the system than the others and therefore, according to the rules, should be the last one to go. The principal tried to get around this rule by submitting the vice-principal's name to the district superintendent. The district superintendent overruled the principal because of the seniority issue. In this case, the principal attempted to avoid compliance to a seniority rule for the benefit of the school. It was the judgment of the principal that the vice-principal he wanted out was incompetent and damaged the welfare of the school.

The second mode of disobedience is called a "gentlemen's agreement." An example would be an agreement between two principals to discourage transfers between their schools. In this situation, the Board of Education had adopted a plan allowing for the transfer of students between an all black and an all white school for part of a day. The principals of the two schools calculated that the time required for the daily transfers would cost the students 20% of their instructional day. They decided that the program was detrimental to the welfare of the students and therefore worked against the orders of the Board of Education.

Planned delinquency of deadlines is the researchers' third mode of disobedience. In this situation, principals react to the overwhelming amount of paperwork required by the central bureaucracy by making decisions about when or when not to meet a deadline. The researchers claim that a great deal of this paperwork seems to be a result of "the realization that it can be collected." The principal must make a decision about which paperwork is important and which paperwork is "for the make-work staffers downtown who look for something to do and therefore generate their own work. . . ."[42]

Disobedience over deadlines can take the form of principals refraining from giving information at an appointed time. This allows them to determine the urgency of the deadline. If the principal receives a telephone call from the central administration requesting the information shortly after the official deadline, the principal knows that he or she should act promptly. On the other hand, if the telephone call takes days or weeks to arrive, the principal can be reasonably certain that the system does not really need the information. In a similar manner, principals will agree among themselves that the paperwork being demanded is pointless and will drag their feet until the request is abandoned.

The final mode of discretionary insubordination involves disobeying an instruction by following it literally. In this situation, a principal might receive a directive with detailed instructions which if followed would defeat the purposes of the directive. The principal understands the objective of the directive but defeats its purpose by following the instructions literally. On one occasion observed by the researchers, principals received forms to conduct a census on the racial composition of the school, and instructions that the forms were to be completed by the students. As the principal in this case knew, the students made a game of the racial question, with one-sixth of the student population indicating their race as Aleuts or Eskimos. In the words of the researchers, "With a straight face and without comment, the principal boxed up the questionnaires and returned them for tabulating to the district office."[43]

There are two ways of viewing discretionary insubordination. One is that taken by the researchers who consider these four forms as essential for the humanization of the system. The assumption is that the objective of insubordination is the welfare of the students. The coined term is "counterbureaucratic behavior" and is seen as "a balance weight to counteract the seemingly anti-educational forces constantly at work in large school systems."[44] Within this framework, the errors of the bureaucracy are corrected at the school level as principals bend the rules and change directives based on their judgment.

The other viewpoint is the one mentioned previously by Rogers where the actions of the principals are treated as a bureaucratic pathology. Within this context, the actions of the principals guarantee that the system will never work properly nor can it ever be reformed. Any attempt to introduce major changes in the system will be defeated by the discretionary insubordination of field staff. This case can be argued persuasively with the examples given by the researchers. Consider the example of the racial census conducted within the high school. It is possible that this census could produce important information on the racial composition of the school district and could have profound implications for any plans regarding school desegregation. If one assumes that correcting racial imbalances improves the quality of learning environments for students, then the action of the principal was not in their best interests. In fact, it is hard to discern how letting the students make a game of the census contributed to their welfare.

It could be easily claimed that all members of a central city school bureaucracy are primarily motivated by an interest in helping students, but this motivation is not enough to explain organizational behavior. A principal might be concerned primarily about the welfare of students, but she or he might also be interested in job protection, a future promotion to district superintendent, a transfer to a better school, or simply reducing the amount of work associated with the job. One cannot dismiss the desire to reduce workload as a motivating factor and a possible cause of discretionary insubordination.

Conclusion: Following the Rules of the Game

There is a danger in any description of organizational behavior that the reader is left with the impression that all bureaucratic actions are concerned with protection of self-interest and collective interests. This emphasis neglects the ideals that often propel people into organizations and guide their actions and decisions. This is particularly true of education which attracts large numbers of people who are dedicated to the improvement and advancement of learning and to the correction of social problems.

The pursuit of an ideal, like the pursuit of self-interest and survival, is affected by the structure of an organization. An individual learns that to accomplish a particular goal there must be some conformity to the formal and informal rules of the organization. With the present bureaucratic structure of central city schools, it is possible to pursue an educational ideal and display the same behaviors as anyone in pursuit of increased status and income. The reason for the possible similarities in behaviors is that the person attempting to actualize a particular goal might find it to her or his advantage to recognize and act within the boundaries of the formal and informal rules of the organization.

As part of the recognition of the formal and informal rules of an organization, someone attempting to accomplish a purely educational goal might consider that her or his colleagues in the organization are concerned about survival, advancement, and control. This would mean a careful development of any plan of action so that it does not threaten the informal networks or the positions of the members of the organization. Of course, this type of careful planning does not usually result in any type of revolutionary change and, in fact, can reduce the speed of change to a snail's pace.

Therefore, both the idealist and the opportunist must deal with the realities of organizational structures and behaviors. Actions regarding these realities can be in two directions. As suggested in the previous paragraph, one option is to attempt to work within the framework of the formal and informal networks of an organization. The other option would be to see fulfillment of ideals about education as being possible only through reform or a complete change in the bureaucratic structure of central city schools. This might mean replacing the authoritarian bureaucratic model with one that makes it easier to accomplish a particular goal. The danger with this approach is that in the midst of battle, the means can often become the end. For instance, in the battle for community control of the schools, the goal for minority groups was the creation of central city school systems that incorporated the beliefs, desires, and interests of the clientele. Community control was only a means of achieving those ends. But it sometimes happened that contestants in the struggle lost sight of these broader ends and just community control became the end.

Even with demands for a revolutionary change in the organization of central city schools there must be some understanding of how organizations have functioned so that past problems are not duplicated in a new context. Recognition has to be given to individual concerns about survival and advancement and how these human traits are shaped by the structure of an organization. Understanding the problems inherent in the present bureaucratic administration of schools might serve as a guide to those who seek reform or revolutionary change in the administration of central city schools.

The idealist and opportunist and the organizational conformist and revolutionary have to understand the advancement of their goals in the context of the realities of organizational behavior. As developed in this chapter, these behaviors in central city school systems can be divided into three major categories:

1. the relationship between the central administration and the community
2. the internal network of control in the bureaucratic structure
3. the relationship between the central bureaucracy and the rest of the school system

These three categories of relationship can be used as guides to action within or outside of the bureaucratic structure. In the first category, there seems to be general agreement that the primary concern of the central administration of central city schools in its relationship to the outside community is the protection of image. This results in behavior characterized by insulation from public pressures and a desire to control. The desire to control public access to the schools, educational programs, and the flow of information is based on a fear of being embarrassed or damaged by public events and a need to enhance the image of the organization for the benefit of individual members. This type of control is often justified by a claim to professionalism which is used to argue that decisions and control should be in the hands of experts and not the general public.

The second category emphasizes the importance of informal networks for understanding the internal workings of the organization. It is true that bureaucrats might often use formal rules as a means of delaying or avoiding action but this is not as important as the development of informal networks that protect individuals within the organization. Understanding the informal networks is often the key to getting something accomplished in an organization. What is important to understand about central city educational systems is that these internal networks are the mechanisms that manage the type of control described in the previous paragraph. Access to the central administration can be accomplished most easily by an outsider using these informal networks. Of course, it is hard for the outsider to know and understand these unofficial forms of organization.

For the third category, there is general agreement among the studies discussed in this chapter that there exists a sense of isolation between the central administration and the real world of the schools. This phenomenon has been explained from a variety of standpoints, including branding it a "bureaucratic pathology" and just describing the system as "loosely coupled." The explanation that seems to make the most sense is the one that stresses that school administrations must conform to external rules as opposed to business, which must conform to the actions of the marketplace. From this perspective, as the amount of external control and accompanying paperwork increases, so will the separation between "downtown" and the schools.

These three categories represent the bare minimum that must be known to act effectively within or outside of a central city school system. The reader must recognize, as has been shown throughout the chapter, that there are many nuances and subtleties in these categories of organizational behavior. Probably the most important thing to remember about any organization is that its behavior has to be understood as the result of the interaction of human beings within a formal structure.

Finally, it seems clear, after the review of organizational behavior in this chapter, that the actions of the bureaucracy must be considered an important part of the general structure of central city school politics. Certainly, the bureaucracy shapes and affects the policies established by Boards of Education and local elites. But more importantly, the bureaucracy can advise boards and community leaders on courses of actions that primarily serve the interests and needs of the organizational structure. This was the case in the decade of the 1970s when demands for community control and greater community participation in the schools were translated by the educational establishment into accountability and local school advisory and budgeting councils. As discussed in this chapter, these changes in the schools can only be understood within the framework of the politics and behaviors of educational bureaucracies.

Notes

1. For a description of the adoption of the industrial model by public school administrators, see Raymond Callahan, *Education and the Cult of Efficiency* (Chicago: University of Chicago Press, 1962) and David Tyack, *The One Best System* (Cambridge, Mass.: Harvard University Press, 1974).
2. Brian Rowan, "The Effects of Institutionalized Rules on Administrators," in Samuel B. Bachrach, ed., *Organizational Behavior in Schools and School Districts* (New York: Praeger Publishers, 1981), p. 49.
3. Paul E. Peterson, *School Politics Chicago Style* (Chicago: University of Chicago Press, 1976), p. 120.
4. David Rogers, *110 Livingston Street: Politics and Bureaucracy in the New York City Schools* (New York: Random House, 1968), p. 215.
5. Ibid., pp. 525–26.
6. Ibid., p. 298.
7. Ibid., p. 274.
8. Ibid., pp. 275–77.
9. Ibid., p. 301.
10. Ibid., p. 267.
11. Ibid., pp. 299–300.
12. Ibid., pp. 475–492.
13. Marilyn Gittell and T. Edward Hollander, *Six Urban School Districts* (New York: Praeger Publishers, 1968), pp. 52–53.
14. Ibid., p. 196.
15. Ibid., p. 197.
16. Joseph H. McGivney and James M. Haught, "The Politics of Education: A View from the Perspective of the Central Office Staff," in *Educational Administration Quarterly*, Vol. 8, No. 3 (August 1972), p. 35.
17. Ibid., p. 23.
18. Ibid., p. 23.
19. Ibid., p. 23.
20. Ibid., p. 30.

21. Ibid., p. 30.
22. Ibid., p. 31.
23. Ibid., p. 34.
24. Rowan, "Effects of Institutionalized Rules," pp. 48–49.
25. Ibid., p. 49.
26. Ibid., p. 61.
27. Karl E. Weick, "Educational Organizations as Loosely Coupled Systems," in *Administrative Science Quarterly*, Vol. 21 (March 1976), p. 3.
28. Rowan, "Effects of Institutionalized Rules," p. 69.
29. Peterson, *School Politics Chicago Style*, p. 112.
30. Ibid., p. 114.
31. Ibid., p. 114.
32. Ibid., p. 222.
33. Ibid., pp. 220–23.
34. Ibid., p. 226.
35. Ibid., p. 239.
36. For a broader discussion of this issue see Joel Spring, *Educating the Worker-Citizen* (New York: Longman, 1981).
37. Leon Lessinger, *Every Kid a Winner: Accountability in Education* (New York: Simon and Schuster, 1970), p. 128.
38. Wayne Barret, "The Politics of Flunking," in *The Village Voice*, Vol. 37, No. 22 (June 1, 1982), pp. 1, 24–26, 38.
39. Van Cleve Morris, Robert L. Crowson, Emanuel Hurwitz, and Cynthia Porter-Gehrie, *The Urban Principal: Discretionary Decision-Making in a Large Educational Organization*, pp. 153–54.
40. Ibid., p. 143.
41. Ibid., p. 143.
42. Ibid., pp. 146–47.
43. Ibid., p. 149.
44. Ibid., p. 149.

4

The Principal as Middle Manager and Entrepreneur

The school principal is successful in his work to the extent that he is able to contain and constrain the forces of change with which he must contend as a matter of daily routine; whatever force he exerts on the dynamics of the school contributes to its stability even when he wants to act or believes he is acting in a way that will encourage an aura of change.

WOLCOTT, The Man in the Principal's Office
(New York: Holt), 1973, p. 307.

If an organization were a car, the top would be the driver, the bottom would be the engine and the drive train, while the middle would constitute all of the electrical and mechanical connections between them.

KANTER and STEIN, Life in Organizations, 1979, p. 80

As a middle manager, the principal occupies an ambiguous position. For, although given only limited access to authority at the top, he or she is entrusted with important leadership responsibilities at the school building level.[1]

The principal's role has been analyzed from a number of perspectives. One approach emphasizes the personal qualities, traits, and skills associated with effective leadership. A second perspective, more recently taken by analysts, is the "behavior approach" which attempts to observe and record in minute detail the conversations, rituals, and other activities constituting the daily round of events in the principal's life. The third approach views the principal's role in a less isolated way than the previous two by seeing the principal's actions in the context

104

of the school system as a whole. Here, the success of the principal is viewed as tied to his or her power and influence as a social actor who must both negotiate with top management's inner circle (the school board and central office) and an oftentimes remote, distrustful, unionized teaching staff.[2] This latter perspective is the one we favor in understanding the principal's position, although we will also present an analysis of the principal's role as a consequence of his or her traits and behaviors. The emphasis made ultimately in our discussion is on the advantages afforded principals whose entrepreneurial savvy and energy maximize organizational resources and minimize the dilemmas, constraints, and ambiguity inherent in their work role.

The world of the principal is not only complex but also has been haunted by the mythology of administrative leadership, a fixed belief that outstanding principals possess readily observable traits and behaviors which can be modeled by and transferred to their less effective colleagues. This mythology has obscured at least three salient dimensions of the real world of the public school principal:

1. the ambiguity of life as a middle manager in a complex public school system
2. the destructive masculine ethic that pervades organizational theory and prevents adequate analysis of the principal's role
3. the dual tracking system that results in differential career opportunities for white males as opposed to women and minorities

Life in the Middle

To provide a context for the analysis of the principal's role responsibilities, day-to-day work life, and differential patterns of career rewards gained by male, female, and minority principals, we must examine life in the middle ranks of the school system. Organizational life, like life in any social group, presents each participant with dilemmas and possibilities that correspondingly delimit and expand choices for action that are open to the individual. Organizational life in a central city public school system is governed by uncertainties and ambiguities, as populations shrink and change and budgets constrict. Problems and options for action are different for actors at the top, middle, and bottom.

Life in the middle has been characterized by Kanter and Stein[3] as the most problematic. Unlike those at the top, middle managers cannot set system policy, and unlike those at the bottom whose jobs are routine, and in the case of public school teachers governed by union structures

and loyalties, they cannot cloak themselves in the anonymity of a unionized monolith. Thus, the most difficult role in the system is that of
middle manager occupied by the public school elementary or secondary school principal.

There is a general pressure for the building principal to "play-it-
safe," as is the case for any organization middle manager:

> Over time, for the middle [manager] . . . powerlessness coupled
> with accountability, with responsibility for results dependent
> upon the actions of others, provokes a cautious, low risk, play-it-
> safe attitude. Those in the middle are often unwilling to jeopar-
> dize the privilege they have attained by rocking the boat. . . . The
> organization's concern with regulations reduces administrators'
> spheres of autonomy and limits their influence and decision-mak-
> ing power.[4]

Thus, were it not for the discretionary power accorded to principals by
the ambiguity and mystery of their jobs, it would be difficult to imagine
any such phenomonon as an effective principal, one who somehow
provides increasingly good pupil performance, smoothly functioning
staff relations, pleasant school atmosphere (free of violence and despair), and harmonious community interaction. Yet, as we will see in the
case studies at the end of this chapter, two principals in the Cincinnati
system, through very different situations, have created effective
schools.

Role Responsibilities of the Principal

Historically, the principal's role in the school emphasized clerical duties
such as maintaining records, filing reports, and managing the physical
facilities of the school building. These responsibilities initially were
assumed by a head teacher but during the nineteenth century became
associated with the post of principal. The incumbent's instructional
duties gradually diminished, although instructional leadership responsibilities were retained.

By the turn of the century, although the responsibilities associated
with the principalship had not changed dramatically, the long fascina-
tion with the role's ideal managerial and instructional leadership skills
had begun. The emphasis on these capacities was nurtured by the
romance of organizational leadership springing from a "masculine
ethic" of rationality and reason that still pervades organizational theory.
Although tempered by a human relations theory that acknowledged
the importance of social interactions among key actors, rational models

of the organization continue to maintain a hold on the popular imagination. The rational organization mythology has roots in early twentieth century thought:

> A "masculine ethic" of rationality and reason can be identified in the early image of managers. This "masculine ethic" elevates the traits assumed to belong to men with educational advantages to necessities for effective organizations: a tough-mined approach to problems; analytic abilities to abstract and plan; a capacity to set aside personal, emotional considerations in the interests of task accomplishment; and a cognitive superiority in problem-solving and decision-making.[5]

The corresponding "feminine ethic" assumes that women's characteristic approach is governed by emotionality and petty concern with interpersonal relationships and responsibilities. Thus, women are dismissed as "managerial material" by the rational model. Instead, women's role in the organization is defined as supportive of the male manager. In schools, women's skills in nurturance best suit them for the role of classroom teacher. In contrast, the role of principal requires an "educational leader" cast in a mold reflecting male values and orientations. This is hardly surprising since leadership research has been based almost entirely on studies of males. Thus, leaders are portrayed as effective when they are "assertive, powerful, productive, strong, have uninterrupted career patterns, definite career goals, and assume positions with increasing prestige and responsibilities."[6]

According to this still widely held notion of the role, the principal functions as the school manager and instructional leader exhibiting the characteristics of the cool and level-headed manager described above. It is commonplace today for handbooks, used by students in graduate courses in educational administration in training for the principalship, to list not only the functions associated with the role, but also to provide inventories of the traits and characteristics thought to be linked with successful performance in the role. For example, Blumberg and Greenfield[7] provide a list of characteristics found by a team of researchers to be associated with administrators who managed schools described as "beacons of brilliance" (as opposed to other schools in the same study found to be "potholes of pestilence"). Apparently believing that students in educational administration can modify their characteristics to correspond to those of the successful leader, the authors list eight characteristics shared by principals in educational "beacons of brilliance":

1. Most did not intend to become principals.
2. Most expressed a sincere faith in children.

3. They had an ability to work effectively with people and to secure their cooperation.
4. They were aggressive in securing recognition of the needs of their school.
5. They were enthusiastic as principals and accepted their responsibility as a mission rather than as a job.
6. They were committed to education and could distinguish between long-term and short-term educational goals.
7. They were adaptable.
8. They were able strategists.[8]

As we indicated at the beginning of this chapter, we do not find the trait approach particularly useful in understanding the principal's role. There are at least three reasons for holding this position. First, a "bag of virtues" approach is hardly a useful training mechanism for aspiring principals. For example, what is one to do if, contrary to the findings of the study just reviewed, an aspiring administrator has long held an intention to become a principal, holds less than a sincere faith in children, has an assertive rather than aggressive nature, and so forth?

Second, and more significant, the trait approach assumes that in fact principals *are* primarily managers and instructional leaders and that earnest performance in these capacities will result in successful career placement, evaluation, and advancement. As we will see, this is *not* the case for women, who are generally denied principalships, *despite* the recorded success of female administrators who have gained access to the role.

The gap between the managerial and leadership traits assumed to characterize the role and the way principals actually spend their time results in considerable role strain and frustration for the role incumbent. In a national survey of senior high school principals, most of those responding identified personnel and program development as their top priorities but also reported spending more time on school clerical duties than on either of these top-rated leadership functions. Unfortunately, the explanation for failure and frustration to meet priorities is usually not tied to either the conflicting demands of a middle managerial position in an uncertain and often faltering school system or to the structural dimensions of the principal's role; instead, it is blamed on the role incumbent's lack of leadership skills and knowledge. Like any middle manager, principals are simultaneously faced with tugs and pulls from above and below. More than having a sincere faith in children, being aggressive in serving the needs of their schools, and so forth, it is imperative that principals know how to establish task priorities and allocate time.

A Day in the Life of the Principal

Recent observations of their daily work reveal that most principals do not behave according to the rationality of a textbook case of educational leadership. Several studies have shown exactly how much time principals invest in specific tasks on a day-to-day basis.

Observational studies or ethnographies of the elementary and secondary school principal reviewed by Manasse[9] present findings that clarify the day-to-day behavior and role responsibilities characterizing the life of the central city school middle manager. The following summary of a set of recent descriptive studies of the principalship is highly dependent on the synthesis of these studies. The primary source of information for Manasse's review is a study of 16 Chicago elementary and secondary school principals who were observed over a two-year period (1978–1980). For some of their sample, the researchers recorded all observed behaviors, activities, and conversations for up to 12 work days. Principals in the study came from varied ethnic and racial backgrounds and included both men and women who worked in schools that varied in size as well as in racial, ethnic, and socioeconomic characteristics.

To compare the behavior of school principals with that of middle managers in business organizations, the Chicago researchers used categories developed by Mintzberg[10] in a study of business executives. Several distinctions between the daily life of the business middle manager and the principal emerged:

> Business executives use written communication much more frequently and handle considerably more mail than principals do. They transact a large share of their managerial business in scheduled sit-down group meetings, while principals spend most of their time in spontaneous one-to-one conversations with colleagues and clients. Unscheduled interchanges accounted for only 10 percent of the executives' time, but 76 percent of the time of high school principals in the Chicago study. Finally, Mintzberg's executives spent little time making walking tours of their premises while the Chicago principals spent most of their time on their feet, seemingly in constant motion.[11]

Thus, unlike business managers, principals face a constant round of interruptions and demands which are usually negotiated in face-to-face interactions with teachers and students.

In fact, the principal's day is strenuous fare, punctuated by brief, spontaneous conversational exchanges as is clear in Manasse's overview of the Chicago study:

Elementary principals in the Chicago study spent 80 percent of their workday in face-to-face interchanges with staff, faculty members, pupils, and others, an additional 8 percent of their time in telephone interactions, and 12 percent in desk work. These daily interactions typically were unplanned and very short; a school day could consist of anywhere from 50 to over 100 separate events and as many as 400 separate interactions. Principals initiated the contact for over two-thirds of their interactions, these exchanges—usually made while the principal was on the run—were typically quite brief. Interactions with parents, on the other hand, tended to be longer, often because they were conferences concerning student misbehavior, or, less frequently, parental complaints about a teacher, other students, or school regulations. Despite wide individual variation, as a group the principals spent more time interacting with students than with any other group, supervising student movement, or conferring with students who had caused a disturbance. (Elementary principals averaged 22 percent of their time with students, while their secondary colleagues averaged 15 percent.) Principals were also in contact with their superiors about 11 percent of their day, but spent very little time interacting with other principals. Finally, the elementary principals in this study were physically present in their offices less than half of the workday, spending about 40 percent of work hours off school grounds, in the corridors, visiting classrooms, or working with clerks and aides in the outer office.[12]

After reviewing the major findings of the Chicago study, the initial temptation is to dismiss the principal's role as unimportant except in ad hoc problem management in the school building. The temptation is especially compelling since both successful and unsuccessful principals displayed similar patterns of behavior in their daily work lives.

However, because middle manager positions have considerable role ambiguity, they are afforded extensive discretionary privileges; for example, the capacity to select and order task priorities, to make contact with others, and to expand time and effort in accomplishing tasks. We agree with Manasse that "effective principals take advantage of the ambiguity of their roles to align them with their own goals and their own mix of skills, strengths, and weaknesses."[13] The Chicago study identified patterned sets of behaviors associated with successful school operations whereby pupil achievement advanced, staff members were accountable and cooperative, school atmosphere was conducive to learning, and community relations were exemplary. Effective principals in successful schools were seen by the researchers as "creative insubordinates," able actors who cut through bureaucratic red tape without upending the system or the school.

The Principalship as a Career

Organizations, including school systems, allocate benefits, privileges, and rewards to employees who are favorably judged by their supervisors and subordinates. Unlike teaching, the role of the middle manager in education can be viewed as a career since careers generally involve a sequence of related training and earlier job-related experience considered essential to skilled, career-line performance. Career mobility is critically dependent on sponsorship, the political support of a heavily invested mentor who actively promotes the career ambitions of his or her protegé. Thus, the principalship is generally rewarded to those who have earned at least a master's degree in educational administration or a related field but who have additionally received the sustained sponsorship of an influential member of the system hierarchy, most often the building principal, more rarely a superintendent, assistant superintendent, or other staff member in central administration.

Although women have considerable difficulty in gaining access to the role, once they have achieved a position as building principal, evaluations of their performance are generally favorable; in fact, there is some evidence that women principals are more successful in their roles than men:

> . . . They are more likely than their male counterparts to involve themselves in instructional supervision, to exhibit democratic leadership styles, to be concerned with students, and to seek community involvement. . . . In addition, schools with female principals have higher student morale, more frequent parental approval of school activities, and teacher morale higher or equal to that of schools headed by men.[14]

Yet, survey data indicate that despite their apparently superior skills in the principalship generally and counter to affirmative action policies and equal opportunity employment legislation, in recent years, women have become an even smaller percentage of assistant principals and principals. The number, never high, has fallen from 15.2% in 1970–71 to 12.9% in 1976.[15] Moreover, minority women face even more discouraging prospects for career mobility in school administration:

> Black women are likely to hold positions as consultant, supervisor, elementary principal, and administrative assistant, while men almost exclusively hold the secondary principals and central office line positions. Women in elementary principalships tend to be found in the so-called tough, predominantly black school(s).[16]

Whereas white male administrators generally are under 40 at the time of their initial appointment as principals, black women usually do not advance to the principalship until their mid to late 40s, reducing their opportunities for further career advancement.

It also appears that opportunities for women are extremely limited in other ways. One recent survey of a national sample of high school principals revealed that although only 18% of all principals surveyed worked in the highly urbanized mid-Atlantic region, fully 35% of all female principals surveyed were located there. There were no female principals reported in the Pacific Mountain region. These and other similar data from the same survey led the panel of investigators to conclude that opportunities for female high school principals were limited to urban centers in the declining cities of the East, Midwest, and West. Although almost half (48%) of all principals work in towns or cities of 24,000 or less, only 14% of female high school principals have positions in cities or towns with populations of less than 149,999, according to the same study.[17] Moreover, attitudes toward women administrators in education at all levels correspond to the patterns of regional placement for secondary principals just described. In a study of a representative sample of adults living in a western state it was found that urbanization and years of education were both associated with more favorable responses toward women administrators:

> Those in rural regions and those with less education express more prejudiced attitudes even when respondent age and acquaintance with a female administrator are taken into account.[18]

Thus, we are left with a troubling inconsistency. Although as we have noted, women principals appear to handle their role responsibilities at least as capably as men, social attitudes, especially in areas outside the central city, remain negative. Moreover, the numbers of women in the principalship as a percentage of those holding that position have actually declined in the last decade-and-a-half despite affirmative action. This latter trend is especially discouraging in the face of increased enrollment in advanced degree programs by women seeking educational training appropriate for movement into school administration. According to Adkison:

> While only 8 percent of the student population in educational administration programs affiliated with the University Council for Educational Administration was female in the late 1960s, women earned 21 percent of the master's degrees in educational administration in 1971–1972 and 29 percent of those awarded in 1975–

1976. In the same period, women's share of doctorates in educational administration rose from 6 percent to 20 percent.[19]

To understand why women and minorities have been given limited opportunities in gaining access to the role of principal, it is important to consider the principalship in the school system context. As Wolcott noted—albeit, in male-biased language—at the beginning of the chapter, the critical determinant of success in the principal's work is her or his ability to sustain the illusion that the ship of the school (and school system) maintains a steady course even when the principal is busy altering the rigging.

As we have seen, the prevailing school organization mythology based on the "masculine ethic" emphasizes the leadership strength of a (white male) rational planner. Thus, it is not surprising that women and minorities have difficulty becoming principals. Research is clear on the point that "authorities are less likely to back up a woman in authority than a man, and consequently subordinates are less likely to accept directives and evaluations from a woman."[20] Because organizations value internal stability, especially in times of change and uncertainty such as those that currently beset schools, the homogeneity of the management structure is likely to become critical to those at the top. As we previously noted, women currently constitute a smaller percentage of middle managers than they did in the late 1960s. Faced with shrinking populations and budgetary shortages, systems become less willing to advance women and minorities to managerial positions. Studies of career mobility patterns for men, women, and minorities support this generalization.

In a study of career mobility patterns in Los Angeles metropolitan area, Ortiz found that in school systems

> [M]en are more likely than women to occupy those positions with greater potential for power and opportunity as well as those at the upper levels of the hierarchy. Male mobility tends to be vertical through a series of line positions entailing the administration of adults (as in central office positions). Women tend to move through positions involving instruction and interaction with children from which vertical movement is rare, while minorities tend to be limited to instructing and containing other minorities.[21]

When minority principals are appointed, they are often given positions in "problem" schools with heavy minority student enrollments. There are at least two negative consequences having implications for career mobility of the incumbent in this situation. First, the minority administrator tends to be identified by the top as a "specialist" in minority school problem-solving as opposed to a generalist, capable of handling a broad range of administrative duties. Second, minority administrators tend to become valued only as crisis managers whose role responsibilities are deemed important to the system so long as there are fires to be put out. The minority administrator is likely to be discouraged from further career mobility opportunities once "problems" are under control.[22]

Thus, the principalship as a career must be viewed as a dual tracking system. Men, specifically white males, are far more likely than women and minority group members to find the way clear to advancement from the classroom (and athletic field) to the principalship and to the top. Women and minorities, on the other hand, must contend with specialized assignments to problem schools or spotty access to a few token positions, usually at the elementary school level.

The Entrepreneurial Principal

Rather than viewing the successful principal who rocks the boat as a "creative insubordinate,"[23] we see the effective public school middle manager as a skilled entrepreneur, allowed by favorable opportunities in the system structure to chance a "career roll," similar to a clever and lucky gambler. The image of a gambler is especially apt. An administrative career that results in successful relations with superordinates, peers, and subordinates is related to differences in "response to opportunities for power existing in the school district."[24]

According to findings in one set of case studies carried out by Greenfield and his associates,[25] unsuccessful principals, particularly females, assumed many limits to their behaviors, tended to look to others for direction in solving organizational problems, and often hid behind regulations when enmeshed in organizational dilemmas. On the other hand, those who were successful in their roles, like gamblers, tended to push the limits.

The entrepreneurial principal is successful in the development of an effective school by virtue of a capacity to (1) understand and manipulate position power and authority while recognizing the persistence of inflexibility at the top and resistance at the bottom; (2) create and embody a highly personalized and school-specific rule structure; and (3) create and manage the "psychic ambience" of the school community through such activities as setting schedules, arranging building maintenance, regulating access to and movement in the building, ordering and obtaining institutional materials, and serving as a buffer between teachers and parents. These organizational strategies are enhanced by a self conscious image-building process that the successful principal uses to "sell" his or her school to the community. These strategies are intuitive as much as they are "rational" and most importantly, bear the personal stamp of the school principal. This description of a charismatic leader fits the most successful principals, those whose schools are acknowledged as the most effective in their systems.

The entrepreneurial capacities we have just considered emerge under a set of specific conditions. First, the principal must have achieved smoothly functioning staff relations. In other words, building operations must be securely entrusted to a capable teaching corps that can function with minimal direction from the principal, allowing him or her to turn attention to issues of leadership in the school system at large. It should be emphasized that staff strength is problematic and not directly under the control of the principal, who often must take whatever comes with the building in the form of a teaching staff. Union controls, teacher autonomy, and inertia in the system can make the most "skilled" principal helpless in the face of resistance, recalcitrance, and low levels of commitment.[26]

Once instructional operations are secure, the principal may devote only minimal attention to staff supervision, curriculum development, and the like. For the most part, these functions are the province of trusted faculty lieutenants who are the principal's allies and the remaining teachers' trusted leaders.

Second, the principal must be located in a system that, by virtue of system-wide instructional programs such as alternative or magnet schools and stable, often external (state and federal) funding programs, has available resources that can be exploited by the entrepreneur. Thus, building staff stability and flexibility of system resources form the minimal set of favorable structural opportunities that allow the principal to chance a set of moves to achieve the "finest building in the system," as one entrepreneur in our Cincinnati study put it.

In an era of scarce resources, the principal's major role responsibilities are directed at two related goals: maintaining a flow of goods and services (office supplies, instructional materials, speciality teachers, guidance counselors, and the like) and holding the customers.[27] It is our observation that effective schools, as we described them earlier in this chapter, have principals who exercise managerial savvy and energetic entrepreneurship to promote school building interests, particularly the needs of children and teachers.

An effective school building operation demands funds. Principals are constrained in the amount of money available to them from local, state, and federal sources; however, the successful entrepreneur is able to augment monetary constributions to school building operating costs, as the following example illustrates.

In Cincinnati, as in most publicly supported school systems, locally generated funds are allocated to each school building on a per pupil basis. Thus, in the 1982–83 school year, Anderson Place Elementary School, with an enrollment of approximately 800 students, received allocations of $1,846 per pupil, in the range of the system average ($1,943) for similar schools. From the system's general fund, Anderson Place was budgeted $1,275,761 to cover all instructional and support services costs including transportation expenses, custodial fees, and the like. This sum does not include monies allocated by the state of Ohio or the federal government for specific student populations. Because Anderson Place has a large student body—the system average at the elementary level is 462—its budget was correspondingly larger than the average sum of $894,071 paid from the general fund to elementary schools that year. Janice Mooney, Anderson Place Principal, raised an additional $6,200 to cover general operating costs by conducting two fund raisers. The first project was a highly successful Christmas trim-a-tree campaign promoted by a pizza parlor chain. The staff (and Janice herself) later regretted the grotesquely commercial character of the firm's sales pitch. Ornaments and promotional materials were displayed during a school assembly by a man in a mouse suit assisted by a garrulous female emcee.

Over the course of her experience in such campaigns at Anderson Place and in two other schools, Janice Mooney has learned that successful fund raising depends upon choosing the right enterprise, one that generates enthusiasm, anticipates loopholes, and manipulates the prize structure to benefit students who establish outstanding sales records. For example, in the Chuck E. Cheese trim-a-tree campaign, Janice made special arrangements with the organization's representative to get $350 for cash prizes rather than the firm's usual "junk" prizes. An "easy" $700 was raised by having individual student pictures taken. Janice considers this an effortless fund raiser since a single bulletin sent home with each child and one hectic day of photo taking are the only requirements for a successful campaign.

Costs for running secondary schools are greater because of the increased complexity of the school program; for example, drivers' training, athletics, and the like. In Cincinnati in 1982–83, the average student enrollment in each of the nine area high schools was 1,614 students. Overall, 14,730 students were enrolled in basic, vocational and special education programs throughout these schools. The amount budgeted per pupil at the School for Creative and Performing Arts (SCPA) was $2,436, placing it in the "normal range" for similar schools. The total allocated to SCPA from the system's general fund was $2,627,970. Approximately $300,000 was added to the school operating budget through income from private donors' gifts, ticket sales for school productions, concession stands operated at school performances, special performances for a variety of groups outside of the school, and a host of other fund raising events.

The previous examples illustrated that even in organizations with rational, equalitarian standards for allocating funds to subunits, that is, a per pupil expenditures formula, there are discretionary avenues available to middle managers. As the examples indicate, school principals, by virtue of both the constraints and possibilities at work in their curricular programs, Parents Teacher Organizations, the system structure, and so forth, can enhance their organization's position in a most critical area—funding.

Closely related to funding, declining student enrollments are a critical issue to central city administrators. Enrollment is important from the organization's perspective primarily because "headcount" determines the level of staffing, distribution of instructional materials, office supplies, and other resources made available to the school from the central office. Even the salaries of principals are keyed to indicators of the number of students enrolled, such as the percentage of students in attendance daily (95% is considered the ideal by most systems). Thus, enrollment loss is translated into redistribution of valued instructional support. To retain students and to gain transfer students, successful principals adopt several strategies to "hold the customers":

1. enhance the attractiveness of the school program
2. court and recruit parents of prospective students
3. once on board, counsel and advise individual student clients[28]

These three strategies can be seen as comprising an image-building strategy that is critical to the principal's foremost role: maintaining a growing student body.

In the Chicago area principal study, the researchers found that effective principals were challenged by the city-wide Access to Excellence program. This program was in actuality a system of alternative schools and facilities established during the 1970s to encourage racially balanced school enrollments. Programs included classical schools, magnet schools, and career development centers. Similarly, in Cincinnati, an array of school programs was developed during the same period. These included college prep curricula and individually guided education (IGE) as well as more exotic formats such as German and French bilingual schools, Montessori Programs, and the School for Creative and Performing Arts, all designed to capture the interest of both the white middle class and black students. Not all programs in either city were capable of attracting and holding racially diverse student clienteles. Those schools noted for their recruitment and retention of students had principals who actively employed the three customer-holding strategies outlined above.

In Chicago, Miller Academy, before its transformation into a magnet school, had been losing enrollment. Like many neighborhood schools in Chicago and in large urban centers generally, it had suffered the usual student exodus associated with a rapidly changing residential community. However, a determined group of young parents was committed to the retention of the school in their neighborhood, convinced that with the proper leadership the school could become a model for the city system. Fortunately, the community successfully recruited a principal with the skills for image building that were necessary to gain students from other city schools to bolster enrollment. The principal, aided by influential citizens with whom he invested much time, developed linkages to the press which frequently reported favorable stories about the school. For example, an exchange program with Italian students was developed in cooperation with local families which gained favorable publicity for the school. Reporters even covered relatively mundane events such as the school's Halloween party, keeping the school visible in the community and maintaining its positive image.

Similarly, Janice Mooney in Cincinnati uses her considerable public relations skills to enhance her school's image in the eyes of the building's full constituency: administration, teaching staff, local neighborhood community, and civic leadership. Not only are the building's hallways bright and clean, they are filled with luxuriant plants, watered by the children, as well as brightly displayed projects completed by the children. At Halloween and other holidays, Janice personally tours the school, stopping in each classroom to ask children about their plans to construct mobiles, drawings, cutouts, and the like to decorate the building corridors. Care is taken to make sure each child's work is on display within the classroom or hall. "Andy Grams" are regularly sent home by classroom teachers to reward children for acts of kindness, classroom accomplishments, and displays of athletic skill. Selected as a site for the visitation of a Chamber of Commerce team of civic leaders, Anderson Place in 1982 received the enthusiastic positive appraisal of influential area leaders which prompted a generous written tribute from the system superintendent. Staff receive teaching awards each year. Teachers are selected by the Anderson Place Building Committee, but the notion originated with Janice.

"Holding the customers" through the construction of a favorable school image occurs in the face of structural contradictions. The principal in Chicago's Murray Academy and Janice Mooney in Cincinnati's

Anderson Place School must negotiate strategies for maintaining and recruiting school enrollment in systems that are caught in a double bind: on the one hand, to avoid unfavorable court action in desegregation litigation, school systems must demonstrate equal opportunity for black minority students; on the other hand, principals of neighborhood schools without special programs accuse their alternative school peers of "raiding" their student populations to achieve racially balanced enrollments. In Cincinnati, this phenomonon has surfaced actively at least twice within the last five years. Principals vociferously complained to the superintendent that a "brain drain" was siphoning off the brightest students from neighborhood schools. In a memo to his Evaluation Branch chief, Joseph Felix, Superintendent James Jacobs referred to principals' complaints as the "issue of creaming neighborhood schools for the benefit of alternatives."[29] Felix's response included a copy of an earlier memo to Jacobs on the same issue. Not only was the "brain drain" a recurrent issue but, contrary to principals' perceptions, students who left neighborhood schools for alternatives had test scores that tended to be lower than the highest stanine scores (7, 8, and 9):

> Approximately one in six (15.5%) of the high achieving students in grades 1–6 in neighborhood schools is attending an alternative program at a different location. A larger proportion of average students (16.3%) and a smaller proportion of below average students (13.1%) are attending alternative programs at a different location. Overall the "brain drain" does not remove a disproportionate percentage of high achieving students from neighborhood schools.[30]

It can be concluded that principals in neighborhood schools resent the loss of students no matter what their levels of tested ability might be. This resentment makes sense because, as we have seen, student enrollment is the key to the principal's access to building resources.

The Cincinnati Principalship in the 1980s

Not surprisingly, in the early 1980s the modal principal at both the elementary and secondary levels is a white male. Although 38% of secondary school principals are black men (there is only one female, a black woman), 12 of the system's 21 positions at the junior and senior high school levels are held by white men. At the elementary level, 53% of those in the field are white men, and black women constitute the second largest proportion (19%). Equal numbers (11) of white women and black men serve as principals at the elementary level. Clearly, white women are the most underrepresented of all racial and gender groups considered. This is consistent with a central administration policy emphasizing racial desegregation issues and instructional leadership at the expense of sex equity issues.

Instructional leadership is stressed in a 1981 memo from Raymond Brokamp, assistant superintendent in Curriculum and Instruction, to all system principals. The memo is actually a 14-page document outlining strategies ("illustrative activities") and resources to be utilized by principals in attaining a set of 14 objectives.[31] The principal's role as instructional leader is seen in three aspects: goal focusing, resource distributing, and program monitoring. A more general description of the instructional leadership role of the principal is set forward in Board Policy N. 2221:

> Each school shall be under the supervision of a principal.
>
> A principal shall be the instructional leader, the administrator and the individual responsible for good communications with pupils, staff, parents, and the school neighborhood. *Instructional leadership is the first priority, but all three of these roles are interrelated and concurrent.*
>
> *Factors crucial to instructional leadership are supervision of the quality of the instructional program including the coordination of curriculum and the development and implementation of necessary programs, staff supervision including appraisal and lesson planning, and communication of school needs to the line officer.*
>
> As administrator, the principal shall be responsible for the organization, administration, and supervision of all school pupils and employees, processes, activities, and property. *He/she shall manage all resources available to the school which support and insure the effective delivery of instructional services to pupils* and shall provide for the welfare and safety of pupils and staff within the school environment.
>
> The principal shall formulate rules and regulations for the operation and management of the school and shall be responsible for the observance and enforcement of the policies and regulations of the Board of Education and directives of the superintendent.
>
> Continuing good communications both within the school and with the outside community are essential for the most effective operation of the school system. Cooperation with the PTA or comparable groups and with neighborhood organizations shall be continually encouraged.

In the case studies that follow, we examine the specific strategies used by two Cincinnati principals in routinely carrying out multiple role responsibilities as instructional leaders, administrators, and individuals "responsible for good communications" with the school's multiple constituencies. Our study took us to schools considered by the central administration in the Ed Center to be the system's most effective schools. Thus, our portraits are of exceptional school middle managers, people considered by their superiors to be the best in the business.

Case Study of Janice Mooney

Janice Mooney, principal of Anderson Place Elementary School, is a strikingly beautiful woman of about 40 years whose personal presence is arresting. A colleague describes her as a "Celtic goddess." She wears stylish clothes because she believes the children appreciate seeing her well groomed. Her office, blooming with plants, decoratively carpeted and furnished (out of her own pocket), reflects its occupant's playfulness and sense of beauty. Two plush animals embrace each other on a book shelf. Pictures of a pet cat and her dog Samantha (a frequent visitor to the school) hang on a wall. A large drawing of Madisonville Elementary School, done by a child, is displayed on another. Her letter of lavish praise from the superintendent is displayed in her small adjoining lavatory. Prominent behind her desk is a makeup table with lighted mirror. The desk itself faces two oak benches covered with soft cushions which Janice fashioned at home. The desk is often covered with correspondence, reports, and other "paper work." Writing memos and filing reports are often deferred to the weekend when Janice comes in to "shuffle papers" for a few hours on Saturday or Sunday.

Janice Mooney's belief is that Anderson Place is what it is because of its "fine faculty." In gratitude to them she plants mums in the fall and bulbed plants in spring close to where the faculty enters the school. In tracing the history of the school (her personal career history did not emerge for some time into the study), Janice pointed out that Anderson Place was the school that was not supposed to work. It is located at the edge of a predominantly black community in a building that had originally housed Lyon Junior High, a school whose program had been widely regarded as a failure. Anderson Place draws most of its student body from the Madisonville and Oakley communities, the same neighborhoods that had sent students to Lyon Junior High. These widely distant neighborhoods contain low and middle income black families (Madisonville) and low and middle income white urban Appalachian families (Oakley). As Janice sees it, Madisonville had nothing to lose since the school was located in the neighborhood and children could walk to school; Oakley on the other hand, had everything to lose. Not only were Oakley children bused in, but Janice herself, though white, was identified with the Madisonville community where she had been school principal before schools in both neighborhoods had been closed.

The school supports a diverse program rather than a single format. Janice described the college prep curriculum as a lure for upper income families, although the college prep program actually enrolls children from a differentiated social class spectrum. The college prep curriculum is a magnet or alternative program that recruits student membership from throughout the city. Approximately 30% of Anderson Place students in grades 1 through 6 are enrolled in the college prep program. Only a small number of these students are bused from neighborhoods other than Oakley or Madisonville. However, Janice has heard by the grapevine that the principal of a nearby elementary school with a predominantly white middle class student body, is upset at the departure of 10 of his students, all of whom had top stanine scores in reading and math achievement. Janice is happy to enroll these students since a major goal is to raise student reading achievement scores. Among Cincinnati elementary schools in 1982, Anderson Place ranked 17th in reading achievement, up from 26th the year before. A major academic goal in 1983 is to be among the top 10.

Although the college prep curriculum with computer-assisted learning and other alluring features may be the flagship program at Anderson Place, the school offers a diversified educational format. In addition to the regular program enrolling an additional 50% of the learners, there are seven classrooms of special education. Programs include four classes of slow learners, one class of learning-delayed children, and one class of severe behavior-problem children. These classes are smaller in size than either the regular or college prep classes and enroll students citywide.

Janice describes her teaching staff as "key" to the school's success. Although she brought some of her staff from Madisonville and subsequently recruited two teachers with whom she had previously worked at other schools, most are at Anderson Place by accident—by virtue of seniority. Not all faculty are superstars. She rates only 35–40% top notch ... "you leave them alone and they will just fly. The next echelon sees what occurs with the top group and they get inspired."

The Teacher Building Committee, elected by the staff according to union regulations, comprises her top leadership who work closely with Janice to "market" innovations. For example, the committee, at Janice's suggestion, organized Community Day, inviting representatives from various civic organizations to spend the day at Anderson Place. Members of the Oakley Community Council, Madisonville Coordinating Committee, and Madison Villa, a retirement home, visited the school. Refreshments were served and visitors spent time in several classrooms interacting with children during reading lessons. Visitors were encouraged to return to the school in the capacity of volunteers. Community Day accomplished at least three goals:

1. spread the good word about the school to the immediate community, including individuals without children enrolled at Anderson Place
2. generated a potential pool of school volunteers
3. served as a pilot test of a similar program Janice and her staff wished to organize for Anderson Place parents

Although mandated by the union as a clearinghouse for grievances (complaints which typically are directed against the principal—teachers' immediate line supervisor), the Building Committee at Anderson Place is in fact a major catalyst for program innovation.

Students at Anderson Place are constantly reminded by their principal that they are number one, and that they attend the best school in Cincinnati. Before the school day begins at 8 A.M., like a cheerleader at a pep rally, Janice starts each morning with a battery-powered bullhorn organizing children in lines by classrooms for entry into the building. All Cincinnati public schools manage pupil entry in a similar manner. However, not all school principals oversee the operation, generally leaving this process to be coordinated by classroom teachers. Janice not only supervises entry to the school but also is on hand at lunch periods, lunch recess, and school leaving times. During these intervals (comprising about 20% of her day), she interacts with the children and is available to hear their complaints, recent accomplishments, family news, and so forth. Janice knows the names of most of the 800 students at Anderson Place, and has considerable knowledge of their family backgrounds and relationships, especially if they have siblings or other relatives in school.

School assemblies, most frequently scheduled during the fall, begin with rousing choruses of "We're the best." At one assembly early in the year of this study, Janice introduced school rules to primary grade (K–3) children. She told the observer beforehand that she was concerned that "young kids were 'smarting off' to the school crossing guards." After briefly introducing the new assistant principal, Mrs. Mitchell, Janice made an elaborate display of the corps of 6th grade crossing guards, smartly decked out in white belts and silver badges displayed on their chests. As they stood beside her, Janice announced, "These are our safety patrol guards, the young men and women who, just like Mrs. Mitchell and your teachers, help you get through the day." With badges gleaming, the guards returned to their seats in the auditorium while Janice asked the crowd of youngsters: "Now there's no one here that would be smart alecky is there?" The voices were one: "Nooooooo."

"I'm asking, she continued, "because some people think that they shouldn't listen to these helpers." Janice continued to "play the crowd" throughout the brief assembly which she purposely kept to 10 minutes, although a similar agenda with older children had lasted twice as long.

Throughout the remaining discussion of line-up procedures, school bus behavior, and rules for play on the grassy acreage surrounding the school, Janice used children to demonstrate rules (and breaking rules), interspersed amusing stories of her dog (e.g., she wouldn't let Janice tell the children what her Halloween costume would be that fall because she didn't want children to recognize her that day!), and presented other pieces of information underscoring traditions, rituals, and events important to the school's image as it exists in Janice's head and in the collective oral history of the group.

Janice's career is characteristic of many women public school middle managers. She rose through the ranks from her first position as an art teacher who floated between assignments in several elementary schools in a suburban school system. During this initial teaching experience in Finneytown, Janice was mentored by a principal who later became a professor at Xavier University in Cincinnati where Janice subsequently earned a master's degree in educational administration. Her career mobility was also associated with two major personal events: (1) a decision to leave a marriage in which her husband expected that her career ambitions would take a back seat to his and (2) a galvanizing experience as a teacher in a predominatly black central city elementary school in Cincinnati during the disruptions following Martin Luther King's assassination. By accepting assignments first at Vine Elementary School, a low income, predominantly black school, and later as principal of the Applied Arts Academy at Highlands, and ultimately as principal of predominatly black Madisonville Elementary School, Janice completed her "apprenticeship" before receiving her current assignment at Anderson Place.

Janice views her early administrative assignments as critical in establishing her credentials with the central administration: "To maintain credibility you set [it] by working yourself to death and keeping still." Now that she has proven her skill at attracting and holding a racially and economically diverse student clientele, raising achievement scores, maintaining a school building as a showplace for the community, and creating high morale amongst staff (as reflected in teacher attendance figures, the second best in the city), Janice has begun her self-styled "year of revolt," undertaking battles she believes will benefit the system. For example, Janice led a battle to reorganize pupil census surveys to cut down on time spent by alternative school principals in clerical duties. She did this by carefully offering criticism and concrete suggestions to school system officers, including the superintendent. Her plan for handling census information was almost immediately implemented system-wide.

Janice does not see Anderson Place as her final career achievement. She wishes to continue to build the school and to see it as an academic mecca in the system. However, she also feels the tug of her own ambitions to rise higher in the system's administrative structure. She realistically believes her opportunities to reach the top (the superintendency) are slim. "A black male will be superintendent before any white female," she forecasts. Her appraisal seems realistic.

Case Study of William Dickinson

William Dickinson, perhaps even more than Janice Mooney, exemplifies the entrepreneurial principal. As head of Cincinnati's innovative School for the Creative and Performing Arts, he operates from a philosophy that combines elitism with a concern about the arts. The arts are viewed as a means of achieving racial integration, with the means being as important as the end. Elitism is essential because the school recognizes and promotes the best talent through its requirement that children are only admitted after a successful audition before the school faculty, and through its selection of only the best talent for public performances and recognition. This general philosophy shaped the school during its early years, having been established in 1973 in the midst of the struggle over racial integration of the schools. It was one of the first of the magnet schools, which were to be the core of the plan for racial integration. William Dickinson assumed command in an unorthodox fashion. Without the proper courses in educational administration he was not eligible for a principal's license. While he took evening classes to meet state certification requirements, the School Board appointed another principal to act as a figurehead while Dickinson made the real decisions about the school's operations. He claims that only one or two of the courses were of any real value in teaching him how to operate the school, but they did certify him to become the official principal.

During the first two years of the school's existence, Dickinson found himself constantly on the move as the school system tried to find a permanent location for its first magnet school. Since construction of a new building was out of the question in the early 70s because of declining financial resources, the answer was finally found in a 72-year-old high school building located downtown in a neighborhood of old red brick buildings that housed part of Cincinnati's poor Appalachian and black community.

The high school building and present location of the school symbolically tie together two centuries of racial concern. Down the hall from the second floor principal's office hangs a plaque, "In memory of the President of the Underground Railroad." On the site of the present high school building, the headquarters of the Underground Railroad operated out of a house originally built in 1832. The remains of the operation is a tunnel which extends from the basement of the school to the Ohio River. The plaque's tribute to the Underground Railroad reads, ". . . for 33 years they received into their home over 100 fugitive slaves each year. They healed, they fed, they clothed them and sent them on to Freedom."

Dickinson states, "I do not do anything without a concern about integration." But this statement must be placed against the background of his concern with the arts. From his perspective, the schools have discriminated against the arts as much as they have discriminated against minority groups. Born in a small town in the Appalachian region of Ohio, Dickinson recalls that in his high school, recognition only went to the athletes and not to the artists. Art programs were always the lowest priority in both school recognition and budget. He began to combine his concern over the arts with his concern for racial integration while attending the Cincinnati Conservatory of Music in the early 1960s. A white supporter of civil rights during this period of widespread activity, he led a demonstration against the exclusion of minority groups from the school's dormitories.

Presently, the School for Creative and Performing Arts reflects this concern with integration by attempting to maintain an evenly balanced student racial population; and for William Dickinson this concern extends into all school activities. Racial balance is maintained in all school performances. If one leading role is given to a white student, then the other leading role goes to a black student. If a classroom is found to have all black students sitting in one area and all the white students in another, then Dickinson immediately lets the teacher know that the seating pattern will not be tolerated. If teachers claim to have let the students select their own seats and the pattern occurred naturally, then Dickinson emphasizes to the teachers that they must take positive action to assure that it does not happen.

Any congregation of students of one race is considered an immediate problem. If, for instance, Dickinson sees a group of only white or only black students in front of the school he immediately reacts by explaining to them that racial separation will not be tolerated. When he found that all the cheerleaders for the school were black, he insisted on the addition of white students. He did not ask any of the black cheerleaders to step down because that he saw as unfair. Instead, the number of cheerleaders was increased to achieve racial integration.

The one difficult area has been the school's basketball team, which is all black. The principal attributes this to the fact that the school attracts more black males than white males. This he attributes to a combination of factors. One is that many white males shy away from the school because of the stereotypic image of the arts as feminized. On the other hand, many black males are attracted to the school because it represents an escape from their neighborhood schools. Since the grade range in the school is from the 4th to the 12th grades, the school is viewed as an escape from neighborhood elementary schools and junior high schools.

In speaking of the unbalanced racial population in the school, Dickinson said this tended to create a situation conducive to interracial dating. He has no problems with interracial dating for his own daughters who attend the school but he would not encourage interracial marriage because of the continual social problems occurring for any couple in that situation. He found that many parents of his students were not tolerant of interracial relationships. When they did occur, many students went to elaborate lengths to conceal their relationship from their parents. One example he gave was of an interracial couple who would go to dances with dates of their own race and then pair up at the dance.

To Dickinson, the problem of discrimination against the arts is as important as racial discrimination. His eyes are as quick in detecting the neglect of the arts as they are in locating potential racial problems in his student body. For instance, a district meeting of secondary and elementary school principals included an in-service program on a new reading series. The books in the reading series contained what would currently be considered the proper mix of racial types and avoided casting girls and boys in traditional roles. Pictures in the reading books showed boys and girls of different racial backgrounds engaged in similar activities. However, Dickinson noticed that there was only one picture of an artist, and that picture was of a female ballet star. Not only had the publishers neglected the arts in a book supposedly providing representative samples of race, but they had also presented a single female dancer. From Dickinson's perspective, this not only reinforces the current image of the arts as feminine, but also that of the dance.

His concern about discrimination against the arts extends beyond the local school system. He has noted that current proposals for state minimum educational standards contain no requirements in the arts. In the past, he has viewed state minimum standards as something one tries to work around to establish an effective educational program. Now he feels it is time to do something about the exclusion of the arts. This will mean attendance at one of the meetings held by the state of Ohio to discuss the proposed minimum standards. Dickinson noted, in discussing his plans to lobby for inclusion of minimum standards in the arts, that all of the meetings to discuss state curricular requirements were being held primarily in vocational schools throughout the state. This was symbolic, he felt, of what state educational leaders thought was important about education.

One of the important values of the School for Creative and Performing Arts, according to Dickinson, is the creation of an educational environment which not only avoids discrimination but actually makes the arts the center of student attention. Football heroes are replaced as the "important people" of the student body by those who have leads in the school's major performance. Student heroes are singers, actors, dancers, writers, and artists, not quarterbacks and cheerleaders. The idea is for students to dream of going to Broadway rather than of joining the National Football League.

Within this context, Dickinson believes the school provides the artistically inclined child with a peer group that cannot be found at other schools. In most schools, he argues, not only is the artist neglected but he or she also lacks the companionship of a peer group that shares similar interests. In educational terms, peer group interaction is an important means of learning. The School for Creative and Performing Arts, he believes, provides a supportive peer group and places the artist on center stage.

An important issue is whether or not the goal of the school should be development of the practicing artist or the development of both the practicing artist and the consumer of the arts. Dickinson argues quite strongly that the emphasis of his school is on practice and not consumption. The education of the consumer, he argues, is a by-product of the actual practice of an art. He has no room in his curriculum for courses like art and music appreciation. He believes that appreciation is a product of practicing an art.

For instance, he argues that if he meets someone who enjoys going to a symphony, it is usually a result of some form of musical training. This training may be only a brief period of piano lessons during childhood, but it will be enough to provide an understanding of the fundamentals necessary to appreciate music. Dickinson gives as an example his own problem of dealing with painting during his early years at the School for Creative and Performing Arts. His own background is in music and he felt inadequate in the area of painting. To solve this problem he took painting courses rather than art appreciation or history courses at the local university. He maintains he learned the technical problems facing painters and their common language. This provided him with the basis for understanding and appreciating painting.

The emphasis on practice is reflected in the curriculum. In Dickinson's words, "Learning scales does not kill creativity." At one time the school had tried free expression as a method of teaching the arts, but it was considered a failure and was displaced by a much more structured approach. For instance, in hiring a teacher for drawing, painting, and design courses, the school specifically looks for one who will emphasize technique and control as opposed to free expression. This approach, he states, has generated heavy criticism from the local art community.

A conservative approach has also been taken for teaching drama. According to Dickinson, "Children must be able to follow a director." The emphasis is on training and technique. Also, he maintains the school is not in the business of turning out child actors. In music, there have been no major disagreements about the curriculum. In fact, during the first year of the school's existence, choir, band, and theory were the core of the arts program. Dance has presented a more complex problem because there is a wide variety of schools on the subject. Therefore the emphasis is on body training, with all dance majors being required to study ballet according to the Russian school. Instructors are brought in from the community to teach modern methods.

William Dickinson also believes in the interrelationship of the arts. For instance, he argues that it is important for a musician to study dance because he or she is often called upon to be an accompanist to dance performances. This argument, combined with the belief that appreciation is the result of practice, is reflected in the school's requirement that all students take at least one class in each major arts area. The school defines these major arts as dance, drama, vocal or instrumental music, and visual arts. In addition, all students must major in one area of the arts, such as creative writing, dance, drama, instrumental music, music composition, vocal music, visual art, fine arts, music theater, and stagecraft.

William Dickinson candidly admits that he must function as a dictator to maintain a successfully integrated school. He assumes that students accept this fact because they know he is working in their best interest. One of the difficulties in this situation is maintaining a balance between elitism and integration. This issue becomes a problem when casting for school performances. Elitism means that only the best are selected. Integration means that the best form a racially balanced group. The decision is not a democratic one but a dictatorial one that must be considered in the best interests of all. So far, Dickinson maintains the school has had enough talent from both races that neither principle has had to be sacrificed for the other. But, maintaining the balance between elitism and integration requires a strong and dictatorial hand.

That being an artist is an important part of William Dickinson's life is reflected in his office furnishings. Speakers to his stereo system flank both sides of the desk and a piano stands against one wall. It is not unusual for him to conduct a quick audition at the piano in the middle of a busy day. At the time of this study, he was composing a piece for the dedication of the school's organ. His previous compositions include the opera/ballet, *The Promise*.

It is the managerial and clerical aspects of the job that consume most of his day. He estimates that 50% of his time is spent worrying about the financial problems of the school and another 25 to 30% with what he referred to as "busy stuff," primarily reports for local, state, and federal agencies. He has four federal reports, eight state reports, and numerous local reports to complete each year. He laments that at the most he has only 10% of his time available for supervision of instruction.

His role as financial manager of the school reflects the economic hardships of central city schools. Although the school system considers the School for Creative and Performing Arts one of its most effective magnet schools, the system does not have the financial resources to provide complete support for the arts program. This means that Dickinson must not only play the usual school principal's role in handling the assigned budget but he must also spend considerable time searching for outside support. As he states, there was nothing in his training that prepared him for this task.

Dickinson feels that without outside support the school would not be able to achieve most of its artistic goals. During the 1981 to 1982 school year, $300,000 was raised through donors, bake sales, candy sales, and money earned through school productions. Outside the administrative offices three framed tributes hang listing the names of the many donors. Pianos have been donated to the school and money has been given for book collections, sound systems, guest artists, props, auditorium seats, underwriting productions, scholarship funds for private lessons, student activities, and other artistic needs.

Of primary importance is the money needed to support the position of the school's artistic director, Jack Louiso. According to Dickinson, Jack Louiso is the "life-blood" of the school's artistic endeavors. Louiso has had a dance performance career in New York, is presently choreographer for the Cincinnati Opera Ballet Company, and has gained recognition as body-movement coach for Notre Dame's football team.

Funding Louiso's position has been a problem because the school system can only pay him according to the teacher's salary schedule since he lacks administrative certification. This means that to compensate Louiso for his full value to the school, Dickinson must find outside funds to supplement Louiso's salary. Of major importance in raising this money and the other monies needed by the school is a private group called The Friends of SCPA, organized in 1973. This group has been a conduit for most of the private money entering the school and has provided salaries for not only the artistic director but also for a costume designer, technical director, production assistant, dance teachers, a strings teacher, and a production teacher.

Because of the need for outside support, Dickinson finds himself in the unusual position for a public school principal of managing a major funds-seeking operation. Of course, these responsibilities are characteristic of an entrepreneurial middle manager. In 1982, the Friends hired a director of development with 15 years previous experience as troubleshooter for the March of Dimes. In addition, there is a business manager and a secretary. Both the director of development and the business manager have offices in the same complex as the school principal.

Conclusion

Rather than assume that paralyzing limitations can affect them in their roles as effective school building middle managers, Janice Mooney and William Dickinson have carefully assessed their limits and possibilities for creating their unique school worlds. Not all principals are similarly effective. We suspect that the majority make do, getting along day to day, caught in a web of competing obligations. Rather than seeing this latter group of principals as personally defective, we argue that role ambiguities, a masculine ethic, and a dual tracking system often conspire to create almost insurmountable obstacles to "effectiveness."

To analyze the probability of locating effective building middle managers in your municipality's school system, you must first determine the extent of system and building-level support that is available to a given principal. Initial questions should be: What kinds of school building programs exist in the system? Which schools within the system have achieved some measure of building success? Has your community system constructed a program of alternative schools? Which specific kinds of building programs have been erected? These questions can be answered by gaining an understanding of the system-wide programs in existence in the district. Magnet schools, individually guided education (IGE), and single-concept curricula (applied arts, fine arts, etc.) are commonly found in central city districts. To determine effectiveness, consult achievement test scores for each building in the district. These are usually published by local newspapers in the spring or summer.

After you have made a preliminary determination of which are the district's most promising "beacons of brilliance," you may wish to arrange an interview with one or two of their building principals. Your interview should focus on the principal's relationships with the central administration, building staff, students, and community. Don't neglect to inquire about the career path the principal has followed to determine if the opportunity structure has in fact resembled a dual tracking system, differentially sorting majority and minority group principals.

By determining the nature of the principal's role and career experiences you will be prepared to understand how the building manager constructs an effective school atmosphere. You will be able to move to an analysis of the lives of teachers and students in the school, keeping in mind that in large part, their experiences are keyed to the managerial success of the building principal.

Notes

1. Bruce S. Cooper, "The Future of Middle Management," in Donald A. Erickson and Theodore L. Reller, eds., *The Principal in Middle Management* (Berkeley: McCutchan, 1979), p. 272.
2. Gary Yutl, "Managerial Leadership and the Effective Principal," in *The Effective Principal*, (Reston, Va.: National Association of Secondary School Principals, 1982).
3. Rosabeth M. Kanter and Barry A. Stein, eds., *Life in Organizations* (New York: Basic Books, 1979).
4. Ibid., p. 95.
5. Rosabeth M. Kanter, "Women and the Structure of Organization: Explorations in Theory and Behavior," in Marcia Millman and Rosabeth M. Kanter, eds., *Another Voice* (Garden City: Anchor, 1975), p. 43.
6. Sandra E. Mark, "Leadership in Higher Education: A Critical Review of Sex Differences," in *Journal of Educational Equity and Leadership*, 1, No. 3 (Fall 1981).
7. Arthur Blumberg and William D. Greenfield, *The Effective Principal: Perspectives on School Leadership* (Boston: Allyn and Bacon, 1980).
8. Ibid., p. 35.
9. A. Lorri Manasse, "Effective Principals: Effective at What?" in *Principal* 61 (March 1982).
10. Henry Mintzberg, *The Nature of Managerial Work* (New York: Harper and Row, 1973).
11. Manasse, "Effective Principals," p. 11.
12. Ibid.
13. Ibid., p. 15.
14. Judith A. Adkison, "Women in School Administration: A Review of the Research," in *Review of Educational Research*, 51, No. 3 (Fall 1981), p. 317.
15. J. Frasher and R.S. Frasher, "Educational Administration: A Feminine Profession," in *Educational Administration Quarterly*, 15, No. 2 (Spring 1979).
16. Adkison, "Women in School Administration," p. 332.
17. David R. Byrne, Susan A. Hines, and Lloyd E. McCleary, *The Senior High School Principalship*, Vol. 1 (Reston, Va.: National Association of Secondary School Principals, 1978).
18. Adkison, "Women in School Administration," p. 314.
19. Ibid., p. 320.
20. Ibid., p. 325.
21. F.I. Ortiz, *Career Patterns in Education: Men, Women and Minorities in Public School Administration* (New York: Praeger, 1981), p. 81.
22. Ibid.

23. Van Cleve Morris, Robert L. Crowson, E. Hurwitz, Jr., and Cynthia Porter-Gehrie, *The Urban Principal* (Washington, D.C.: National Institute of Education, March 20, 1981).
24. William D. Greenfield, "Research on School Principals: An Analysis," in Blumberg and Greenfield, *The Effective Principal: Perspectives.*
25. Ibid.
26. Seymour B. Sarason, *The Culture of the School and the Problem of Change* (Boston: Allyn and Bacon, 1971).
27. Morris et al., *The Urban Principal.*
28. Ibid.
29. Superintendent James Jacobs, Memorandum on "brain drain," 21 October 1982, Cincinnati Public Schools, Cincinnati, Ohio.
30. Cincinnati Branch Director, Joseph Felix, Response to memorandum on "brain drain," 21 October 1982, Cincinnati Public Schools, Cincinnati, Ohio.
31. Assistant Superintendent Raymond Brokamp, Memorandum on instructional leadership, September 1981, Cincinnati Public Schools, Cincinnati, Ohio.

5

Teacher Power:
A Study of Labor

By the 1980s, "teacher power" had become a reality in central city schools as teacher unions expanded their demands from economic issues to participation in school management. The most dramatic change took place with the establishment of union-negotiated teacher building committees. The traditional paternalistic role of the principal towards teachers has been replaced by a more adversarial relationship, with teachers being quick to complain about working conditions and managerial actions. These changes have taken place against a background of concern that increased union power meant a decline in public control of the schools.

The issue of teacher power and unions will be explored by first considering the evolution of issues and teachers' demands. Of particular interest is how union contract demands affected the relationship between teachers and school managers. The chapter will include a description of the life and philosophy of a president of a central city teachers' union.

The Evolution of Teacher Power

The modern era of teacher power can be dated from 1960 when New York City's United Federation of Teachers (UFT) conducted a successful one day strike for bargaining rights and changes in the salary schedule. Prior to this time, strikes had been considered unprofessional and beneath the dignity of the job. In fact, a no-strike policy had been maintained until the 1960s. But the pressures from members and the independent actions of local teachers' unions throughout the 1950s finally forced the American Federation of Teachers (AFT; the national union affiliation of the UFT) to accept the right of teachers to strike.[1]

It was logical for the AFT to be the pioneer in teacher militancy. As a member of the AFL-CIO it was influenced by the strikes and militant actions of the other union members. The rival organization to the AFT, the National Education Association (NEA), had no tradition of union affiliation and for many years had been dominated by school administrators. But all this changed as the actions of the AFT gained widespread recognition and support. Under pressure from the militant activity of the AFT during the 1960s, the NEA was reorganized to give greater control over the organization to teachers and it adopted a policy of supporting collective bargaining. By the 1970s, the NEA was willing to declare itself a union and support teacher strikes. By the 1980s, it was difficult to tell which was the more militant and progressive of the two organizations.

The emergence of teacher militancy in the 1960s occurred at the same time that teachers were beginning to fight against the traditional control that school boards and officials had exerted over their personal lives. Since the nineteenth century, teachers had been expected to lead exemplary lives so that they could serve as moral models. This meant that school officials often attempted to regulate the dress of teachers, their personal lives, and their associations. In a sense, teachers were treated in the same manner as students. In the 1960s and 1970s, teachers went to court to find legal protection from the intrusion upon their personal lives by school systems.[2]

Union militancy and court protection of civil rights gave teachers a new sense of power and freedom. This occurred against a background of school systems which were usually unwilling to make organizational changes that would allow teachers greater participation and control. This meant that teachers had to fight through their union organizations to force organizational changes that would end the paternalistic practices of the past.

The development of teacher power in school systems can be traced in the contract demands made by the unions. It is through these contract demands that teachers have hoped to force a reorganization of the distribution of power in school systems. Contract demands can be divided into economic and noneconomic issues. In general, economic issues deal specifically with wages and benefits, and noneconomic issues with items ranging from class size to teacher participation on system-wide curriculum committees. Of course, issues tend to overlap with many noneconomic issues having some economic consequences.

Of primary concern in teacher bargaining have been wages and benefits. Ironically, studies on the effects of collective bargaining tend to find little positive influence on teachers' salaries.[3] A major reason for this is the difficulty of separating salary gains caused by union activities from salary gains caused by the simple supply and demand of teachers. In addition, salary increases resulting from collective bargaining in one city might cause salary increases in another nonunion city as both school systems attempt to attract and retain teachers.

One of the striking facts about changes in teacher salaries between the development of militant teacher unionism in the 1960s and the present is the relationship to teacher supply and demand. There was a national teacher shortage of varying degrees from the end of World War II to approximately 1967. During this period, the ratio of teachers' salaries to the average United States per capita income steadily increased. In 1945, the ratio was 1.60 and by 1960 it was 2.36. During the early days of the 1960s, as the winds of teacher unionism spread across the country, the ratio sharply increased to 2.47 by 1963 and then it began to decrease, falling below the 1960 ratio to 2.31 in 1966. After 1966, except for a couple of years, the ratio decreased at almost the same rate as the previous increase. By 1973, the ratio of 2.15 was the same as 1955 and by 1978 the ratio of 1.98 was getting close to that of 1945.[4]

The figures given above suggest several things. First, changes in the ratios can help to explain teacher union activity. The ratio provides an index of the possible feelings of financial well-being of teachers in relationship to the rest of the population. During the 1950s, teachers could feel a general improvement in their financial well-being as their salary increases improved their economic conditions compared with the rest of the population. After the middle of the 1960s, however, teachers lost financial ground compared with the rest of the population. It would seem logical that after the acceptance of militant union activities in the early 1960s teachers would, by the end of the 1960s, be rushing to unions to protect their declining economic status.

Secondly, the changes in the ratios suggest a close dependency between salaries and teacher supply and demand. As mentioned above, there was a national teacher shortage until the late 1960s. It was not until 1967 that the demand for additional teachers was approximately equal to the supply of new teacher graduates. In fact, the 1960s had witnessed a marked decrease in the demand for teachers in relationship to the supply. In 1960 there were 1.4 teaching positions open for every new teacher graduate. After supply and demand became equal around 1967, available teaching positions declined to approximately .50 for each new teacher graduate in 1974.[5]

Thirdly, changes in supply and demand might also provide another clue for increased union activity over the last two decades. As the availability of jobs began to decline, older teachers became more concerned with protecting their teaching positions. Collective bargaining provided a means for protecting jobs through seniority rules and negotiated reduction-in-force policies. This is particularly important during times when school districts are suffering budget problems and it is cheaper to replace older teachers who earn more money with new teachers who start at the bottom of the salary schedule. Therefore, there does seem to be a relationship between supply and demand, teachers' economic conditions, and increases in unionization. That is, teachers seek the protection of unions when there is an apparent decrease in their economic conditions and when the supply of teachers outstrips demand. In fact, it was in the late 1960s and 1970s that both the NEA and the AFT experienced their most rapid growth in membership.[6] In the context of these figures, one could argue that teachers primarily joined unions in the late 1960s and 1970s to protect their economic gains and jobs rather than to increase their economic gains.

National averages sometimes obscure differences between local unions. In this case, national averages tend to overlook the superiority of certain union locals in winning benefits for their members. Sometimes the economic gains made by local unions cannot be totally explained in terms of supply and demand. When this occurs one must seek an explanation in either the organization and activities of the union local or in the peculiar circumstances of the school district.

The most outstanding union local in terms of winning economic benefits has been the Chicago Teachers Union. Prior to 1967, the minimum salaries for teachers in Chicago were below the average for salaries in the 14 largest central city school districts. After 1967, Chicago teachers' salaries rose rapidly so that by 1973 they were paid far better than teachers in other big city school systems including New York, Los Angeles, Detroit, and Philadelphia. By 1973, the minimum salary for teachers in Chicago was 11% higher than the minimum salary in these four other big cities. Comparison of maximum salaries shows an even greater advantage for Chicago teachers with maximum salaries being 20% higher than those in the average big city.[7]

The key to the success of the Chicago Teachers Union is in the political style of the city and the traditional relationship between the political machine and Board of Education. Since the school board in Chicago is appointed by the mayor as opposed to direct election, it has often reflected the composition of the mayor's political machine. During the 1960s, an important part of that machine was organized labor which received positions on the Board of Education by appointment by the mayor. During this time, the mayor was forced by public pressure to appoint a reform faction. It was the machine faction which included union leaders that gave strongest support to the demands of the teachers union. In addition, the mayor saw the union as an important new member of the Democratic political machine for the area and helped to support its demands. However, both the reform faction and superintendent of schools were opposed to most salary demands and saw the union as ruining attempts to introduce new educational programs into the system. But the alliance between the teachers union, the machine faction on the board, and the mayor's office proved too powerful for the reform faction. Teachers' salaries increased more rapidly than any other city, outstripping any increases that might have been predicted strictly by supply and demand.[8]

Whether teacher unions are increasing economic gains for teachers or just protecting economic gains, they do have an effect on the distribution of resources within a school system. The distribution of resources does affect educational programs and policies. In other words, the economic demands of unions do have an effect on noneconomic issues. This is why it is sometimes difficult to separate economic from noneconomic issues during negotiations. For instance, reform members of the Board of Education in Chicago complained bitterly that union demands were making it difficult for the system to reduce its class size and introduce new educational programs. Also, they objected to making educational policy through the bargaining process. They felt that union demands were forcing them to abandon sound economic and management policies to the detriment of the school system.[9]

Effects of Collective Bargaining

There has been some attempt to determine the effect of union economic demands on educational policy in a school system. Although this type of study is difficult because of the variety of variables affecting educational policy, there are certain things that can be said about decisions regarding the distribution of resources in a school system. One of the best studies dealing with this issue is by Eberts and Pierce. Their study was conducted during the period of declining enrollments and budgets of the 1970s using data from 1,336 school districts in Michigan and New York.[10]

In designing their study, they wanted to find out the possible consequences of collective bargaining on decisions regarding resource allocations by school administrators. They felt that during periods of declining enrollments and budgets, school administrators had a number of options for dealing with the situation:

1. Administrators could decide not to fill vacant teaching positions
2. They could defer any salary increases for teachers
3. They could cut nonprofessional staff

4. Expense could be reduced by requiring teachers to teach more and larger classes, reducing or eliminating teacher preparation periods and eliminating inservice
5. Teaching supplies could be cut
6. Older more experienced teachers could be replaced with a younger and cheaper teaching staff

If one considers these options in light of union concerns, it is easy to see the possible effect of union demands on resource allocations and educational policy. For instance, unions would certainly fight against the option of replacing an older staff with a younger staff. In fact, union contracts would definitely contain language protecting the seniority rights of teachers. Unions would also fight any attempt to defer salary increases for teachers. Protection of seniority rights and salaries are the most important priorities of most unions and have been major issues in most strikes. This would mean that with a strong union in a district school, authorities would have to select other means for reducing the budget. Most teachers' unions would fight against larger class sizes and elimination of teacher preparation periods, but these issues would not have as high a priority as salaries and job protection; no teachers' union has conducted a strike just over class size and preparation periods. Indeed, it is hard to imagine a teachers' union striking because of a hiring freeze, the cutting of nonprofessional staff, or a reduction in supplies.

What this suggests is that in school districts with strong union requirements, cutting the budget might result in fewer supplies, larger classes, and fewer nonprofessional staff. Larger class sizes and decreased supplies would seemingly result in a poorer quality education for students but Eberts and Pierce argue that retaining an experienced and educated teaching staff, which is the union's top priority, is related to student achievement. In fact, they found in their study of school districts in Michigan and New York that unionized school districts keep more senior teachers, whereas nonunionized districts tend to replace older teachers with junior teachers. "This results," Eberts and Pierce concluded, "in larger spending per pupil, larger teacher–student ratios, a slightly older and more educated staff, and a slightly higher percentage of the budget spent on instruction in declining enrollment districts. . . ."[11]

Therefore, when economic demands are considered against the background of declining enrollments and shrinking budgets there emerges an interesting picture. Teachers, faced with a reversal of the previous decade's trend of increasing salary gains compared with the rest of the population, rushed to join unions in the late 1960s and 1970s to protect their salaries and jobs. This action was made possible by the fight for collective bargaining in the early 1960s. The threat to teacher welfare has been caused by a combination of an increasing teacher supply and a declining number of students, and shrinking school budgets. As school systems attempt to cope with these financial and demographic trends they must, for the first time in history, give consideration to teacher union demands. The consequence is educational policies that protect teacher seniority at the possible expense of class size, supplies, and nonprofessional staff.

Unions might also be spurred into greater concern about noneconomic issues. For instance, if school systems increase class sizes in order to balance budgets, then teachers would begin to react to this decline in working conditions. If school systems were forced to actually reduce their teaching staffs, then teachers would be concerned about explicit contract language dealing with reduction-in-force. In other words, declining enrollments and shrinking budgets would force teachers into bargaining over noneconomic issues.

These motivating factors, combined with a union ideology that stresses greater teacher control, help to explain the growth of teacher power through collective bargaining in the 1970s and 1980s. The trend in teacher union concerns with noneconomic issues during the 1970s has been documented by McDonnell and Pascal in a 1979 report. Together with a team of hired researchers, they evaluated changes in 151 teacher union contracts between 1970 and 1975, and visited a sample of 15 school districts to study the effects of contract items. They found increases in all categories of noneconomic items included in teacher contracts during this period.[12]

Noneconomic Issues

For the purposes of discussion in this chapter, the noneconomic issues identified by McDonnell and Pascal will be divided into the categories of job protection, protection of a specific teaching assignment, working conditions, and participation in school management. It should be understood that all these categories affect educational policy decisions within a school district. In job protection, the number of contracts in the 151 school districts studied containing a provision giving teachers the right to formally respond to an administrator's evaluation increased from 42% to 64% between 1970 and 1975. An administrator's evaluation can, of course, be the basis for firing a teacher. Protection against arbitrary and capricious evaluation is important for job security. The issue of teacher evaluation is also important from the standpoint of professional power. During the 1980s, there developed a trend in union contracts to give teachers a direct role in evaluating other teachers. This most often took the form of master teachers evaluating and helping new teachers.

There were also increases in the number of contracts which included items dealing with seniority and procedures for reduction in force. In 1970, only 11% of the contracts contained language dealing with the procedures to be followed when reducing the size of the teaching staff. By 1975, after the effects of the decline in student enrollments and budget cuts had begun to be felt, the number of contracts containing reduction-in-force procedures increased to 37%. The number of contracts giving specific recognition to credentials and seniority increased from 20 to 33%.

Within the category of protection of a specific teaching assignment two items began to appear more frequently in union contracts. One provision, which appeared in 21% of the contracts in 1970 and 27% in 1975, gave teachers the right to refuse an assignment outside grade and subject matter area. This provision touched on one of the long-standing complaints by teachers that they were often forced to teach subjects for which they were not qualified. This meant more work in preparation for the teacher and often a poorer education for the student. The other provision that increased in contracts from 19 to 29% required specific criteria for the involuntary transfer of teachers from one school to another.

The working conditions category contains four important provisions affecting general educational policy within a school district:

1. The number of contracts specifying the length of the school day increased from 39% to 58%.
2. The right for teachers to exclude disruptive students appeared in 28% of contracts in 1970 and 46% in 1975. For teachers in urban areas who felt threatened by school violence this was considered a very important issue. Before this, teachers were often forced by administrators to try and deal with disruptive students during class hours. This often meant class disruption and a potential physical threat to the teacher and other students.
3. Contract provisions for maximum class size increased in number from 20% to 34% during this period. As mentioned previously, this item became important when school administrators faced with budget problems tried to reduce costs by increasing class sizes.
4. There was an increase from 11 to 29% in contracts requiring a minimum number of aides per classroom.

Both the class size and classroom aides provisions reflect the problems administrators were having in balancing budgets in the context of union demands to protect wage gains.

The last category of participation in school management includes two important provisions giving teachers increased power in school management. The first provision, and the most widely included in contracts, specifies that all grievances are subject to arbitration. This provision increased in contracts from 70 to 83%. It provides an important mechanism by which teachers can be sure that the school district complies with all provisions of the union contract. It establishes a formal grievance procedure that a teacher or group of teachers can follow to assure an adequate hearing of their complaints. It should be noted that grievances can go beyond the language of the contract and can also involve a broadening of interpretation of contract items. Arbitration also guarantees that the school administration will be forced to hear an outside opinion before making a decision. An arbitration provision requires that if the grievance procedures within the school district do not provide a solution satisfactory to all parties then a professional arbitrator will be hired to make a decision on the facts of the case. The usual process involves the union and school administration agreeing upon a professional arbitrator who hears all sides of the case and renders a judgment. Some contracts specify that the arbitrator's decision will be binding.

The second provision deals with what McDonnell and Pascal call an instructional policy committee in each school. This committee has been given a variety of names including teacher building committee, and its primary function has been to provide a forum for teachers to raise issues on management and conditions within individual schools. This item jumped from 16 to 31% during the period under study and is one of the most important items to give teachers increased power at the building level. As we shall see in the concluding section of this chapter, teacher building or instructional committees have become an important means for ending the traditional paternalistic role of principals.

The figures given above for the increase in noneconomic items in union contracts only deal with the period of the early 1970s. What these increases indicate is the trend in union negotiations that continued through the 1980s, with an increasing emphasis upon noneconomic issues and teacher power. By the 1980s, as we shall see in our study of the modern union president, noneconomic issues have increased to include provisions for teacher participation on system-wide curriculum committees, on book selection committees, and in decisions regarding educational programs.

The extent of these provisions in any given contract depends on the particular school district. McDonnell and Pascal found that large school districts often acted as flagships with contract provisions spreading to smaller districts. In terms of differences between the two unions, the AFT was found to be more likely to gain contract provisions dealing with instructional policy committees, class size, and exclusion of disruptive students, and the NEA was more likely to get a clear definition of promotion rules.

McDonnell and Pascal also found that the noneconomic provisions had their greatest effect at the school building level. They wrote, "The noneconomic effects of collective bargaining are more perceptible at the school than the district level. Because of contractual provisions . . . principals have less latitude then before in managing their own buildings."[13] This statement takes on greater meaning when placed within the context of the power politics discussed in the chapter on central city school bureaucracies.

The argument has been presented in a previous chapter that demands for greater community participation in educational policy-making resulted in many central city school systems establishing community advisory groups for each school. By responding to the demand for greater community participation in this manner, administrators were able to protect the central bureaucracy and place the burden on the school principal. The same thing seems to have happened with regard to teacher power. Central office administrators usually control the negotiating process and they can assure that the burden of teacher power falls on the shoulders of the building principal.

The effectiveness and degree of activities of teacher building committees varies greatly between school systems and between schools within systems. In some situations the committees actually co-administer schools; in others, they exert no influence. This range of activity appears to depend on the willingness of teachers to become actively involved and the type of reaction to these activities exhibited by school administrators. McDonnell and Pascal write, "In one district with contractually mandated committees, a central office administrator noted that they are 'all over the map' in terms of effectiveness ranging from adversarial to cooperative working conditions."[14]

One of the important consequences of the expansion of noneconomic items in teacher union contracts is the possible loss of public control. It can be argued that during negotiations, the public is represented by the Board of Education. The assumption is that the board functions as elected representatives of the public in bargaining with teachers' unions. The major problem with this argument is that Boards of Education tend not to play an active role in negotiations and give the majority of responsibility to either professional negotiators or members of the administrative staff.

McDonnell and Pascal think it is naive of the public to assume that the Board of Education plays a major role in union negotiations. They argue, "Citizens may simply assume that their elected representatives on the school board take an active part in negotiations, but we have seen that this rarely happens."[15] They found a lack of community participation in most contract negotiations and discovered that school boards were often divorced from negotiations except for approval of the final contract. In many districts, it was found, collective bargaining was being handled by a director of personnel and/or an employee in public relations.

One of the main reasons given for the lack of involvement of school boards in collective bargaining has been inexperience resulting in an overdependence on expertise. When school boards are first faced with the prospect of union negotiations they seldom are ready to deal with the complexity of labor law and usually seek the aid of outside consultants who train staff members in collective bargaining technique. In addition, there are arbitrators, mediators, and fact finders who act as neutral third parties and can exercise quasi-judicial power.

Collective bargaining also involves a battery of lawyers for both sides who increasingly play an important role in decisions about which issues should be accepted or rejected in a contract. For instance, it is reported that most of California's 1,172 school districts had to hire private law firms after county law offices, which normally provide advice to school districts, declared their inability to handle cases dealing with labor relations. The amount of litigation is exemplified by the fact that after a public employees collective bargaining law passed in California, one law firm reported 63 cases and another 58 cases in one year before the state employment relations board.[16]

Whereas collective bargaining has decreased public control of the schools it has increased the complexity of internal governance of school systems. Charles Kerchner has used the term multilateral to describe the style of governance resulting from collective bargaining. He argues that the traditional hierarchical structure of schooling with a unitary command structure has broken down and been replaced with one that involves continuous negotiations between a variety of actors in a school system.[17]

Kerchner uses one incident in a California elementary school to depict both the changes in the command structure in education and the role of teacher building committees. In this particular school a group of vandals had entered over a weekend destroying equipment and stealing the master key for all the classrooms. The teachers became concerned that the thieves could enter their classrooms and steal personal property. The principal called the central office to have the locks changed and received a firm refusal because of the expense. As Kerchner points out, before there was a union that would have been the end of the issue. But in this case the building representative for the California Teachers Association got on the phone and told the central office that if they didn't change the locks there would be a major grievance. The locks were changed within a few days.[18]

In this example the union representative, even though a teacher, was able to exert more influence than the principal. The central office administration found itself in the position of having to deal with two different parties over the same issues. This multilateral bargaining can be seen in a broader framework when looking at the functions of a single school district. For instance, the 1976 California public employees bargaining law requires that initial proposals by management and labor be given a public hearing. In Los Angeles, this has resulted in the establishment of a citizens' advisory committee for collective bargaining. The purpose of the committee and the intention of the law is to increase public control and input into collective bargaining. The result, of course, is to make the bargaining process even more complex with teachers being represented by the union, and the public by the Board of Education and the citizens' advisory committee.[19]

As mentioned previously, collective bargaining affects decision-making in school districts about major issues like budgets and enrollment declines. Kerchner used the example of integration in Los Angeles. Obviously, an integration plan has to receive some support from the teaching staff to be effective. But before unionization, a school district could simply impose an integration plan and if it affected teachers negatively there was little they could do. When an integration plan was initiated in Los Angeles in 1979 the concerns of teachers had to be considered because of the power of the combined NEA-AFT United Teachers of Los Angeles. The leadership of the union tended to favor the plan and the rank and file had mixed feelings. The union actively provided workshops to train member teachers and more importantly, from the standpoint of teachers, the union has tried to deal with the delicate issue of involuntary transfers.

For Kerchner, the most important thing was that the development of integration plans required the active participation of the union. In fact, the union worked actively behind the scenes to form integration plans that would be both acceptable to the court and the school board. In this case, the union protected its own constituency and at the same time acted as a mediator between the courts and the school board. This placed the union in the direct role of helping to formulate educational policy and as an important participant in a multilateral decision-making process.

The above example also demonstrates the range of activities of teachers' unions. They are not only involved in the formal bargaining process, but they also are continually negotiating over other issues with a variety of public and private agencies. Any educational issue affecting a school system becomes a concern of the union. Teachers' unions must fight at the national level to assure federal legislation which they feel is beneficial to their constituency. At the state level, unions are active in issues dealing with minimum state standards, teacher certification, funding, and any legislation affecting public employees' unions. At the local level, unions often defend the school system against outside attacks and will give active support to attempts to raise additional money for the schools.

The President of a Local Union

The range of actions and philosophy of teacher power is exemplified in the following sketch of the president of the Cincinnati Federation of Teachers (AFT). The sketch conveys a picture of the internal political life of a teachers' union and the ways in which unions become involved in a variety of political activities. The president, Tom Mooney, describes his youth as being propelled by political activism and a compulsion to become self-supporting. He breezed through high school and college and in 1974, at the relatively young age of 20, earned his diploma from Antioch College. During the period of his attendance, Antioch College was known for its politically oriented student body in support of a variety of social causes. Mooney's political activism found its place in work for the Farm Workers Union and provided his first major involvement in a trade union movement.

Within a short time of his graduation from Antioch, Mooney took the plunge into school politics by working for a Cincinnati group called Concerned Citizens for Quality Education. The major focus of his work was research into the problems of local school desegregation and school funding. While working for this group, he achieved his goal to become self-supporting by landing a teaching job with the Cincinnati Public Schools at an inner city junior high school. As Mooney describes his entry into teaching at the age of 20, it was a classic case of being pointed toward a classroom and having to sink or swim. His college work had not prepared him for the realities of an inner city junior high school nor did he receive much help from the school administration. He even had a difficult time understanding the language of the black students who made up the majority of the school's population.

With hindsight, it seems natural for a young teacher like Tom Mooney to direct his interest in political and social causes toward teacher union activities. He claims that his major motivation at the time was low teacher salaries and the fact that the school system had fouled up the operation of the schools. Mooney argues that school systems have traditionally expected teachers to dress and act like members of the middle class but have never provided a high enough salary to allow a teacher to achieve a middle class life-style. From the perspective of a young inner city teacher, the school system failed to provide decent working conditions and the services and supplies required to provide education to inner city children.

His movement through the union organization was as swift as his high school and college career. During his first year of teaching, he had a chance to experience briefly a union position when he served as building representative for one week. The following year he transferred to another junior high school and joined the union's Educational Policy Committee. Using the knowledge of school funding and desegregation he had acquired while doing research for the Concerned Citizens for Quality Education, he wrote a critique of the superintendent's five-year plan for the school system. Mooney's report was adopted by the union as their official position. By 1976, he had become an area coordinator with the responsibility of coordinating union representatives from the various schools. When the Cincinnati Federation of Teachers conducted a major and successful strike in 1977, he served on the union's bargaining team.

In 1979, when the president decided not to run for re-election, Mooney launched a campaign for the position. The major parts of his platform were building a united bargaining council and influencing school board elections. A united bargaining council, which was later achieved, was to bring together other workers in the system (like office workers) with teachers so that a united front could be presented to the Board of Education. As will be discussed later, attempting to influence school board elections is part of Mooney's general concern with increasing teacher power.

Mooney won the election in 1979 and at the age of 25 became head of a major local of the American Federation of Teachers. At the time of this study in 1983, the offices of the Cincinnati Federation of Teachers were located in a building occupied by other trade unions. Mooney's office reflects a dedication to trade unionism and progressive politics. On the wall directly in front of his desk hangs a picture of union leader Big Jim Larkin giving a speech to a group of workers in Dublin in 1913. On top of a bookcase sits a picture of Mooney with Senator Edward Kennedy. A picket sign from the successful 1977 strike hangs on the wall.

Mooney now sees improving working conditions for teachers and increasing teacher power as his most important job. To understand his position on teacher power, one must also understand his general philosophy with regard to social action. He believes that the key to social action is convincing people that they have the power to make a change and a difference. This means overcoming the apathy and sense of powerlessness that pervades modern societies. One way of convincing people that they can make a difference is to engage them in collective activity where they learn that working with others can bring about social and political change.

This philosophy placed in the context of teacher unionism means overcoming the sense of powerlessness that has tended to dominate the teaching profession. Through the collective work of the union, teachers learn that they can make a difference in the control and operation of a school system. This does not mean that the teachers' union can leap immediately into major attempts to exert control over the system. What must first take place is the gradual unfolding of awareness that greater influence is possible through collective action. One of the things Mooney claims he has learned since being in office is that things take time and that social and political goals require hard work and incremental steps.

This belief in social change through collective action based on incremental steps and a growing awareness of ability to affect social change is reflected in what Mooney states as his goals for teacher unionism. He feels that the union has accomplished major gains in salaries and working conditions, but that it needs to exert more control over educational policy. This he believes is the next stage in the gradual unfolding of teacher power. Rather than stressing wage issues, the current union negotiating items center around policy issues. Included in the negotiating goals are a firm class size; the assignment of art, music, and physical education teachers to each school with ratios for the number of specialists per pupil; the banning of extracurricular activities as a factor in surplusing; a maximum of five teaching periods in secondary schools; 45-minute prep time; paid time for writing and conferences for special education; and faculty meetings limited to one hour.

These rather concrete negotiating items, which can only be fully appreciated by a person understanding the daily work routines of teachers, represent for Mooney only a stage in the evolution of teacher power. When asked how extensive teacher power should be, he stated that there should be school administrators to maintain the general organization of the school but that teachers should control and make educational policy. In terms of long range plans for extending teacher power, he considers the contract negotiated by the Toledo Federation of Teachers as the model he would like for Cincinnati. Just achieving that type of contract he believes is a long range goal. The ultimate goal he believes would be for the teachers to share joint decision-making power over the local school district.

An examination of the Toledo contract gives some indication of Mooney's long range planning. The contract, like many others being written around the country, touches about every aspect of a teachers' day and increases the role of the teacher as policy-maker. The contract contains very tight language regarding class size, teacher layoff, and recall procedures. It almost guarantees that the school board will adhere to the class size agreement by requiring that the school system make overload payments to the teacher for each student above the class size agreed upon. But more importantly, the contract calls for teachers selected by the union to serve on all committees relating to curriculum, testing, and staff development. In addition, it calls for a system-wide curriculum committee to be composed of eight members, four each appointed by the union and school board. The contract also states that the union should be consulted before any new educational programs are initiated or adopted by the school system.

Mooney finds the last item somewhat weak because it does not explicitly provide a means for assuring that the school board will in fact consult the union on all new educational programs. He finds that contract language that only states "should be consulted" is too loose and that the school administration or board can always find some way of avoiding compliance. But even with this objection he would still find this type of contract an important step forward for the Cincinnati union.

Regarding the ultimate goals for teacher unionism, Mooney would like to see Teacher Building Committees sharing equal decision-making power with the principal. Presently, the Cincinnati union contract calls for the establishment of a Teacher Building Committee elected by secret ballot to "meet monthly to discuss and to make recommendations with respect to implementation and interpretation of this contract, educational policies and programs in the building, and other matters relating to terms and conditions of employment." Mooney realizes that it is a major step from making recommendations to sharing equal power. On the systemwide level, he would like to see the union sharing equal power with the Board of Education on issues involving educational policy.

Any discussion of teacher power leads to the issue of the potential conflict between the interests of teachers and the educational welfare of students. This issue is most often raised with regard to possible union protection of incompetent teachers, but it also includes union support of educational policies that might be detrimental to students.

The protection of incompetent teachers, Mooney argues, is a false issue usually raised by those who do not understand how school systems work. In the first place, most school systems put new teachers on appraisal for three or four years before giving them a permanent contract. Even after receiving a permanent contract, teachers can still be dismissed. According to Mooney, if incompetent teachers exist within a system, the guilt is on the shoulders of the administration and not the union. Clearly, continued employment of poor teachers has to be blamed on the inaction and failure of the school administrations to evaluate teachers adequately. The union's role in these situations is to assure that the appraisal system is fair and to provide the teacher with help. Mooney describes the dismissal process as adversarial, with the administration presenting its case and the teacher organizing his or her case, but the decision rests with the administration. If the union feels that a teacher is unfairly dismissed, then it can find some means of appeal through arbitration proceedings or through the courts.

Of course, the broader issue is union support of educational policies based on self interest and not the interests of students. For instance, Tom Mooney recognizes the negative effects of magnet schools and vocational education. In the case of magnet schools, the concern is with the draining off of talented youth from neighborhood schools. With regard to vocational education, the issues have been the use of vocational education as a dumping ground for disadvantaged youth, the failure to fulfill the promise of finding the graduate better jobs and higher pay as compared with the regular high school graduate, and the high cost of vocational programs.

Magnet schools and vocational education do employ teachers who are members of the union. The issue then is whether or not the union should represent the interests of its members or seek changes in educational policies that might result in the loss of jobs for some members of the union. Mooney's response to this situation is that one must work within the framework of the interests of one's constituency. There must exist a base that allows one to bring about educational change. To go against the interests of that base would render one totally ineffective. To plunge ahead without collective support or work against the interests of one's constituency and expect significant results is politically unrealistic and utopian. What one must do is seek change in programs and policies so that individuals are not hurt.

One aspect of teacher power is improving the public image of teachers. Mooney believes that competency tests for teacher certification might have that effect by answering public complaints about illiterate teachers. At the time of this writing, Ohio was considering a competency test emphasizing educational methods for applicants of teacher certification. Mooney strongly objects to this approach to testing because of the variety of educational methods being taught and his own negative experience with the practical value of teacher education courses. He also objects to competency tests that cover subject matter because of the danger of standardization of knowledge. In a controversial field such as social studies, it would be difficult to construct a test that did not reflect a political, economic, or cultural bias. The only competency test that Mooney feels would avoid some of these problems and still help the image of teachers would be one on the basic skills of reading, writing, and arithmetic.

Mooney's objection to the type of state examination being proposed reflects a growing distrust of the involvement of state government in local education. For instance, he claims that at one time he was very much in favor of greater state financial support of local schools. This attitude changed when he became more knowledgeable about the tax system in Ohio. What he discovered was that local property taxes were more progressive than the state income tax. While working with a state-wide tax reform group it became clear that local property taxes compared with the state income tax forced upper income groups and corporations to carry a larger percentage of the tax burden than lower income groups. A shift to state funding would mean that lower income groups would have to shoulder a larger percentage of the costs of local schools. In addition, Mooney feels that state funding of education might make it more difficult for local unions since every time an economic issue occurs, the union would have to bargain within the halls of the state capital.

The emphasis upon supporting the existing local school organization is reflected in his attitude toward the pending school desegregation case in Cincinnati. The union has supported the local NAACP in their local school desegregation suit which includes Cincinnati and a majority of the local suburbs. One of the possible consequences of involving suburban communities is a metropolitan school desegregation plan. Mooney opposes such a plan because it would involve busing minority children to often hostile suburbs where their treatment within schools might be far worse than anything they are experiencing within the central city schools. In addition, each suburb would probably only receive a small number of minority children. This situation, Mooney feels, could have negative consequences because there is often strength in numbers. From this perspective, metropolitan desegregation might result in small groups of minority children being isolated in the hostile environments of suburban schools.

The variety of issues and concerns related to the growth of teacher power and unionism are reflected in the types of activities Mooney engages in as union president. There is no such thing as a typical day for a union president because of the cyclical nature of some issues and the way other issues will suddenly burst onto the scene. The issues that generally follow a cycle involve negotiations with the local school board and meetings over the school budget. When these occur, they generally absorb a majority of Mooney's time. Some issues can appear suddenly, like a recent challenge from the local branch of the NEA which required a special election for teachers to determine their bargaining agent. When this occurred, Mooney found the majority of his time devoted to campaigning.

Although it is difficult to give a typical daily schedule or a schedule showing how Mooney's time is divided, it is possible to describe a general range of his activities. These fall into seven categories that not only reflect the life of a union president but also the major concerns and involvements of the union in general.

The first category involves conferences with school administrators and school board members over educational policy or grievances. The policy issues can range from the establishment of middle schools to the retraining of surplused teachers. Grievances can include violations of the contract between the union and the school district or an issue involving a teacher evaluation. Sometimes grievances result in formal arbitration hearings before an arbitrator who is agreed to by both the union and the school district.

The second category involves writing for union publications. Many hours are spent at the president's desk writing descriptions of union events and other items Mooney feels are important for his constituency. Mooney must also represent the union before the public media and the community. This third category of activity can be very demanding. Local newspaper people often call him for his opinion on some new educational development or event. He is often asked to speak before local groups dealing with educational issues and before classes at local universities.

He must also spend a great deal of time in the schools listening to teacher complaints and grievances, and recruiting new union members. This part of his job is politically very important because he must stand for election every two years and, like any elected official, is constantly campaigning. Also, there is a constant need to convince non-union members to join in order to strengthen the bargaining position of the union.

The fifth category is negotiations which absorb a majority of the union president's time when they occur. Time must be spent preparing the union case for the negotiation process and constantly revising that case as the negotiations proceed. In addition to the actual time spent in formal negotiations, there is constant lobbying and negotiation behind the scenes. Both the formal and informal negotiation process absorbs a great deal of time and can consume weekends and nighttime hours.

Lobbying local and state government varies with the issues involved. Tom Mooney has found it necessary over the years to spend time lobbying the city government over tax issues, particularly those involving tax abatements. Tax abatements have been frequently given in recent decades as a means of stimulating the development of new businesses. But abatements do mean less tax revenues and consequently less money for the schools. In recent times, Mooney has found himself in the state capital lobbying over state minimum standards, competency testing, and state funding of the schools. Consequently, he has become involved in state politics and was invited to the inauguration and ball of the Democratic governor of Ohio.

The seventh and last category of activities involves the supervision of the union staff. This includes other elected union officials and an office secretary. Like any other organization, this supervision can involve countless problems that are not directly related to the goals of the organization but have to be solved to assure the smooth running of the union. In addition to the regular staff, there were, at the time of the study, two extra people who had been assigned by the state organization to help with recruiting new members both in Cincinnati and surrounding areas.

This range of activities requires that the union president maintain a constant awareness of political and economic issues affecting the schools, changes in school policies, union politics, and the needs of teachers. How these concerns are blended together could be seen during a typical campaign day when the local branch of the NEA challenged the union for representation of Cincinnati's teachers. The NEA had been able to collect enough signatures to require a special election to be called in which teachers could determine their bargaining agent.

On a typical day during the campaign, Mooney met with two groups of teachers at different elementary schools. The first meeting was scheduled during the first hour of school when teachers were free for their preparation period. It was held in the school library, with the head of the Teachers Building Committee acting as chairperson of the meeting. The other meeting was held informally in the teachers' lunchroom during their lunch break. In this situation, Mooney ran the meeting and answered questions from teachers.

Mooney's general strategy was to begin the meetings by emphasizing the benefits that had been gained by the union. He was able to do this in an indirect manner by asking if the teachers had any questions about the new dental and medical benefits the union had negotiated with the board. Because of the newness and complicated nature of the choices under the new medical and dental plans, Mooney was guaranteed a stream of questions and an interest on the part of the teachers. After a lengthy discussion of these benefits, Mooney moved directly into a general campaign speech that emphasized the bargaining goals of the union and why a strong show of support by teachers in the coming election would strengthen the union's position at the bargaining table. Mooney was able to campaign by linking past negotiated gains with the hope of future benefits.

The campaigning in these two schools did not stop with the discussion of present and future benefits. Mooney's presence provided an opportunity for teachers to express their individual and collective problems. As a union leader and good politician, Mooney had a responsibility to respond and act on these concerns. At the school visited in the morning, teachers were upset by the conduct of their principal who they complained was often late to school and managed discipline poorly. Mooney recommended in this situation that the Teacher Building Committee meet with the principal and express their concerns, and pressure the principal into making formal rules to handle the discipline problems.

Following the morning meeting at the first school, Mooney was invited to the classrooms of two teachers to discuss their individual problems. The first had a complaint about the way the principal was handling her evaluation. He had not explained any of the procedure nor given her any written information about the appraisal process. Mooney assured her that the union would send her information and have a union representative stop by and check on the matter. The second teacher wanted to join the union but was hesitant about doing it in public. She was an older teacher who had never thought she would join a union. She wondered aloud why administrators made so much more money than teachers. After Mooney explained the payment of dues, she asked about the pension fund and the contribution made by the Board of Education. This led to a general discussion about retirement in which she voiced the opinion that teachers used to be able to teach 30, 40, and sometimes 50 years but that this was no longer possible because they could no longer stand the stress of the job.

At the second school, Mooney greeted teachers on their lunch hour with discussions about benefits and the future election. The teachers did not have any general complaints about the school, but one did request a private meeting over a personal problem. The teacher's husband had been fired from his job just prior to requiring hospitalization. When he was fired, he lost his hospitalization insurance. She had called the Board of Education and asked that he be put under her insurance plan and was guaranteed immediate inclusion over the telephone. It had not occurred and now the couple had a $5,000 hospital bill with one member of the family still unemployed. Mooney copied down the details of the problem and promised to check with the board and insurance company to see if anything could be done about the bill.

This combination of concerns with union survival, teacher welfare, and educational policy were expressed at meetings of the union Educational Policies Committee. The major issue of the meeting, as observed by the author, was the organization of middle schools to replace existing junior high schools. Mooney had expressed a concern to the author before the meeting that middle schools might be one way the school administration had for attacking the union. The argument was that the administration was planning on requiring middle school teachers to have elementary certification. In the past, junior high schools had been staffed by teachers with secondary certification, who usually were new teachers waiting for a position in a high school. It was from this pool of young junior high school teachers that the union received its strongest support and most active participation. Middle schools staffed by older elementary teachers would eliminate, according to Mooney, this most active element in the city's teaching staff.

What is of general interest about the meeting of the Educational Policies Committee was how teacher welfare issues, educational concerns, and union politics had to be balanced in dealing with the issue of the middle school. The major concern of the meeting was that most industrial arts and home economics teachers in the remaining junior high schools and middle schools would lose their jobs because there was no room in the planned schedule for those subjects. Of primary interest to the union was the protection of those teachers' jobs. In addition, the teachers composing the committee argued that students of that age needed those types of educational experiences. The task the committee felt it had to perform was the creation of an alternative schedule that would allow for the inclusion of those courses. The plan was to take this alternative schedule to the administration and try to achieve some modification of their plans.

One plan that the teachers developed did seem to work but it required all teachers to increase their workloads with the addition of one extra class. Mooney rejected this plan because it would not receive support from other middle and junior high school teachers. Or, in political terms, it would put Mooney in a difficult position to advocate a change of that nature. The safest plan politically required the hiring of extra staff so that the number of classes could be expanded without requiring teachers to work an extra class. Though politically a sound plan, it had its major drawback in the fact that the school system was short of cash and had stated several times that it would not be hiring new staff.

Over issues of this type Mooney most often negotiates with members of the school administration rather than the Board of Education. From the perspective of his position, he has witnessed a real shift in power in recent years between the central administration and the Board of Education. Mooney argues that the Board of Education became stronger during the desegregation battles of the early 1970s, but that in recent years the board has retreated to its former position of giving back most power to the central administration. But this occurred after the board had selected a figurehead for superintendent. Consequently, the real power is in the hands of the middle managers who became stronger as the board became weaker. It is these middle managers, Mooney claims, who are now becoming the major adversaries of local union power.

Conclusion

The political picture that emerges from the above discussion is one that shows a competition for power between the union, the school board, and the central administration. If we add the role of the principal discussed in the previous chapter we have a four-way struggle over educational policy. Each of the four actors in the struggle attempt to balance his or her own self-interests with what is believed to be good educational policy. For the union president, self-interest means assuring continued election by union members, which in turn means protecting the interests and welfare of the teachers. In this context, teacher power is both in the interest of preserving the union and considered good educational policy. It is the two priorities of teacher welfare and good educational policies that the union president must balance when dealing with the problems of central city schooling.

Any individual wanting to understand the role of unions in the struggle for power in a local central city school district should consider the following factors. First, there should be a determination of how the union's economic demands have affected the distribution of resources within a school system. As suggested earlier in the chapter, supplies, class size, and other educational items might be affected if a central city school district is forced to protect older teachers and maintain salaries during periods of declining budgets. On the other hand, this might be positive for student achievement in that union protection assures an older and more experienced teaching staff.

Secondly, the noneconomic items in the union contract should be carefully considered when evaluating local union power. Does the local contract specify teacher participation on system-wide policy committees, curriculum committees, and textbook committees? Does the contract require union approval or review before the introduction of new educational programs? The inclusion of these items in a contract indicates a potentially high degree of union involvement in the decision-making process of the school district. Of course, how effective this participation is depends on the participants. The union and teacher representatives might show little interest in the affairs of these committees or there could be very active participation.

The same thing is true of teacher building committees. Just because they are specified in the contract is no guarantee that they are active and effective in every school in the system. Their existence indicates at least the potential for teachers to share power with principals in the management of school buildings. But, as indicated before, there seems to be as much variation in the activity of these committees between school buildings in a particular district as there is between school districts.

A close look should also be taken at those items in the union contract that specify length of school day, teacher approval of the school calendar, class size, inservice, faculty meetings, assignments, and reduction-in-force procedures. In essence, these contract items are educational policies that have been decided during negotiations. Decisions like these that end up in union contracts indicate a direct participation of the union in the determination of educational policy through the collective bargaining process.

A more difficult area to investigate when evaluating local union power is union participation in informal meetings with school administrators and board members. While the author was preparing the sketch of Tom Mooney, Mooney was contacted by the school system's treasurer to meet and discuss informally the budget and school calendar. Essentially, the treasurer wanted to prepare the union for budget decisions and gain union input into those decisions. There was nothing in the union contract that required this type of meeting and discussion. It developed as an informal meeting because of concern about union response to the budget and calendar. In cities where the union is strong and vocal, there are probably many informal meetings between school and union leaders to settle differences before confronting the public.

Another way of looking at local union power is in terms of the participants in the collective bargaining process. Of basic concern is the degree of public participation in the negotiations. For instance, are board members actively involved? If not, is there any other representative of the public directly participating? If the answer to both questions is negative, then one can assume there is little public control over the educational policies decided upon during negotiations. The majority of control in this case is probably in the hands of professional negotiators working for both the union and the school system.

One can show the variation of teacher power between school districts by comparing contracts, union activities, informal meetings and the degree of public control, but there is no doubt that teachers' unions have become an important part of the structure of power in most central city school districts. This transformation of the role of the teacher which has taken place over the last two decades can be both condemned and praised. It can be condemned because of the possible loss of public power over the schools and the sacrifice at times of the welfare of students for teachers' self-interests. It can be praised for giving those who most closely work with students an important role in educational policy. For many years teachers were powerless at the bottom of a hierarchical administrative structure. With militant unionism teachers have been able to assert a role of leadership in the shaping of educational policy.

Notes

1. A history of the National Education Association and the American Federation of Teachers can be found in Joel Spring, *American Education,* 2nd ed. (New York: Longman, 1982), pp. 198–219; William Eaton, *The American*

Federation of Teachers, 1916–1961 (Carbondale: Southern Illinois University Press, 1975); and Edgar Wesley, *NEA: The First Hundred Years* (New. York: Harper & Row, 1957).

2. For a review of the court litigation related to teacher rights and personal life see Louis Fischer, David Schimmel, and Cynthia Kelly, *Teachers and the Law* (New York: Longman, 1981), pp. 112–268.
3. For a study and review of this issue see Richard Wynn, "The Relationship of Collective Bargaining and Teacher Salaries 1960 to 1980," *Kappan,* Vol. 63, No. 4 (December 1981), pp. 237–244.
4. Ibid., p. 241.
5. Ibid., p. 241.
6. Anthony M. Cresswell and Michael Murphy, *Teachers, Unions, and Collective Bargaining in Public Education* (Berkeley: McCutchan Publishing Co., 1980), pp. 53–104.
7. Paul E. Peterson, *School Politics Chicago Style* (Chicago: The University of Chicago Press), pp. 212, 214.
8. Ibid., pp. 186–216.
9. Ibid., p. 190.
10. Randall W. Eberts and Lawrence C. Pierce, *The Effects of Collective Bargaining in Public Schools* (Eugene, Or.: Center for Educational Policy and Management, 1980).
11. Ibid., p. 179.
12. Lorraine McDonnell and Anthony Pascal, *Organized Teachers in American Schools* (Santa Monica, Ca.: Rand Corporation, 1979).
13. Ibid., p. ix.
14. Ibid., p. 77.
15. Ibid., p. 87.
16. Charles T. Kerchner, "Unions and their Impact on School Governance and Politics," in Cresswell and Murphy, *Teachers, Unions, and Collective Bargaining,* p. 395.
17. Ibid., pp. 382–87.
18. Ibid., pp. 384–85.
19. Ibid., 393–94.

The Changing Curriculum
of Central City
School Systems

Colonel George Bailey, former director of continuing education for the army, argues that "during the next decade, the military, the colleges, and business and industry will all be competing for the same limited supply of people."[1] It is expected that between 1980 and 1990 there will be a 25% decrease in the number of high school graduates. This shrinking pool of young workers seeking entry level occupations has led urban employers to be more concerned and involved with the operation and curricula of central city schools to assure that they will have a well trained labor supply. This involvement by business, in combination with the growth of magnet schools in the 1970s, has resulted in more specialized curricula linked to particular careers.

The development of magnet schools was a result of the implementation of both voluntary and involuntary desegregation plans. Most of these plans for city schools have included the establishment of alternative or magnet schools which are designed to maintain racial balance by creating innovative programs to attract students of all races. The development of magnet schools was also stimulated by the availability of money from the federal government in the late 1970s and early 1980s. The result has been the creation of specialized school programs in both central city elementary and high schools.

In addition, the financial problems of central city schools and shifts in population have led to closer ties between the schools, and business and industry. Business has responded to the financial crisis by providing direct aid through the establishment of private foundations and Adopt-a-School programs. In many cities, business has provided executives to help in the management and reform of central city school administrations.

The ties between business and the schools have been made even stronger by the decline in the number of high school graduates. Whereas in the past employers could find enough adequately skilled employees without worrying about the large number of urban youth who were graduating with inadequate basic skills, they have now been forced to dip into that population. Consequently, business and industry have become highly critical of central city school graduates and have sought ways to improve basic skill training and career preparation. Magnet schools and business concern with career preparation have tended to dovetail. Some of the magnet schools have become career preparation centers for particular businesses with potential employers directly involved in the organization of the curriculum and preparation of the students.

Concern with basic skills coupled with the growing difficulty of desegregating central city schools as the percentage of minority population increases in cities has created what has been called the "more effective schools" movement with curriculum changes that have been directed primarily at improving reading and arithmetic skills in central city schools. The broad claims of the promoters of effective schools has influenced other curricula and aspects of school organization. The effective schools literature will be discussed in more detail in the next chapter.

Concern about the education of urban youth has not entirely been concentrated on job preparation and basic skills. A variety of programs designed to aid college bound youth have developed over the last decade. In some cases these programs are part of magnet schools and directly linked to industrial needs.

Magnet Schools

Magnet schools have been components of both voluntary and involuntary plans for the desegregation of central city schools. In voluntary plans, they have often been considered an alternative to forced busing of students. As a voluntary means of desegregation, it is assumed that parents will make rational choices between the curriculum offered in their local neighborhood schools and the special programs offered in the magnet schools. It is hoped that enough parents make the choice not to send their children to a local segregated schools so that the integrated magnet schools will achieve a racial balance equivalent to the racial balance of the entire school district.

Several problems have plagued magnet school programs. First, magnet programs placed in minority neighborhoods have a difficult time attracting whites. In voluntary majority to minority busing arrangements white parents are more willing to send their older children to secondary magnet schools than send younger children to elementary magnet schools. Second, it has been difficult to devise a wide range of curricular offerings so that a large number of unique alternatives can be made available. This has been particularly true at the elementary level where magnet schools have tended to offer special learning styles rather than special curricula. Third, there has been the problem of cost. Organizing and supporting a variety of programs has been an added burden to already strained central city school system budgets. Part of the financial burden was eased by the 1976 amendments to the Emergency School Aid Act (ESAA) which provided financial support specifically for magnet school programs.[2]

Magnet school programs as part of involuntary desegregation plans are considered a means of reducing the potential hostility of parents. In these situations, the choice is not between a segregated neighborhood school and a desegregated magnet school, but a choice between a forced reassignment to a desegregated school, leaving the school system, or selecting a desegregated magnet school. Christine Rossell reports that in Boston, where magnet schools were part of a court ordered desegregation plan, they "reportedly have long waiting lists, . . . and were perhaps the only 'successful' aspect of the plan despite greater busing distance and numbers bused."[3]

A major result of magnet school programs has been a broadening of central city school curricula and in some cases the adoption of different teaching styles. Philadelphia is an example of one city that strongly resisted mandatory desegregation plans in favor of some form of voluntary desegregation. The result was a plan that relied upon magnet schools and federal support through ESAA funds. What is important to understand is that the Philadelphia school system did not start out with the intention of creating specialized curricula and schools, but only chose magnet schools as a means of avoiding mandatory desegregation. In other words, major curriculum changes occurred as a byproduct rather than as a direct product of concerns about curriculum.

Philadelphia

The Philadelphia story begins in 1968 when the Pennsylvania Human Relations Commission mandated that a plan be prepared to desegregate the Philadelphia public schools. The Philadelphia school board devised a series of desegregation plans between 1968 and 1976 which were either rejected by the Human Relations Commission, the State

Department of Education, or the state courts. In 1976, the Philadelphia School Board refused to adopt any mandatory desegregation plan, or to promise to adopt any mandatory plan if voluntary attempts failed. The commitment was to a completely voluntary desegregation plan.[4]

Finally in 1977, a voluntary desegregation plan was accepted by the Pennsylvania Commonwealth Court. The school board immediately directed the superintendent to apply for ESAA funds and the district received $307,907 for magnet schools. The first priority of the school system was the establishment of a Magnet School for the Performing Arts. In 1978, the superintendent was authorized to apply for over $7 million in ESAA funds and to develop a High School of Engineering Technology. By the 1978–1979 school year, the voluntary desegregation plan was implemented. A guide to the Philadelphia magnet schools in existence by 1983 is given in Table 6.1.

The magnet schools in Philadelphia can be simply divided into special admission and nonspecial admission schools. Special admission schools require that students formally apply and meet admission requirements which include academic performances, attendance and behavior requirements, testing and interviewing, and maintenance of racial balance. In practice, all special admission schools are high schools and middle schools; the elementary grades are nonspecial admission schools. The magnet schools can be further divided into those that exist as separate programs within regular schools and those that are completely separate schools.

For instance, there are 11 separate high schools with specialized programs and seven magnet programs within regular high schools. Of the 11 separate magnet high schools two are college preparatory, four are vocational, and the other five have specialized curricula. The two college preparatory high schools, Central High School and the Philadelphia High School for Girls, admit only students who have a high percentile ranking on the California Achievement Test and a high grade point average. The school system claims that "95% of the graduates of these schools attend four year postsecondary institutions. Many of the alumni have achieved eminent success."[5] These two academic high schools existed before desegregation plans but were brought under the umbrella of magnet schools to enhance the variety of special offerings.

The five high schools with specialized curricula range from a High School for Health Sciences to a High School for International Affairs. The High School for Health Sciences is mainly a vocational program and is described by the school district as preparing students "for careers in medicine, nursing, medical technology, research, and medical record keeping."[6] The first high school specifically designed as a magnet school, the High School for Creative and Performing Arts, offers programs in the visual arts, drama, creative writing, and vocal and instru-

TABLE 6.1

A Guide to Magnet Schools in the School District of Philadelphia

Magnet Program	Grades
Academics Plus Learning in carefully structured, well-disciplined educational surroundings.	K–8
Academy for Academic Excellence A program for academic excellence with a focus on basic subjects, science, foreign languages, and enrichment.	K–8
Basic Skills/Unified Arts Programs This program makes use of individualized educational programs and learning laboratories.	K–6
Child Development Centers Full-day program serving children of kindergarten age and offering a family grouping curriculum.	K
Instructional Enrichment Centers Major emphasis is on the enrichment of the basic academic skills.	K–6
Shawmont Academic Music Program Provides an opportunity for instruction in voice, music composition, and musical instruments.	K–8
Alternative for Middle Years Individualized instruction and emphasis on basic skills.	6–8
Middle Years Alternative for the Humanities An in-depth study of ancient and modern cultures.	6–8
Academic Academy for Middle Years Curriculum emphasizes basic academic skills.	6–8
Girard Academic Music Program Combines academics and special instruction in music.	5–11

163

TABLE 6.1 (continued)

Magnet Program	Grades
Conwell Middle Magnet School Dedicated to the educational and social development of preadolescents.	5–8
Masterman Laboratory and Demonstration School Emphasis on acceleration and enrichment.	5–12
Academy for the Humanities Emphasis on basic skills, science, development of self-esteem, and development of world cultures.	6–8
Bok Preparation for the world of work with training offered in 20 trade areas.	9–12
Dobbins Trade exploratory program and training.	9–12
Mastbaum Programs in vocational and technical areas.	9–12
Saul High School of Agricultural Sciences Specialization in agricultural areas.	9–12
Central High School *Philadelphia High School for Girls* College preparatory program.	9–12
Franklin Learning Center Comprehensive program with flexible progression of students.	9–12

High School for Creative and Performing Arts
Emphasis on visual arts, drama, creative writing, and vocal and intrumental music. — 9–12

High School for Engineering and Science
Academic program in science and engineering. — 9–12

High School for International Affairs
Academic program emphasizing a global education. — 9–12

The Parkway Program
Community-based learning opportunities. — 9–12

John Bartram High School
Education for specialized business careers. — 9–12

Germantown High School
Social studies magnet program. — 9–12

Northeast High School
Medical, engineering, and aerospace sciences magnet program — 9–12

Overbrook High School
Scholars, fine arts, and music magnet programs. — 9–12

William Penn High School
Communications magnet program. — 9–12

South Philadelphia High School
Foreign language magnet program. — 9–12

University City High School
Science/mathematics magnet program. — 9–12

mental music. The High School for Engineering and Science is located on the campus of Temple University and offers mathematics, science, and computer science courses which prepare a student to either enter a college course in engineering or science, or to directly enter a technical vocation. The Parkway Program, which also existed before desegregation plans, is a high school without walls which utilizes 150 community-based learning opportunities such as the local zoo, Independence National Park, and art and scientific institutions. The High School for International Affairs is one of the more ambitious magnet high schools with students working through the World Affairs Council of Philadelphia to visit the U.S. Department of State, the United Nations, and the Goddard Space Flight Center. The curriculum emphasizes global education, foreign language instruction, business and computer studies, and international finance and business.

The vocational high schools included in the magnet programs are very much like any traditional vocational-technical high school. Their inclusion is justified because they do offer a curriculum different from that of the traditional comprehensive high school. Three of the schools, Bok, Dobbins, and Mastbaum, provide a general career education program and training programs for employment in business and industry. The fourth vocational school, the Saul High School of Agricultural Sciences, is considered unique because of its agricultural program in an urban setting.

The seven magnet high school programs within schools reflect the constant search for unique and varied programs to provide a large enough number of options to assure voluntary desegregation. The titles of most of these magnet programs indicate the curricular emphasis. There is a business magnet program, a social studies program, a medical, engineering and aerospace program, a foreign language program, a science/mathematics program, and a communications program. The scholars, fine arts, and music program has three separate components with the scholars program providing accelerated academic classes, and the fine arts and music programs emphasizing those special areas.

The limited number of magnet schools for the middle and elementary school years demonstrates the difficulty of creating specialized programs for those age groups. The three special admission middle schools include the Girard Academic Music Program, the Conwell Middle Magnet School, and the Masterman Laboratory and Demonstration School. The Masterman Laboratory School is for the gifted child with an emphasis on academic acceleration. The Conwell Middle Magnet School "is dedicated to the educational and social development of pre-adolescents in an integrated setting."[7] Rather than emphasizing a special curriculum, emphasis is placed on different instructional styles such as team teaching, modular scheduling, individualized instruction, and open education. The Girard Academic Music Program represents one attempt to provide a specialized curriculum for this age group with special instrumental lessons, and instruction in music theory and history. Two nonspecial admission middle schools also try to provide a special curricular emphasis. The Middle Years Alternative for the Humanities provides in-depth instruction in the study of ancient and modern cultures. The Academic Academy for Middle Years places special emphasis on the basic academic skills of language arts and mathematics. The Alternative for Middle Years Program simply provides individualized instruction in basic skills.

There is only one specialized program at the elementary school level and that is the Shawmont Academic Music Program. Three other magnet school programs emphasize basic skills. In addition, there are 13 Instructional Enrichment Centers located in elementary schools throughout the city. These centers are designed to provide elementary school children with special work in basic skills in small group settings.

The Pennsylvania courts have considered the magnet schools a successful method of school desegregation. As we have seen from the review of magnet school programs in Philadelphia, there has been a significant addition of specialized high schools which have added to the variety of curricula available to the city's students. Some of those specialized schools, vocational and academic, did exist before the magnet school plan. Philadelphia seems to have had less success in developing magnet programs for the middle and elementary years. But whatever the limitations, there has been an increase in the number of options available to the student in Philadelphia. Whether that variety is good or not is another question.

Houston

The Houston Independent School District has been more successful in developing magnet options for the elementary school years. Unlike Philadelphia where the desegregation case was handled by state courts and human relations commissions, Houston adopted magnet schools under pressure from the federal courts. The Houston Independent School District is one of the six largest school districts in the United States and the largest in the South. Prior to the 1954 *Brown* v *The Board of Education* decision by the U.S. Supreme Court, Houston operated a dual school system with specific schools reserved for black students. After the Brown decision, the school district went through a series of desegregation activities similar to those of most other southern school systems.

In 1960, the Houston Independent School District tried desegregation by a grade per year transfer plan. In 1967, the district tried to desegregate by allowing parents freedom of choice in the selection of schools for their children. In 1971, a plan was implemented for desegregating by pairing schools. None of these plans produced any significant desegregation.[8]

Finally in 1975, the Federal District Court approved the substitution of a magnet school program for the unsuccessful school-pairing plan. Like Philadelphia, the major goal of the magnet school proposal was not the introduction of curriculum options but desegregation. Magnet schools were only the means to achieve a desegregated school system. In fact, in 1975 the Federal District Court approved four objectives for the magnet school plan which were all related to desegregation goals. These objectives were to reduce the number of schools with a 90% minority or majority population, reduce the number of students attending schools with a 90% minority or majority population, provide free transportation for all magnet school students, and report enrollment and teacher assignment by ethnic group in each magnet school.

By 1983, Houston had developed one of the most extensive magnet school programs in the country with approximately 33 elementary school programs, 13 middle school programs, and 15 high school programs.

An example of how an elementary school magnet works is the MacGregor Music and Science Academy in Houston. Parents can choose for their child either an emphasis on music or science. All students at the academy receive instruction in language arts, math, and social studies complemented by health and physical education programs. In addition, there is an accelerated academic program for 3–6 grade students who test above average on the Iowa Test of Basic Skills. For those students in the music program, there are six full-time instructors to teach brass, percussion, woodwind, string, guitar, chorus, piano, and organ. Small classes of no more than 12 are taught in soundproof rooms. For those in the science program there are laboratories equipped with laboratory specimens, professional grade microscopes, and closed-circuit television.[9]

Of particular interest are the Extended Day programs which give recognition to the important role of the schools in baby sitting children for working parents. The school day for children in this program extends from 7:30 a.m. to 5:30 p.m.; children studying a regular school curriculum have regular hours. After regular school hours, the children can choose between enrichment programs in gymnastics, music, art, dance, health, languages, literature, and sports.

The middle school years seem the most neglected in the magnet school plan for Houston, with fewer magnet school options available for this age group than for high school students. For the most part, programs for this age group continue studies begun in elementary school in math, science, music, basic skills, and physical education.

It should be mentioned that career education is an important part of the Houston schools beginning in the elementary grades. The system has cluster centers, designed to give students exploratory and simulated work experiences, where elementary school children can be sent from their regular schools for a day's activities. The object is to allow students to understand various careers and to gain good social attitudes toward all types and levels of careers. Each week a new group of 100 students from the fourth, fifth, and sixth grades are received from three elementary schools representing different ethnic groups. This combines career education with an integrated learning experience.[10] It is at the high school level that we begin to see the linkages between local industry, the schools, and career education. At magnet high schools career education is part of the curriculum and in many cases linked to local industry. One example is the Petro-Chemical Careers Institute located in the heart of the refining industry in Houston. The school offers three programs for students from the ninth to twelfth grades, all designed for training students for technical level jobs as chemical laboratory technicians, plant technicians, and mechanical technicians. Similarly, the High School for Health Professions is a cooperative venture with the Baylor College of Medicine and located on that campus for the purpose of providing entry-level skills for such jobs as dental assistant, practical nurse, medical assistant, and physical therapist. Also, the vocational high schools, the High School for Engineering Professions, the School of Communications, the Aerodynamics Academy, and the Community High School are all oriented toward some form of career preparation. The purely academic schools are the Foreign Language Academy, the Vanguard program for the gifted, the Fundamental Education program and the College Prep High School. The only high school that boasts unique instructional techniques is the Contemporary Learning Center. The High School for the Performing and Visual Arts is typical of similar schools found in most magnet programs with an emphasis on community performances.

One of the most unique magnet schools in Houston is the High School for Law Enforcement and Criminal Justice. This is a school designed to specifically train high school students for government occupations in law enforcement and criminal justice. In this particular case, one government agency, the Houston Police Department, links with two other government agencies, the Houston Independent School District and the Texas Education Agency, to train students to meet their specific needs. The school claims career opportunities for its students in a broad range of occupations including, police officer, narcotics investigator, border patrol, parole officer, game warden, and prison guard. The school building contains a firing range, a functioning Justice of the Peace court facility, and a court reporting center.[11]

The High School for Law Enforcement and Criminal Justice represents the constant search for the new and unique in developing magnet school programs, the growing linkages between magnet schools and specific occupations, and the potential danger that the goals of American schooling are being distorted by an overemphasis on careers and specialized schools. It is hard to fit the goal of training for a specific career in law enforcement with the traditional goals of public schools to train democratic citizens.

The same issue was raised when in the late 1970s the Cincinnati Public Schools proposed the establishment of a public high school military academy. This school, which planned to prepare students for any of the branches of the armed forces, did not get past the final planning stages because the Defense Department withdrew promised support. Like the High School for Law Enforcement and Criminal Justice, the plans for the military academy raised the issue of the goals of American education and reflected the growing occupational specialization of the magnet schools movement.

Cincinnati

Cincinnati began its magnet school program in the middle of the 1970s to avoid any form of mandatory desegregation plan. A liberal school board in the early 1970s had adopted a resolution calling for the immediate and mandatory desegregation of the Cincinnati schools. A conservative reaction led to the defeat of liberal board members and the rescinding of the mandatory desegregation plan. In its place was substituted a plan for voluntary desegregation of the school system. The two key components of the plan were a freedom of transfer plan for all students based on racial balance and the establishment of magnet schools. Unlike Philadelphia and Houston which adopted magnet school plans under direct pressure of either the state or federal courts, Cincinnati adopted its plan free of direct intervention by the courts. In this sense it was a truly voluntary plan.[12]

An interesting feature of the Cincinnati magnet school plan is its lack of attention to traditional separation of students according to age and grade. For instance, the School for Creative and Performing Arts and the Cincinnati Academy of Physical Education include students from grades 4 through 12. The uniqueness of the Cincinnati Academy of Physical Education should be noted by the reader. At the time of this writing, Cincinnati appeared to be the only city in the country to offer a program concentrating on physical education for grades 4 through

12.[13] There is a total of 21 different magnet programs at more than 40 different locations.

As one can see from the examples of Cincinnati, Houston, and Philadelphia, magnet school programs have opened the central city school curriculum to a wide variety of offerings and instructional techniques. Evaluating the impact of these changes is difficult because the original intent of the magnet school programs was desegregation although the programs themselves raise basic questions about the goals of American education.

In evaluating the desegregation aspect of magnet schools, a distinction must be made between mandatory and voluntary desegregation plans. According to the most recent review of 51 desegregation plans by Mark Smylie of Vanderbilt University, "Districts implementing mandatory plans achieved over three times the racial balance among schools achieved by districts implementing voluntary plans."[14] As noted at the beginning of the chapter, magnet schools tend to be more successful in attracting students in mandatory as opposed to voluntary plans.

As for achieving racial balance within magnet schools, there is a great deal of variation between magnet programs within a school district. For instance, in 1981 Philadelphia had a student enrollment of 47.1% minority and 52.9% nonminority at the High School for Creative and Performing Arts, and a student enrollment of 54.8% minority at the High School for Engineering and Science. On the other hand, the Communications Magnet program was grossly segregated with a student enrollment of 98% minority and 2% nonminority.[15] In Houston, integration is a more difficult problem since in 1982 its student enrollment was only 23.3% white. But even with this small percentage of white student population there were some major differences in the racial composition between different magnet programs. The student enrollment in 1982 at the Barbara Jones High School for Careers was 94% minority and 6% nonminority; at the High School for the Performing and Visual Arts it was 33.3% minority and 66.7% nonminority.[16] The above figures suggest an unevenness between magnet programs in maintaining and fostering racial balance. Although a thorough study has not been made of this issue, one can hypothesize that parental choice, location of program, nature of the program, peer group, and counseling are all factors in the unequal distribution of racial groups between magnet school programs.

The general effect of magnet schools on the central city school curriculum raises the issue of the role of specialized curricula and instructional techniques. This broader question will be discussed after an examination of increased business involvement in the schools and the resulting career orientation of central city school systems. As we have seen, many of the specialized curricula in magnet schools are geared toward specific career training.

Corporate Involvement in the Schools

Beginning in the early 1980s, American business began to forge increasing links with central city schools primarily out of a concern about the employability skills of school graduates. Corporate involvement took several forms including financial support, administrative help, and planning of career education programs. Through this aid, business expected that it would be able to hire school graduates with a good understanding of basic skills and the right attitudes toward work. But this expectation has meant that the curriculum of central city schools has been increasingly directed toward preparation for the labor market as opposed to preparation for citizenship, for protection of political and economic rights, and for increased personal pleasure. In addition, these developments occurred against a background of an increasing body of research questioning the value of vocational and career education programs.

In the early 1980s, Michael Timpane, Dean of Teachers College, Columbia University, set out with a grant from the Carnegie Corporation to investigate the growing links between corporations and public education in the cities. He conducted on-site interviews with corporate and educational leaders in 10 large cities, read extensive reports and talked on the telephone to individuals in 9 other cities, and interviewed the leadership of organizations with an urban or business focus. He found that the reasons for corporate involvement ranged from a concern with "recruitment and retraining of a skilled work force" to "keeping school-related taxation at reasonable levels." Between these two conflicting interests there was also corporate concern with community goodwill, retraining employees, and promoting research of benefit to corporations.[17]

The heart of the issue, and one that would be of increasing concern to corporations as the 1980s progressed, was demographic changes affecting the recruitment of skilled employees. Timpane argued that over the decade of the 1980s there would be a 14% decline in the number of persons between 14 and 24 years old and a 20% decline in high school enrollments and graduates. In addition, there would be disproportionate declines of this group in cities as compared with suburbs and an increase in the proportion of minority and disadvantaged youth. Added to these demographic changes are the growing number of youth going on to higher education or entering the armed forces.

Timpane concluded from the above set of facts that, "For the first time in a generation there will probably be, in several urban locations, an absolute shortage of labor supply for entry level positions. Urban employers already report great difficulty in locating qualified employees for entry level positions."[18] As further proof of his argument he presented the following statements by corporate leaders around the country.

Yes, we have been increasingly concerned with the problem of our city schools, but we have been able, basically, to get by by excluding their failures. We 'cream' the city schools, screening 10 applicants to find one qualified. (Sometimes we simply decline to hire anyone under 20, to let age and experience season our prospects.) We use Department of Labor training programs to recover an additional few and satisfy affirmative action requirements. But our bread and butter recruiting is carried on in the suburban and private high schools, and among women reentering the labor force.

What scares us now is that this equilibrium is breaking down. We who are tied to the cities (principally financial institutions, public utilities and large and small service establishments) cannot compete for recruits with the suburban shopping malls and high technology industries, let alone with the colleges. . . . If a way is not found to improve substantially and quickly the proportion of qualified youngsters graduating from the city school systems, we will face unpleasant but unavoidable alternatives: moving job requirements out of the city (or the state, or the nation!); or making capital substitutions for labor (i.e., technological innovation) more quickly or more extensively than we want."[19]

Concern with the quality of graduates from central schools has resulted in forms of financial aid from businesses to economically strapped school systems by the establishment of foundations and Adopt-a-School programs. The creation of nonprofit foundations for the purpose of providing direct financial aid to public schools is a rather recent phenomenon. In California, after severe budget cuts in the late 1970s, over 100 independent, locally controlled foundations were created to channel money into local public schools. For example, the San Francisco Education Fund awarded $800,000 for 201 school projects over a three-year period. The Allegheny Conference Education Fund in Pittsburgh, a part of the business-supported Allegheny Conference on Community Development, directs its grants toward the classroom level to aid teachers in curriculum projects. The BankAmerica Corporations' Educational Initiatives Program has provided money for creative local programs. It is possible that if the financial problems of public schools continue there will be an increasing development of these types of foundations.[20]

Adopt-a-School Program

A more popular form of business aid to public schools has been the Adopt-a-School programs. The idea of the program is that individual businesses will work cooperatively with a particular school to help improve and enrich the school program. This creates a situation in which a business is identified with a particular school. For instance, in Denver in 1981–82, $21,000 in special projects were funded and 7,684 volunteer hours were provided to local schools through the Adopt-a-School program. The range of groups adopting schools in Denver included banks, businesses and civic organizations such as the Central Bank of Denver, the Samsonite Corporation, the Lions Club and the Denver Broncos. In Denver, 29 different organizations have adopted schools.[21]

A great deal of the cooperation developed through Adopt-a-School programs has centered on career education programs. In Denver, a monthly school calendar is printed listing monthly Adopt-a-School activities. Most of these involve on-site tours of businesses, mock job interviews, economic education lectures, and career days. But it would be incorrect to portray all Adopt-a-School activities as just serving the employment needs of business. In Dallas, Fidelity Insurance Company employees give violin lessons and art instruction for two hours at the end of each school week. In Minneapolis, General Mills uses its research lab for training advanced math and science students in chemical research. And in Atlanta, Sears provides printing services for all special events at a magnet school.[22]

Foundations and Adopt-a-School programs represent forms of direct financial and other support that businesses are giving public schools thus creating direct linkages between individual schools and companies. One must assume that these activities are not the result of pure benevolence, but are reflective of business concern with the quality of the schools. It is therefore logical that a great deal of the Adopt-a-School activities are geared toward career education and introducing the student to the world of work.

In Chicago, businesses have organized career centers to introduce students to the world of work. Rather than giving aid directly to the schools, corporations have essentially organized alternative educational centers where students are brought during school hours. The Continental Bank and Harris Bank of Chicago have organized two centers for Economics and Business Studies. The Holiday Inn-Lake Shore and Holiday Inn-Mart Plaza have two centers for Hotel/Motel Careers, and

Montgomery Ward operates a Center for Marketing and Retailing. Illinois Bell's Center for Urban Communication has the very specific goals of exposing students to a real work environment, teaching appropriate behavior and dress and teaching career awareness and economics. The president of Illinois Bell stated in reference to the Center, "Career education can't just happen by accident . . . the way it did when I was in school. There has to be a systematic way to get information to students. Business can help clear the smoke in the career decision-making process."[23]

A logical step in the development of career centers and Adopt-a-School programs is for companies to participate directly in the operation of schools that are specifically designed to train youth to meet labor market needs. This has occurred in Hartford, Connecticut where 75 companies have worked with the school system to establish alternative high schools called Hartford Workplaces. The program is specifically designed for disadvantaged minority students and to meet the labor market needs in Hartford. The Workplaces are nontraditional school settings with an educational program that includes vocational training, jobs, and career counseling relevant to the city's blue collar needs. In addition, Hartford has five career centers supported by local insurance companies, banks, hospitals, and business equipment companies.[24]

JAG Program

Jobs for America's Graduates, Inc. (JAG) is another plan, developed in Delaware, that provides private business involvement in the schools to increase the employability of all students. The plan was introduced in 1979 under the leadership of Governor Pierre S. duPont IV, and because of its supposed success, was implemented in 1981 in Arizona, Massachusetts, Missouri, and Tennessee. The JAG plan, with offices in Washington, D.C., was organized into a national nonprofit corporation with funding from the Rockefeller, Aetna, and Mott Foundations, and the U.S. Department of Labor. Its board of directors includes a list of impressive names from the political, educational, and business worlds. The chairman of the board is Governor Pierre S. duPont IV and the vice-chairmen are Governor John D. Rockefeller of West Virginia and Governor Lamar Alexander of Tennessee. The secretary is William Pierce, executive director of the Council of Chief State School Officers, and the treasurer is James Howell, senior vice-president of the First National Bank of Boston. The rest of the board of directors is composed of three corporate leaders, one labor leader, one senator, one U.S. representative, two governors, the vice-president of the United States, a former vice-president of the United States, and two state superintendents of education.[25]

Beginning in 1981, JAG established a three year goal to promote "a comprehensive concept of motivation, job preparation, job placement, and job retention in the private sector for *all* public high school graduates throughout the nation." In practice this means concentrating on those youth who have been identified as potentially unemployable.[26] The concept was tested in states around the country for the possibility of using it as a national approach to reducing youth unemployment.

The JAG program is organized around several basic features. The first is the creation within a community of a public service agency to administer the program. Its board is composed of leaders of business, government, education, labor, and the community. This group is supposed to accept personal responsibility for the success of the program. Second, potentially unemployable youth are to be identified before they become unemployed. At a ration of 30/50, these youth are to be assigned to staff members of the locally organized public service organization. They are then to receive motivation for employment through participation in a vocationally-oriented motivational student organization. In addition, the youth are to receive preparation in basic "employment skills" as identified by employers for entry level employees, and the youth are to receive an orientation to the "real world of work." Thirdly, the staff members of the public service agency must identify known job opportunities in the local labor market with a special focus on employers of 20 or fewer workers. The youth are then to be placed in these private sector jobs with continous follow-up for nine months after graduation from high school. And lastly, there is an attempt to change the status of the youth on the job by promotion or raise during the nine-month follow-up study.[27]

The JAG program is designed to work through local high schools. Initiated in 1979, by 1982, it was in place in Delaware, Tennessee, Arizona, Massachusetts, and Missouri.

JAG has claimed considerable success during its early years. In a study conducted by Educational Testing Service under contract from the Department of Labor it was found that for Delaware graduates who has been through the program there was, in relationship to a control group, a more than twice as likely chance to get a job interview, a 61.5% greater chance of being employed full-time three months after graduation, and a 26% greater chance of having a job after nine months. With reference to increasing the employability chances of students weak in basic skills, the study found that poor readers in the program were 32.5% more likely to have a full-time job than were nonparticipant poor readers and that at the end of nine months, 81.1% of the programs' poor readers were employed as compared with 32.4% of the poor readers in the control group. In terms of minority employment, the study claimed that black youth were 36% more likely to be employed full-time than black youth not involved in the program. The JAG program also claims to be more cost effective than similar government programs. It estimated its cost per placement after three years was approximately $1,500 as compared with the national CETA Title II average of $6,000 and Title IV (youth) average of $9,200.[28]

Jobs for America's Graduates creates the interesting situation of a national elite (as represented by JAG's board of directors), requiring for implementation of their program that local elites organize into a public service organization to work with the schools in improving the employability of youth. In a similar manner, local elites have organized on their own initiative in several cities to influence local schools for the purpose of career education. The result of this activity in Boston was the signing by the school system and business community of the Boston Compact in 1982. In Atlanta, the Atlanta Partnership of Business & Education was formed in 1981 under the hopefully inspirational banner of "A Community of Believers." And in Chicago, Chicago United, a consortium of business people formed in 1974 to work with the public schools, joined formally with the school system in 1979 to conduct a systemwide study.

The Boston Compact

The Boston Compact is one of the most formalized agreements between a city school system and a business community. It includes several agreed-upon actions to be taken by the school system and the business community to achieve certain measurable goals. The two business organizations forming the agreement with the schools are the Tri-Lateral Council and the Private Industry Council. The Tri-Lateral Council originally had been formed in 1974 by representatives from the Greater Boston Chamber of Commerce, the National Alliance of Businessmen, and the Boston School Department for the purpose of aiding in the implementation of school desegregation.[29]

The Boston Compact is very specific about it's economic goals. It states that "as the largest school system in Massachusetts, the Boston Public Schools must improve to sustain economic growth in the city."[30] The Compact argues that Boston has recently experienced a period of prosperous growth because of the availability of a well-educated work force, but poor and minority residents have not benefited because of a lack of skills in reading, writing, math, and self-discipline. This argument placed in the framework of Michael Timpane's thesis discussed earlier in the chapter suggests that Boston has reached its limits in availability of qualified workers and must focus on minority residents to increase the labor pool.

The problem that business and the school system faces is that only half of the students entering the ninth grade in Boston are still in school in the twelfth grade. And, in the words of the Compact, "Only a third of the system's high school students read at grade level equal to their counterparts across the country. Only half of those who graduate from the city's high schools go on directly to college or a full-time job."[31]

The agreement between the school system and business involves academic and employment problems. The Boston Public Schools have agreed as their part of the bargain to achieve a "five percent increase per year in the number of students who graduate as compared with the number who entered ninth grade."[32] In addition, the school system will try by 1986 to have all graduates demonstrate reading and math skills needed for employment. Also, there is to be a 5% increase per year in the number of graduates who are placed in jobs.

To aid in the accomplishment of the goal of increasing the skills required for employment, the school system has begun to test a Boston Youth Career Development Model which includes measurable competencies for employment as determined by local businesses. This model has specific steps leading to employability and results in a career passport to be issued to graduating students. Ties between the business community and the schools are to be increased through the Tri-Lateral Council's business-school pairings (similar to Adopt-a-School). Specific career and vocational education are to be linked to the magnet school program initiated under school desegregation plans in the 1970s.

As it's part of the bargain, the business community has agreed to initiate a campaign to give hiring priority to job applicants residing in Boston. To aid in the work of the schools, the Tri-Lateral Council has agreed to strengthen its relationship with each high school in the city and to expand a Job Collaborative program designed to introduce students in all high schools to the work world through part-time and summer internships and jobs. The business community also has agreed to loan executives to the schools for special projects.

The Boston Compact contains a description of what the future education of a student might be like as a result of this partnership between business and the schools. In the model, a student entering the ninth grade would be tested for skill level, interests, and career knowledge. If the student needs remediation in a skill area, special help is provided until the student is able to pass a competency test in the subject. The level of basic skills to be required will be based on the determined requirements of entry level jobs. The student would also participate in a career education course taught in her or his high school and take field trips to local businesses. Between the summer of the tenth grade and graduation, the student would be required to have a part-time job which would be used to introduce the student "to the performance and attitudinal requirements of the workplace." If the student is not planning on going on to college, the student would receive career counseling and job placement help through the Job Collaborative program. In the senior year, a career passport would be prepared showing the student's success on competency tests, school attendance records, academic and vocational courses, and actual job experience. Interviewing for jobs would begin in March of the student's senior year and continue, under school auspices, until September or October after graduation. The Compact states, "For all students who have qualified, support services would be available for nine months after graduation."[33]

The Atlanta Partnership

Like the Boston Compact, the Atlanta Partnership of Business & Education, Inc. was chartered by the state of Georgia for the purpose of linking improved schooling with economic development. The one stated goal of the Atlanta Partnership is "To enhance the economic development potential of Atlanta and to improve the standard of living of its people by raising the educational achievement of its citizenry." More specific goals can be found in what the Atlanta Partnership felt it had accomplished between 1981 and 1983. They claimed that during this period, the student attendance rate had increased by 0.5%, the dropout rate had declined by 25.4%, the test scores in 1981–82 on basic literacy skills for Atlanta students were "the highest yet recorded," and in 1982, the crime rate in Atlanta had decreased compared with a month-by-month rate in 1981. A decline in crime rates was one of the major objectives established by the Atlanta Partnership during its first year. The assumption was that education would not only aid in the solution of the economic problems of Atlanta, but also in the reduction of criminal activities.[34]

In a rather picturesque analogy, the Second Anniversary Report of the Atlanta Partnership likens the "community of believers" to a body of water with four ships moving in formation. The flagship (the Atlanta Partnership of Business & Education) is responsible for its own maintenance and direction, and the other three ships are self-maintaining but in constant communication with the flagship "to assure that the fleet stays in formation." The other three ships are the Atlanta Council of PTAs, the Superintendent/Deans' Breakfast Club, and the Religions Community Partnership. The result of this relationship, according to the report, is "that the 'ships of the fleet' all move in the same direction and with a common plan."[35]

The phrase "community of believers" originated from an article written by the Atlanta School Superintendent Alonzo Crim and published in a 1981 issue of *Daedalus*. Crim argued that school improvement had to be based on a belief in the ability of the system to improve the educational achievement of poor and minority students. A community of believers, he argued, had to demonstrate a commitment to students in four different ways. First, he stated, all students "must feel that people who are important to them must believe in the goal." In other words, all four ships in the fleet must believe in the improvability of the students in Atlanta. Secondly, all students must be shown evidence that they are doing something worthwhile by either seeing themselves or other students secure jobs and college placements. Thirdly, students must be able to express their opinions regarding the goals set for them. And finally, students must "be challenged to improve their own performances."[36]

Crim described the challenge for the community of believers in very concrete terms. In 1981, the Atlanta school system had a student population that was 90 percent black with 123 of 126 schools qualifying for Title I money from the federal government. Atlanta public school students, in general, scored below national norms in the basic skills of reading and math. As Crim stated, "My students have usually been poor and predominantly black, and without exception have always achieved below national norms in literacy skills."[37]

The hope of the Atlanta Partnership has been to improve the basic skills of Atlanta students and to enhance their employability so that poverty can be reduced and economic development increased. One of the model schools in the Atlanta system, George Washington Carver Comprehensive High School, is attempting to accomplish these goals with what is considered the most disadvantaged student population in Atlanta. The high school draws its primary student body from a nearby public housing project where the median income of families in 1981 was $3,700 with 80 percent of the families headed by single parents and more than 80 percent on welfare.[38]

The economic and racial philosophy at George Washington Carver seems to reflect the underlying assumption of the Atlanta Partnership: that the days of racial problems are over and that the only barriers to the successful advancement of poor and minority students is their learning basic academic and social skills. In the words of writer Sara Lightfoot, the message conveyed at the school is "that blacks have been treated unfairly, but that the system is basically fair. To overcome the profound injustices, Carver students need to learn how to successfully negotiate the system, must refuse to become discouraged by the barriers they will face, and must become exemplary models of discipline and civility."[39]

George Washington Carver High School shares with the Atlanta Partnership a belief that the most important means to negotiate the system is to learn skills required for employment. As a first stage in the accomplishment of this goal, all tenth grade students at Carver are required to join an Explorers program modeled after the Explorer Scouts. The Explorers program is "designed to provide an initial linkage to the world of work." Every month the students are taken to the business and financial section of Atlanta to explore how business functions and to receive career orientation. The goal is for students to gain "an awareness of vocation, accurate image of work life, awareness of the full range of job settings and opportunities available, motivation for learning, increased access to job opportunities, and a broad base for vocational and career decision-making." The experience in the Explorers program is to provide help for students in making curricular and vocational decisions in the eleventh and twelfth grades.[40]

Most of the programs at Carver reflect the alliance between the schools and business. Of primary importance is the Work-Study program which places juniors and seniors in skilled jobs throughout Atlanta. Students spend a half day at school and the other half day is spent at jobs at "banks, hospitals, offices, service stations, and fast-food establishments." The Work-Study program ends in a ritualistic ceremony called Free Enterprise Day where students tell a gathered audience about their jobs and future career plans. The event is staged to present the values of "discipline, perseverance, punctuality, and civility for rising in the world of work."[41]

Carver's link with the business community is through David Tanner, vice-president of a major trust company in Atlanta. The visits to the downtown area have mostly been scheduled by Tanner and he has acted as master of ceremonies at the school's Free Enterprise Day. One might consider Tanner's viewpoints as reflective of the general business community in Atlanta. He believes that lack of industriousness and seriousness in today's youth will lead to violence and social chaos. His involvement in George Washington Carver originated out of a concern about the deterioration of the urban environment. He believes that students must be shown that with opportunity comes responsibility.[42]

George Washington Carver is but one example of the Atlanta Partnership which, according to the above, seems based on a fear of rising urban crime, social chaos, and economic collapse. The answer to these problems in Atlanta is to educate students to be responsible workers. The Atlanta Partnership has five major programs to accomplish this goal which are all directly related to linking the business community to the schools. These programs are Adopt-a-School, Magnet Schools, Work/-Study, School Without Walls, and the rather unique program called Career Orientations for Public Educators.

In Atlanta, the Adopt-a-School program is directly connected to career education. The Atlanta Partnership's report specifically states, "A school may be adopted by any business, industry, civic, social, or professional organization interested in sharing the responsibility of career education of students." In addition, the school system has an Adopt-a-Student program where businesses may adopt individuals, small groups or classes, rather than entire schools.[43]

The Magnet Schools program in Atlanta is organized so that individual programs will be continually influenced in the direction of career development. Each magnet school has an advisory committee which is formed from the membership of the Atlanta Partnership. This committee, according to the report of the Atlanta Partnership, "provides continual counsel so that the curriculum and its delivery stay attuned to developments within the industry."[44] There are six magnet schools in Atlanta: the Northside School for the Performing Arts, formed in 1972; the Henry Grady School for Communication, the Harper Center for Financial Services, the Mays Academy of Science and Mathematics, the Fulton Center for International Studies, and the Roosevelt Center for Information Processing and Decision-Making, all more recently formed.

The Harper Center for Financial Services and the Roosevelt Center for Information Processing and Decision-Making reflect the growing demand for these types of workers in certain labor-intensive businesses found in urban centers. Business appears to be using the schools primarily as a means for training workers for their specific needs. This is most evident in the Harper Center for Financial Services which is designed to train workers for the banks and finance industry. The school has represented on its advisory board eight different banks, including the Federal Reserve. Not only have the banks worked with the school system to develop the curriculum but they have also contributed as much as $150,000 in direct or in-kind contributions.[45]

The Work/Study program, previously described at George Washington Carver High School, and the School Without Walls are both designed to introduce students to the world of work. The Atlanta Partnership helps place students in half-day work programs during their junior and senior years. The School Without Walls is designed to provide students with instruction "while gaining experience in the real world of work." In this program, high school juniors and seniors are selected to study business courses over a period of weeks at a business location. This allows students, according to the report of the Atlanta Partnership, to learn from business people who must daily apply their skills to actual work situations. The report of the Atlanta Partnership specifically recognizes and applauds the fact that businesses are using the School Without Walls program to train for their specific labor needs.

The report states, "Businesses, of course, profit from the experience, too. They are training youngsters to be valuable employees for their own businesses."[46]

Career Orientations for Public Educators (Cope) is designed to provide public school teachers and counselors with firsthand information about entry level jobs in the Atlanta area. It is hoped that this experience will shape the attitudes of school personnel and prepare them for influencing the career education of their students. Counselors and teachers in the program spend four weeks during the summer working at entry level jobs in restaurants, banks, factories, wholesale houses, hotels, hospitals and department stores. In these settings they are to study "work places and jobs, nonacademic working factors, employer manpower needs, and other on-the-job career data." After their work experience, teachers and counselors meet with researchers to compile data for the development of a career guidance curriculum.[47]

If the Atlanta Partnership of Business & Education continues on its present course, it might result in the majority of curricula objectives and content being designed to meet the specific needs of Atlanta's economic development and labor market. All of the various programs backed by the Atlanta Partnership almost guarantee business influence and control of the public school system. The same thing has occurred in Chicago through the organization of Chicago United.

Chicago United

The power of Chicago United was evidenced when they proposed an 11-person school board slate to the mayor who appointed the entire group to serve on the board.[48] Chicago United's extensive involvement in the Chicago school system began in 1979 when a severe financial crisis hit the school system. It had been organized in 1974 as a consortium of business people and private citizens interested in being involved in helping the school system. When the financial crisis occurred in 1979 a series of summit meetings were held between the state of Illinois, the city of Chicago, the Board of Education, and the banking communities to plan a financial rescue of the educational system. It was decided at these meetings that the problems of the school system were not just financial but included serious management problems. It was at this point that Chicago United offered to conduct a comprehensive study of the school system's operation.[49]

Eighty-three executives and professionals on loan from their companies comprise the Special Task Force on Education assembled by Chicago United. The individuals and companies involved in this task force represent the elite of the business and financial community in

Chicago. The chairman of the task force is from Inland Steel and the cochairman from Commonwealth Edison. The task force is composed of eight representatives from the financial community, eight from business, two from industrial concerns, one from a utility company, two from civic organizations, five from educational organizations, and one from a labor organization. The overwhelming majority on the task force from the business and financial community, as opposed to civic and labor organizations, is reflected in the membership of the team that conducted the actual study and proposed recommendations to the school system. The study team is composed of sixteen representatives from the financial community, thirty-three from business, three from utilities and two from industrial concerns. On the other hand, there are only six representatives from education institutions, four from civic organizations, one from government, and five private citizens.[50]

The Special Task Force of Chicago United presented its set of recommendations to the school system in March 1981. The overwhelming majority of the twelve recommendations made by the Special Task Force were related to the administration of the school system. The recommendations called for a decentralization of the authority of the central office, an upgrading of management information systems, improved research and evaluation functions, improved quality of pupil personnel services, improved community relations, better personnel practices, an early beginning to labor negotiations, and changes in food service delivery. These recommendations reflected the expertise of the team members.[51]

In addition, the Special Task Force made a recommendation that would not only assure their continued involvement in the school system but also threatened the time-honored practice of promoting teachers through the ranks to administrative positions for which they are not trained or qualified. The Task Force recommended that the school system "continue to welcome on-going help from the Chicago business and professional community in modernizing operating functions." This recommendation was specifically related to school management in areas like real estate, pupil transportation, warehousing, recordkeeping, and food service. With reference to teachers who had been promoted through the administrative ranks to manage these areas, the Task Force stated, ". . . the practice of promoting teachers who lack management training to operating departments should be discouraged."[52]

The major recommendation regarding the curriculum dealt with vocational education and reflects the general concern of the financial and business community with vocational education. In fact, the recommendation on vocational education was highlighted as one of the "most important task force recommendations," along with twelve others. The recommendation was that the school system "Upgrade vocational education training by providing the people, money and status it requires." The Task Force argued that vocational education must serve a larger segment of high school students and become a mainstream activity with up-to-date equipment.[53]

More specifically, the Task Force defined as one of the primary purposes of vocational education "... to provide students who enter the work force upon graduation with entry-level employment skills." It was recommended that a detailed study be conducted to determine present and future entry-level skills required by the business community, and the degree to which the current curriculum taught those skills. The study, it was proposed, should be conducted by the business community.[54]

In March 1983, the Chicago Public Schools issued a slick pamphlet with the revealing title, *Chicago United and the Chicago Board of Education: Partners in Change,* containing a brief summary on the efforts to implement the recommendations of the Special Task Force. Of the total of 253 specific recommendations, it was claimed that 165 (65%) had been completed or were under way and that 69 (27%) were approved but remained unassigned for implementation. Only 19 (8%) of the recommendations were rejected.[55]

What this means is that between 1979 and 1983 Chicago United was able to take over all 11 positions on the Chicago Board of Education and "can" acceptance of 92% of its recommendations for organizational change in the school system. In addition, Chicago United aids in the coordination of career education programs and the career centers discussed earlier in the chapter. Like the Boston Compact and the Atlanta Partnership, Chicago United has increased business influence and power within the school system and over the curriculum.

The partnerships between the business community and central city schools through the creation of private foundations, Adopt-a-School programs, Jobs for America's Graduates, and the various compacts and alliances springing up around the country received added support in federal legislation passed in 1982. The legislation, Job Training Partnership Act, has as its stated purpose "... to establish programs to prepare youth and unskilled adults for entry into the labor force and to afford training to those economically disadvantaged individuals . . . facing serious barriers to employment. . . ."[56] The program requires that the training money be channeled through state agencies to local service areas.

Of importance to strengthening the ties between educational institutions and the business community is the requirement in the legislation that the local administrative unit should be a private industry council composed of representatives of the business community, educational agencies, labor organizations, and community-based organizations. The legislation guarantees that the majority of influence will be exercised by the business community. The legislation specifically states that the private industry council shall consist of "representatives of the private sector . . . who shall constitute a majority of the membership of the council. . . ." Listed as representatives of the private sector are owners of business concerns, chief executive officers of nongovernmental employers, and other private sector executives. Not only does the legislation require that a majority of the members on the private industry council be from the business community but also that "The chairman of the council shall be selected from among members of the council who are representatives of the private sector."[57]

Thus, the legislation not only mandates a partnership between the schools and the business community but it also mandates that business shall have majority control over the job training programs for disadvantaged youth and indirectly over those schools participating in the program. The Job Training and Partnership Act is specifically designed to support programs that will teach the basic entry level skills business has been demanding since the early 1980s. The legislation specifically states that the performance standards for youth employment training programs shall be "attainment of recognized employment competencies recognized by the private industry council." In other words, for those training programs in schools, the performance standards are to be established by an outside agency (the private industry council) which is dominated by local business.[58]

Issues Regarding the Business–School Connection

The growing linkages between the central city schools and the business community in the education of disadvantaged youth raises a number of issues. First, of course, is the issue of public versus business control of school systems, previously discussed in Chapter 2. Second, and more importantly for this chapter, is the issue of whether or not the creation of these linkages and the emphasis on teaching basic skills in specialized schools for entry-level jobs is the answer to the employment problems faced by disadvantaged urban youth. And thirdly, should the general public pay the bill for schools to train urban youth to meet the labor needs of local business and industry?

In considering whether teaching skills for entry-level jobs is the answer to the employment problems of disadvantaged youth, two questions arise. Does the graduate of a vocational curriculum have a lower rate of unemployment, higher wages, and longer periods of employment than the graduate of the general curriculum? Do males and females, different racial groups, and different socioeconomic groups receive different benefits from vocational education? Now there has been an assumption that vocational education is more valuable for gaining employment than a general curriculum. This assumption is based on a belief that if students leave school with a particular set of skills they will have an easier time finding employment than those who leave with only a general education. One argument against that assumption is that the student with the general education will be better able to adapt to the changing needs of the labor market than the student trained in one particular area.

Determining the outcomes of vocational education is very difficult because many factors other than the school curriculum can affect a person's experiences in the labor market; for example, family background, cognitive ability, and the quality of the school. Most studies attempt to take these factors into consideration. Also, most studies compare vocational graduates with graduates of a general curriculum as opposed to an academic or college preparatory curriculum. The usual assumption is that if a student were not in a vocational curriculum, he or she would probably be in a general curriculum. This assumption could affect the interpretation of results, because it is possible that some vocational students might choose a college preparatory curriculum which could possibly lead to higher wages and less unemployment.

The most consistent finding of such studies is that vocational education is economically more beneficial for women than it is for men; this is specifically related to business and office courses. Female students who take vocational education courses, as opposed to the general curriculum, are more likely than men to have higher hourly, weekly, and annual incomes. In addition, they work more hours per week and more weeks per year. Therefore they are less likely to be unemployed, more likely to receive higher wages, and have longer periods of employment.[59]

The above finding should be considered in relation to a sex-segregated labor market. The pattern is for females mostly to enter vocational programs in office and business skills and subsequently jobs in these areas which are primarily occupied by women. This means that these particular programs reinforce patterns of sexual segregation in the labor market. From the standpoint of the urban employer dependent upon large clerical and secretarial staffs, vocational programs are essential for filling jobs. On the other hand, this linkage between office and business vocational programs and the labor market might lock women into employment patterns that offer little hope of advancement or high wages.

For men the picture is more mixed. Male graduates of vocational programs tend to experience less unemployment and are employed at a particular job longer than graduates of a general curriculum. On the other hand, vocational graduates tend to earn lower wages than general curriculum graduates. One possible reason for this is that because of longer job tenure and decreased educational attainment, vocational school graduates are less likely to be socially and financially mobile during their lifetimes than graduates of the general curriculum. In addition, vocational graduates are less likely to be unionized and this results in lower wages.[60]

The findings are slightly contradictory for differences between socioeconomic and racial groups. The summary of research in *The Vocational Education Study: The Interim Report* concluded that black male and female graduates of a vocational curriculum were less likely to be unemployed than black male and female graduates of a general curriculum.[61] Daymont and Rumberger investigated this issue in terms of both racial differences and socioeconomic differences. Rather than make a distinction between vocational, academic, and general curricula, they measured "the relative effects of taking more courses in one area (e.g., vocational) versus another area (e.g., academic)."[62] Using this method they also found that "the strongest vocational training effects were associated with training in office occupations."[63] With regard to race and socioeconomic status, they found that vocational training had less positive effect on hourly wages for blacks and disadvantaged groups than for whites and advantaged groups. They concluded that this "contradicts the hypothesis that the disadvantaged are the primary beneficiaries of vocational training and suggests that perhaps the most important need for disadvantaged students is training in basic skills."[64]

These findings suggest that if jobs are available (this is a crucial assumption), then disadvantaged and minority youth participating in these programs will have a higher employment rate than those not participating in these programs. But if all minority and disadvantaged youth participated in these programs then such a comparison obviously becomes meaningless and unemployment rates would depend on the labor market. In other words, if all students receive the same type of training then the issue of unemployment is not one of training but of the availability of jobs in the marketplace.

The above raises a fundamental issue for the labor needs of urban employers. Is the problem one of lack of training of potential employees or the lack of job seekers? Unemployment rates in the 1980s, which have ranged into double digit percentages, suggest that the problem is not the lack of people seeking jobs but the skills of the job seekers, so that if all minority and disadvantaged youth received vocational training for entry-level jobs, employers would be happy because they would get a better-educated worker but unemployment rates might stay the same. This will be considered again with the issue of whether or not the public should pay for training of workers for specific industries.

The findings also suggest that vocational training for minority and disadvantaged youth will lead to employment in jobs with lower wages and less potential for upward mobility than if they had proceeded through an academic or general education. This is particularly true for females (for whom vocational education has the greatest impact) who enter and are locked into a sex-segregated labor market.

If we return to the issue of whether or not the public should pay for the training of workers for specific industries then we must consider the potential impact of specific training for entry level jobs for disadvantaged and minority youth. Consider the example of the previously discussed Harper Center for Financial Services in Atlanta. This is a school organized by six banks and the Federal Reserve to train workers for the banking industry. There are no problems for the graduates of this school as long as jobs are available in the banking industry. But let us assume that there are limits to the number of graduates that can be absorbed. This situation would clearly work to the advantage of the banking industry and not the individual who had graduated from the vocational program. A larger pool of trained workers would mean that the banking industry could keep wages at a low level. Also, the banking industry could select better-trained workers. For the individual who graduated from the school but could not find employment in the banking industry there would be a problem of learning new skills or trying to transfer learned skills to another job. For the disadvantaged minority youth who had gone through this training with the hope of future employment, this could be a devastating blow. Essentially, the school provided better-trained and cheaper workers at the public's expense.

This is one of the potential dangers of the business-school linkage where business is clearly gaining the dominant role. The public is being asked to pay the bill for training workers to meet the specific needs of industry without any guarantee or hope that all graduates will be hired. Should business and industry assume a greater share of the cost of these programs? Should they run their own training programs, assuming the full cost of those programs?

The Paideia Proposal

There has, in fact, been a proposal that American elementary and secondary schools completely eliminate vocational training and adopt a single curriculum for all students. This is the argument of the *Paideia Proposal*, which has been hailed by such education leaders as Albert Shanker, president of the American Federation of Teachers, and Ruth Love, superintendent of the Chicago Public Schools. The basic argument of the *Paideia Proposal* is that it is undemocratic to divide students into separate curricula and that equality of educational opportunity should mean that all students receive an equal education. The goal of schooling in this proposal is to prepare all people for life-long learning. This rejects the idea that public schools should train for industrial needs and favors the idea that schools should educate for individual needs. Vocational training or learning should occur after secondary school when the individual has gained the skills to learn and adapt to a changing labor market. This would also decrease, according to the argument, the tendency to give children of the poor one type of education and the children of the rich another type of education.[65]

It does not seem likely that the *Paideia Proposal* will reverse the present trend in urban schooling. It is more likely that business, in its search for better-trained workers and the hope that vocational education will end poverty and unemployment, will lead to even greater links between the business community and the schools. But the pattern of development does create the specter of the schools training the urban poor for entry-level jobs that lock them into a particular class in society or, if unable to use those skills, leave them without the means of learning new skills. It also denies to them the original promise of American education which was to produce an educated citizen capable of participating in the control of a democratic government and society.

The College Bound

Not all of the present trends in central city education have centered around training for entry-level jobs. For instance, many of the magnet schools discussed earlier in the chapter were oriented toward college preparation. Some have specialized curriculums designed to prepare students for professions. But, like the preparatory programs for entry-level jobs, many of the college preparatory programs for minorities and the disadvantaged tend to be tied to particular careers and industrial needs. This is particularly true in the fields of engineering, science, and mathematics.

In the early 1980s, Gene Maeroff, the education writer for the New York Times, was hired by the Carnegie Foundation for the Advancement of Learning to conduct a national study of the relationship between colleges and secondary schools. He looked at the changing relationship between colleges and the schools, and at new experiments in college preparatory curricula. One of his concerns centered on efforts to increase the number of minority and disadvantaged students attending college.

In a chapter from his report, "Minorities: A Shared Mandate," he was able to divide neatly the categories of aid given to disadvantaged and minority students into engineering, math and science, and medical careers. These are the areas receiving the greatest attention in the attempt to increase the number of minority and disadvantaged youth attending college. One such program he found was the Minority Engineering Program, started by the Alfred Sloane Foundation in 1973 to boost the number of minorities in engineering by organizing efforts between schools, colleges, and industrial organizations "to sponsor tutoring, field trips, and clubs for minority students in junior and senior high schools." The primary goal of these activities is to increase student interest in the field of engineering.[66]

A similar program, Maeroff found, was being conducted by the Illinois Institute of Technology in Chicago with an effort being placed on recruiting for engineering careers beginning in the sophmore year of high school. During their sophmore years, selected students are brought to the college campus to attend workshops on preparing for engineering careers. In their junior year, they return to campus to be tested by completing a series of projects. Those students selected from these project tests are given a seven-week summer school course. Illinois Institute of Technology's program is tied to summer jobs provided by such companies as Amoco, Atlantic Richfield, Cummins Engine, Eastman Kodak, and U.S. Steel.[67]

Maeroff argues that the above programs are essential for increasing the number of minorities in engineering. According to his figures, "Of the 62,839 bachelor's degrees awarded in engineering in 1981, only 4.7% went to blacks, Hispanics, and American Indians." Only 2.5% of the master's degrees and 1.4% of the doctorates in engineering went to these three minority groups. Comparable figures can be found for the number of minority physicians and medical students. In 1975, 7.5% of the nation's medical students were black, marking a significant increase from the 2.7% in 1968.[68]

The key Maeroff found in his survey for increasing the number of minority students in medicine was better preparation in high school. Two colleges that have been working with secondary schools to better prepare minority students are the City College of the City University of New York and the University of Alabama. The City College works with a local secondary school in operating a minischool called the Macy Medical Professions Program. Students are enrolled in the ninth grade after extensive recruiting in junior high schools. The University of Alabama's program operates in two of the poorest counties in the United States with students being brought to special campus programs and given a special six-week summer program to improve their basic skills.

As models of science and mathematics programs designed to increase the number of minority and disadvantaged in those areas, Maeroff used New York's West Harlem Magnet Junior High School Project and the Boys Harbor Senior High School Program. The West Harlem Magnet School is specifically designed for students with ability in science to receive special training at the school and to receive college enrichment courses at the City College twice a week. The same thing occurs in the Boys Harbor Senior High School Program which sends high school students to the City College Campus for special instruction each Saturday.

What Maeroff found in his national survey was a combination of magnet schools directing minority students into specific professions requiring a college education, associations between colleges and schools to attract and prepare minority and disadvantaged students for college, and regional organizations promoting college education for minorities, particularly engineering.

One of the important regional organizations not discussed by Maeroff is Mathematics, Engineering, Science Achievement (MESA) first organized in 1970 with minority students from the Oakland Technical High School. By the early 1980s, the program included over 3,300 students from 130 California high schools and from schools in Colorado, New Mexico, and Washington. A major purpose of the program is to provide minority students with role models. In a particular participating school, a science or mathematics teacher is selected to organize and advise a MESA club. Through the club the students take field trips, receive special tutoring, visit working scientists and engineers, and receive special college counseling. Students participating in the clubs are required to take mathematics through trigonometry, chemistry, physics, and four years of English.[69]

Funding of the MESA program has been tied to both private foundations and private industry. Like private industrial involvement in the schools to improve entry-level job skills, the MESA program is considered a future source of engineering talent to meet industrial needs. Dennis Laurie, director of community relations for the Atlantic Richfield Company, acts as chairperson of MESA fundraising. Laurie says the reason 15 industrial sponsors are willing to give $920,000 is "The corporations we're talking to understand that talented, capable people are coming out of the system. It is ensuring that minorities will not be left behind in this race we're all caught up in. For the purest and the most selfish reasons, it makes sense to support MESA."[70]

MESA represents a particular type of program designed to entice minority students into engineering and science; the majority of preparation of minority and disadvantaged urban youth is taking place within regular and special programs in central city school systems. Many of the magnet schools are specifically designed to motivate urban youth into professional occupations. For instance, Houston's High School for Engineering Professions, with a minority student enrollment of 73.1% in 1982, received special attention in the national black community in an article in *Ebony* magazine. According to the article, the school is "the nation's only predominantly black public school designed to prepare students for college-level engineering studies" and it "has established a national reputation for excellence...."[71]

A quick review of the magnet schools discussed earlier in the chapter indicated the number of special programs designed to promote college preparation. Not all of these schools prepare for science, mathematics, and engineering. Philadelphia has a High School for International Affairs and a Foreign Language Magnet Program. In addition, the traditional college preparatory programs at Central High School and the Philadelphia High School for Girls are offered to larger numbers of minority students than in the past. Houston also offers a Foreign Language Academy and a College Preparatory High School. In Cincinnati, there is the college preparatory high school, Walnut Hills, and the International Studies Academy. All of these programs must attempt to maintain racial balance which in general means increased recruiting of minority students. In these situations, magnet school desegregation plans have probably increased the number of minority students entering colleges.

Even with the consideration of these programs, a large number of magnet school programs oriented toward college preparation are emphasizing mathematics, engineering, and science. Philadelphia has a High School for Engineering and Science, a Medical, Engineering, and Aero-Space Sciences Magnet Program, and a Science/Mathematics Magnet Program. Besides the High School for Engineering Professions, Houston has a High School for Health Professions, an Aerodynamics Institute, and special math and science magnets for elementary and junior grades. Cincinnati has an Academy for Math & Science and special elementary programs in science and mathematics.

Though the relationship of these college preparatory programs to business and industrial influence is not as clear as it is with those programs emphasizing entry-level skills, the programs do seem to be geared toward industrial needs. This is particularly true in medical, engineering, mathematics and science programs. Logically, it can be argued, this is important to do not only because of a limited number of minorities in these professions, but also because of the availability of well paying jobs. It is hard to criticize programs that can provide a major step forward for the disadvantaged and minority youth.

On the other hand, one can raise the issue of industrial and business needs determining college preparatory curricula in public schools. The best way of understanding this issue is to consider other alternatives that would probably not be adopted in the climate of the increasing

relationship between business and schools. For instance, why not a
college preparatory high school emphasizing the protection of political,
civil, and economic rights? The curriculum could be heavily weighted
in the direction of political science, economics, history, and sociology
courses.

This curriculum could be justified since it was a major civil rights
movement that resulted in increasing opportunities for minorities and
the poor in the United States. What preparations are the public schools
making for the continued protection of those gains and increased protection of civil rights? The little chance that a business community
would sponsor such a magnet program indicates the boundaries that are
set once a close partnership is built between the schools and a particular
part of the community. Free Enterprise Day is celebrated in Atlanta
with students talking about their job experiences, but there is no Civil
and Social Rights Day when students speak of how they have worked
for protection of political, economic, and civil rights.

Like the training for entry-level jobs, the major problem with current trends in college preparatory programs in public schools is that
they are geared toward industrial needs. It is possible that the shortage
of medical workers, scientists, engineers, and mathematicans might
turn into a surplus. This has happened before in the professions. When
a surplus does occur it is to the advantage of institutions, businesses, and
industry, which can pay lower wages for better trained workers, not to
the advantage of urban poor and minority groups.

Conclusion

The shaping of the central city school curriculum by the growing linkages between city school systems and business creates a perplexing
situation. It has resulted in curricula linked to specific needs in the labor
market which might work primarily for the benefit of the employer by
providing better trained workers at lower salaries. It might not work for
the benefit of the disadvantaged and minority groups if there continues
to be high levels of unemployment. If this occurs, urban disadvantaged
and minority youth might find themselves unemployed with training
for a specific industry and without a general educational background
that would allow for adaptation to the needs of a changing labor market.

These issues should be considered in the context of the real problem
of unemployment among American youth, particularly minority youth.
Between 1979 and 1982, unemployment for young white adults between 20 and 24 years of age increased from 7.6% to 12.8%, whereas
unemployment rates for blacks in the same age group increased from
20.6% to 30.6%. The same contrast holds for the age group between

16 to 19, with whites having an unemployment rate of 14% in 1979 and 20.4% in 1982, and blacks having an unemployment rate of 36.5% and 48% during the same years.[72]

These figures do not tell the whole story for urban youth. According to Janet Norwood, U.S. Commissioner of Labor Statistics, many teenagers in metropolitan areas are responsible for contributing to the support of low-income families. In addition, according to Norwood, during periods of economic prosperity since the 1950s, employment rates for white teenagers have increased whereas those for black teenagers have decreased. One of the results is that compared with the past, fewer black teenagers are seeking jobs. Consequently, argues Norwood, (as quoted in an article in *Education Week*), these young people who have not had success in the labor market "may later encounter more difficulty."[73] It could be argued from the above figures that schools need to teach basic work skills because of the difficulty of disadvantaged and minority youth learning those skills in the labor market. This might avoid the creation of a permanent class of unemployed.

On the other hand, the steadily declining number of youth entering the labor pool through the 1980s will actually improve the possibilities of employment for young adults and decrease unemployment rates. If this occurs then the issue might be what form of education will most enhance the employment opportunities of disadvantaged and minority youth? A specialized education might limit the possibilities for mobility and increased wages at a time when there is a shrinking labor pool. A general education stressing basic academic skills might improve the chances for mobility in this type of labor market.

For women this is a particularly important issue because of the tendency of vocational and career education programs to train for a sex-segregated labor market. The schools might flood the urban labor market with well trained female secretaries at a time when many other employment opportunities are opening to women. This situation would work to the advantaged of employers, but not to the women entering the labor market.

The real danger is that business will use the schools to its advantage to assure cheap and well trained workers, and that this will not be to the advantage of the worker in a shrinking labor market. This situation reflects the type of issue that occurs when one part of society, the business community, becomes a dominant factor in the public schools which were meant to serve all of society.

The readers interested in investigating these issues in their own urban community might begin by contacting their local school district about magnet school and Adopt-a-School programs. If an Adopt-a-School program exists, the reader might investigate the types of relationships established between individual businesses and schools. Have businesses just contributed time and money or have they also had a direct influence on the curriculum? In investigating magnet school programs, the reader might want to determine how many of the magnet schools are tied to particular careers.

Also worth investigating is how much, if any, financial aid has been given to individual schools or the school district by the private sector or foundations. It is important to determine whether or not this money resulted in the school or school system following a course of action that might not have been pursued without the money. In other words, did this money influence the school system in the direction of the needs and interests of the private sector? The reader might also want to determine if local businesses have provided aid in the form of loaned executives to the school system. As mentioned previously, this often occurs with regard to problems of management and administration.

To gain an understanding of employment training programs, those interested should contact their local Private Industry Council. Close attention should be given to the composition of this organization to determine which members of the private sector are exerting the greatest influence. The employment needs of the local labor market should be investigated to determine if these programs will be producing a surplus of workers relative to local needs.

And finally, the reader might reflect on what all this means in relation to the traditional goals of American education. For the last two centuries there has been a continuing tendency to try to use the schools to solve social problems including reducing crime, eliminating poverty, and improving the national economy. So far there has been little evidence of the school's success in solving any of these problems. In fact, it can be argued that the reason the school is turned to so often to solve social problems is because it represents the most conservative approach. Using the school avoids trying to solve social problems by dealing directly with the social and economic structure. By using the school one is saying that the problem is with the way individuals act and not with the organization of society.

Maybe the goal of schooling should be limited to that of providing a sound basic and general education without any claims to solve major economic problems like unemployment. This is an important consideration since there is no proof that schooling can solve the problems of unemployment and poverty in American society.

Notes

1. Quoted by Anne C. Lewis in "Washington Report: The Military Enters the Competition for Technically Trainable Graduates," in *Phi Delta Kappan* (May 1983), Vol. 64, No. 9, p. 603.

2. For an analysis of magnet schools see Christine H. Rossell, "Magnet Schools as a Desegregation Tool," in *Urban Education* (October 1979), Vol. 14, No. 3, pp. 303–20.

3. Ibid., p. 308.

4. "Chronology of Interactions Between the School District and the Pennsylvania Human Relations Commission Desegregation Plan and Funding Fact Sheet," undated fact sheet issued by the School District of Philadelphia.

5. "Golden Opportunities for Students: Information about Special Admission Schools," fact sheet issued by the School District of Philadelphia, Fall 1982.

6. Ibid.

7. Ibid.

8. Cheryl Stanley, *Magnet Schools Seventh Annual Final Report 1981–82,* undated report issued by the Planning, Research, and Evaluation Department of the Houston Independent School District.

9. "MacGregor Elementary School: Music and Science Magnet Program," undated pamphlet issued by the Houston Independent School District.

10. "Cluster Centers," undated pamphlet issued by the Houston Public School District.

11. "High School for Law Enforcement and Criminal Justice," undated pamphlet issued by the Houston Public School District.

12. See Chapter 2 for a discussion of these events.

13. *Detail Budget Presentation: Cincinnati Public Schools* (Cincinnati: Board of Education, 1982), pp. 252–53.

14. Mark Smylie, "Reducing Racial Isolation in Large School Districts: The Comparative Effectiveness of Mandatory and Voluntary Desegregation Strategies," in *Urban Education* (January 1983), Vol. 17, No. 4, p. 485.

15. Office of Research, Planning and Evaluation, "Voluntary Desegregation E.S.A.A. Program Evaluation 1980–81" (Philadelphia: School District of Philadelphia, 1982), p. 22.

16. Stanley, *Magnet Schools Seventh Annual Final Report,* p. 15.

17. Michael Timpane, *Corporations and Public Education,* Report distributed by Teachers College, Columbia University (May 1981).

18. Ibid., p. 8.

19. Ibid., pp. 8–9.

20. Thomas Toch, "Time for Private Foundations for Public Schools," in *Education Week* (November 3, 1982), Vol. 2, No. 9, pp. 1, 15.

21. "Adopt-A-School 1981–1982," pamphlet distributed by the Denver Public Schools.

22. These activities are described in the "Adopt-A-School Handbook" distributed by the Atlanta Public Schools.

23. "Chicago: 404 Businesses Support Career Education Drive in Schools," in *You & Youth,* published by Vocational Foundation, Inc. (November 1980), Vol. 2 No. 11, pp. 1–4.

24. Ibid., p. 5.

25. "JAG: Jobs for America's Graduates, Inc.," undated pamphlet distributed by JAG.

26. "Synopsis: Jobs for America's Graduates," fact sheet distributed by JAG.

27. Ibid.

28. "Initial Research Results," in *Crossroads,* published by JAG (March 1982) Vol. 1, No. 2, p. 3.
29. For a discussion of the forming of the Tri-Lateral Council, see the Civil Rights Commission report, *Desegregating the Boston Public Schools* (Washington, D.C.: U.S. Printing Office, 1975), pp. 175–80.
30. *The Boston Compact. An Operational Plan for Expanded Partnerships with the Boston Public Schools, September 1982,* booklet distributed by the Boston Public Schools, p. 2.
31. Ibid., p. 1.
32. Ibid., p. 4.
33. Ibid., pp. 47–48.
34. "A Community of Believers," in *The Atlanta Partnership of Business & Education, Inc. Second Anniversary Report,* undated booklet distributed by the Atlanta Partnership of Business & Education, Inc., p. 6.
35. Ibid., p. 1.
36. Alonzo A. Crim, "A Community of Believers," in *Daedalus* (Fall 1981), Vol. 110, No. 4, pp. 146–47.
37. Ibid., p. 150.
38. Sara Lawrence Lightfoot, "Portraits of Exemplary Secondary Schools: George Washington Carver Comprehensive High School," in *Daedalus* (Fall 1981), Vol. 110, No. 4, p. 19.
39. Ibid., p. 32.
40. Ibid., p. 32.
41. Ibid., p. 31.
42. Ibid., p. 33.
43. "A Community of Believers," in *Atlanta Partnership,* p. 5.
44. Ibid., p. 5.
45. Ibid., p. 9.
46. Ibid., p. 7.
47. Ibid., p. 9.
48. Timpane, *Corporations and Public Education,* p. 34.
49. *Chicago United and the Chicago Board of Education: Partners in Change* (March 1, 1983), booklet distributed by the Chicago Public Schools, p. 1.
50. *Special Task Force on Education: Chicago School System* (March 1981), report distributed by Chicago United.
51. Ibid., pp. vii–ix.
52. Ibid., p. ix.
53. Ibid., p. viii.
54. Ibid., p. 30
55. *Chicago United and the Chicago Board of Education,* p. 2.
56. *Public Law 97–300 Job Training Partnership Act* (October 13, 1982), Sec. 2.
57. Ibid., Sec. 102.
58. Ibid., Sec. 106.
59. John A. Gardner, Paul Campbell, and Patricia Seitz, *Influences of High School Curriculum on Determinants of Labor Market Experiences* (Columbus, Ohio: The National Center for Research in Vocational Education, 1982), pp. 169–171; Robert Meyer, "Job Training in the Schools," paper

prepared for the Policy Forum on Employability Development at The National Center for Research in Vocational Education, Ohio State University, October 14–16, 1981; Thomas Daymont and Russell Rumberger, "The Economic Value of Vocational and Academic Training Acquired in High School," paper submitted for review to The National Center for Research in Vocational Education, 1983.

60. Gardner et al., *Influences of High School Curriculum,* p. 169.
61. *The Vocational Education Study: The Interim Report* (Washington, D.C.: U.S. Printing Office, 1980), pp. vii–4, vii–5.
62. Daymont and Rumberger, "Economic Value of Vocational and Academic Training," p. 2.
63. Ibid., p. 3.
64. Ibid., p. 22.
65. Mortimer J. Adler, *The Paideia Proposal* (New York: Macmillan Publishing Co., 1982).
66. Gene Maeroff, *School and College* (Princeton, NJ: The Carnegie Foundation for the Advancement of Teaching, 1983), p. 57.
67. Ibid., p. 58–59.
68. Ibid., p. 57.
69. Susan Walton, "Mesa Advances Minorities Toward Technical Careers," in *Education Week* (March 9, 1983), Vol. 2, No. 24, pp. 1, 19.
70. Ibid., p. 19.
71. Ron Harris, "Inner City High School Trains Top Engineering Candidates," in *Ebony,* reprint distributed by the Houston Independent School District.
72. Charles Eucher, "High Youth Unemployment Cited as Major U.S. Social Problem," in *Education Week* (April 27, 1983), Vol. 2, No. 31, p. 8.
73. Ibid.

Teaching and Learning
in Elementary Schools

*There are differences between the teaching and learning style in the
family and community, or informal education, and the style employed in school, or formal education. Specifically, in school every
child acquires new strategies for language use, learns out of context,
and learns how to learn.*

JOHN U. OGBU, *"Cultural Discontinuation and Schoolings,"*
1982, p. 12

During the late 1970s and the early 1980s, the national agenda for
educating central city elementary school children emphasized instruction in the basic skills of reading, mathematics, and, to a lesser extent,
writing. This curricular emphasis can be seen as a response to pressure
from numerous groups including employers of youth and parents, not
to mention secondary school teachers, burdened with ill-prepared students who were unable to read beyond the third grade level.

This chapter will analyze the consequences of this emphasis, the
underlying assumptions of the "back-to-basics" movement, and the
central city school's accountability for students' academic achievement.
The linkages between the "back-to-basics" movement, the social consequences of schooling, and the teaching and learning of elementary
school children will also be discussed.

National Trends in Reading and Mathematics Achievement

Local, state, and national agencies maintain programs of academic testing to monitor the progress of students. These programs allow analysts
to speak of general patterns or trends in various areas of achievement

such as reading, mathematics, and language skills for different groups of children. Gains in "low order" skills such as word recognition and literal comprehension have been dramatic for particular groups, especially minority group children from low income families whose previous academic performance has been poor.

As seen in Table 7.1, performance by a national sample of sixth graders on the Iowa Test of Basic Skills in reading, language, and mathematics suffered a decline from the early 1960s to 1970 after showing an improvement over the 8-year period preceding 1963. This downward trend reversed itself in the latter part of the 1970s and by 1981–82, test scores had climbed close to their mid-1950s level. However, long-term trends are difficult to assess precisely because other tests, such as the California Achievement Test (CAT) have recently been adopted by some cities in place of the Iowa Test of Basic Skills. Considering CAT data only, whereas 39.2% of students in grades K–8 in Cincinnati performed at or above national reading norms in 1981, one year later 42.8% had achieved this standard. In mathematics achievement, the figures were 42.3% in 1981 as compared with 45.4% in 1982.[1]

According to analysts, gains in basic skills reflect a growing and sustained programmatic thrust in nationally sponsored education policies such as Head Start and the Federal Elementary and Secondary School Act (1977), the enforcement of minimum competency laws in a majority of the states, and a commitment to a "back-to-basics" philosophy on the part of parents, teachers, and educational administrators and researchers.[2]

The Social Structure of School Knowledge

The Effective Schools Movement

The commitment to a back-to-basics curriculum is tacitly imbedded within programs of "effective schooling." We say "tacitly" because researchers, school administrators, and others caught up in the effective schools hoopla typically have not examined assumptions underlying projects to enhance school productivity put forward under the effective schooling banner.

The effective schools agenda targets central city schools, and from 1978 to the present has been introduced into the school systems of several declining central cities in the East and Midwest: New York City, New Haven, St. Louis, Chicago, and Milwaukee. Although a program of effective schooling may be adopted systemwide, implementation is carried out at the school level.

The aims of effective schools programs vary but incorporate one preeminent objective: ". . . to bring an equal percentage of . . . [the

TABLE 7.1
Nationwide scores from the Iowa Test
of Basic Skills in the Sixth grade

	Reading	Language	Math
1955	6.20	6.20	6.20
1963	6.42	6.41	6.54
1970	6.16	6.27	6.20
1977	5.86	5.69	5.84
1981–82	6.12	6.02	6.02

The 6.2 scores in 1955, the base year, mean that an average sixth-grader's skills were at the level of a sixth grader in the second month.
Source: University of Iowa.

school's] highest and lowest social classes to minimum mastery."[3] In other words, the final criterion by which effectiveness is gauged is the equalization of achievement test performance at the basic skills level by the most and least economically advantaged groups within a particular school. Current effective schools projects are based on previous research showing linkages between improved academic performance, school-level planning to improve instruction, and a number of school and school system factors.

The effective schools literature is replete with descriptions of the characteristics of unusually productive or effective schools. A set of factors were identified by seven teams of researchers who investigated schools characterized as unusually successful in reversing the downward spiral of academic achievement. Of particular note were six dimensions of effectiveness: principal's belief systems, personal qualities and behaviors; teachers' characteristics and behaviors; school instructional climate; instructional emphasis or "time on task"; pupil evaluation; and resources, including community support. The findings of these and other related research studies focus attention on the school and its potential for enhancing student learning. This is a notable change and, we believe, an important correction of two damaging trends.

The first trend stems from an ideology clearly associated with federal policies flowing from the so-called Moynihan Report entitled "The Negro Family: The Case for National Action."[4] According to Moynihan's analysis of family household functioning, severe and persistent problems in areas such as school achievement and health are associated with particular forms of family structure. By far the most "deficient" form is the single parent household located in a large central city and headed by a black female. So long as problems faced within these families are left untended, schools and other societal institutions remain impotent in their efforts to improve the well-being of all family members including schoolaged children. The policy strategy of "blaming the victim," implied in the Moynihan Report, excuses the school and other social institutions from being ultimately responsible for children by holding the family responsible for children's school failure and lack of motivation.

The stress on within-school factors that is present in the effective schools literature redirects this focus. In Milwaukee, for example, the effective schools program, Project RISE (Rising to Individual Scholastic Excellence) is based explicitly on the following three assumptions:

1. Virtually all students, regardless of their family background, race or socioeconomic status, can acquire the basic skills.
2. Inappropriate school expectations, norms, practices, and policies account for the underachievement of a preponderance of low-income and minority students.
3. The literature on effective schools and classrooms has identified expectations, norms, practices and policies that are associated with high achievement; it is reasonable for schools to emulate these characteristics.[5]

In order to shift the burden of academic performance from the family nexus to the school, the implementation of Project RISE in Milwaukee's 20 lowest performing elementary schools began with training sessions and workshops for staff of participating schools. The central issue pursued during the initial year of debate in these groups was "the premise that low socioeconomic status need not be as important to academic achievement as in-school factors."[6]

The second trend reversed by the effective schools movement (in combination with a back-to-basics and accountability emphasis) is associated with a view of the school as a highly quantifiable entity, a "black box" whose impact upon student achievement can be gauged by taking account of such features as expenditures per pupil, teacher-pupil ratios, the number of books in the school library, and other tangible resources. This econometric model most closely associated with research in political economics and sociology reduces the school to a ledger of input-output features. By far the most influential source for this view is the large scale survey of the schools entitled *The Equality of Educational Opportunity Survey* (EEOS),[7] conducted by James S. Coleman and his colleagues.

The major objective of the EEOS was to determine the educational opportunities and school performance of majority compared with minority group children. The 500,000 children studied were racially, socially, and geographically diverse. The results of Coleman's study indicated that there were:

1. substantial and persistent test score differences among the six racial groups studied

2. increasingly large gaps between minority and majority students' scores from the first to the twelfth grade

3. no differences between minority and majority group children in the value they attach to school and academic achievement; material resources were judged to be of little consequence to achievement differences.

A notable accomplishment of the effective schools movement is that it has altered our view of schools as "relatively static constructs of discrete variables," a view implicit in the EEOS, by allowing us to view schools as individual and unique social organizations whose structures are built upon both contents and processes aside from formal organizational features. The literature on effective schools consistently argues for school-based change by holding the six factors mentioned earlier accountable for student achievement or failure. It has forced a consideration of "roles, norms, values and instructional techniques of a school . . . [as well as] the information taught in the curriculum," i.e., the contents of the school.[8] In addition, the processes characterizing the day to day interaction of various "communication networks" (teachers, students, administrators, parents) are seen as critical to the achievement of students.

In their investigation of effective school projects in Chicago, St. Louis, Milwaukee, and New York City, Eubanks and Levine identified several factors associated with successful student academic performance in elementary school project sites in these cities.[9] Resources, including both expenditures and time spent by staff in the initial planning stages, were particularly critical since a resource base provided teachers with the opportunity to acquire skills in direct instruction or mastery learning, two teaching strategies associated with increased student achievement in basic skills.

Resources also allowed schools to maximize administrative assistance in instructional support and in monitoring student learning. Frequent and formal evaluation of student progress (usually once a week on Friday) is associated with achievement gains. Some cities, St. Louis, for example, received external monetary support from private sources. In that city, the Danforth Foundation provided $200,000 to cover start-up costs involved in the training and supervision of teaching staff. Other cities, for example, Chicago, were given monies allocated through local school districts. The 45 participating schools in Chicago received an average of $100,000 to supplement their regular budgets.

Additional monies were used in a number of ways to bolster Chicago programs. Among the supports most frequently acquired by project schools were the following:

A full time person to work with staff in improving reading; employment of a teacher for art, music, science or social studies; a variety of activities to improve school climate and time-on task; more intensive use of support services in implementing instruction; introduction of in-school suspension programs or other components to improve attendance; and purchase of staff development and in-service training resources. Eighteen of the schools conducted or helped conduct summer schools in 1982 and eight others arranged to send their students to other locations.[10]

Thus, resources to support both administrative and instructional assistance are seen as key to the improvement of school effectiveness. As we have seen in Chapter 1, the capacity of central city schools to generate an adequate resource base is problemmatic and thus improvement efforts in these schools may be hampered.

According to Eubanks and Levine, allocating sufficient planning time prior to program implementation is a second critical factor. Lengths of time ranged from more than a year in Milwaukee to only two months in Chicago. Sufficient advance time allows the development of both leadership and consensus in the ranks of school personnel. More specifically, increased student achievement in basic skills is linked to two organizational features in particular: directive leadership in specifying topics and providing concrete illustrations of school organizational and instructional components drawn from the effective schools literature; and consensus of individual school teaching staffs on school objectives in terms of what form of direct instruction will be used, how schedules and teaching assignments will be organized, and what supplementary materials will be used.[11] Directive leadership and staff consensus do not occur overnight, but demand sufficient time to develop and flourish.

A third, more ephemeral factor tied to programmatic success is what Eubanks and Levine term "school improvement potential." An indifferent, complacent faculty, a hostile community, and lack of zeal in the principal's office can conspire to deflate an effective school project despite the infusion of additional resources. However, the authors argue that from their knowledge of effective schools projects, and especially from their observations in Milwaukee where projects have been established longest, there is room for considerable optimism over improvement potential for virtually all central city schools. Careful monitoring of programmatic change, reassignment of change-resistant staff, reliance on staff seniority for leadership, and especially voluntary (as opposed to mandatory) project implementation at the school level are tied to gains in student achievement. School staff who elect to participate in a school effectiveness campaign are much more likely to achieve success than those who are drummed into the ranks. Eubanks and

Levine advocate a voluntary rather than mandatory decision on both the school improvement potential issue and the participation decision itself. Both are tied to traditional organizational development strategies which argue that meaningful institutional change occurs when participants elect to change and monitor their own activity, as opposed to when participants are being directed by bureaucrats removed from the day to day scene.

Although the central administrative office must take a clear, consistent, and supportive role in directive leadership, schools should elect to participate or should be nominated on the basis of "neutral indicators" such as the amount of Title I or Title IV Federal assistance granted the school. In addition to their role in resource allocation and project monitoring, central staff are key in assisting project schools in utilizing available knowledge in effectiveness. Rather than re-inventing the wheel at the school level, successful programs exhibited "a relatively high degree of structure and specification" emanating from the central office. Eubanks and Levine observe that participating faculty in project schools need "something concrete to plan" flowing from the central office in order to avoid haziness of purpose and lack of direction. Nonetheless, faculty in project schools in all locations had an important role in deciding on schedules, teaching assignments, and the like, all of which they perceived as best implementing such concrete goals as teaching via direct instruction.

Finally, a fourth factor contributing to programmatic success is what Eubanks and Levine term "parent involvement." Here, the central issue in project schools was the extent to which parents and other representatives from the school community should be involved in school program planning and indeed if they should be involved at all. Here the authors found mixed evidence of success.

> In some locations, such as Milwaukee, parents and community representatives generally have not been heavily involved in the initial stage of school level planning, in order to avoid possible problems with respect to school-community polarization and to focus accountability for improvement on the professional staff. In other locations, such as the LSDP in New York, parent and community representatives are full participants beginning in the first stage of the planning process. On the other hand we found evidence indicating that the Milwaukee approach worked quite well and increasing parent involvement was evident at some locations as schools began to implement their plans. On the other hand, we also heard of New York schools at which parents and community representatives had helped in moving schools off dead center during the early planning stage.[12]

A major concern in constructing effectiveness programs as we have seen clearly in the case of RISE, is that the schools rather than children's parents remain accountable for children's academic progress. Eubanks and Levine also express the fear that "community polarity" may disrupt school planning efforts.

Eubanks and Levine's evaluative study is a cautious and reasonable view of effective school projects. Although their report encourages increased installation of similar projects in other central city schools, they argue that the implementation process is far from easy and not without problems. First, they reason that political forces and local norms may prevent the realization of effectiveness in central cities. Second, the authors express the caution that "higher order" cognitive skills may be ignored in both existing and in future effectiveness programs which emphasize direct instruction: ". . . direct instruction raises the danger that curriculum and instruction will be too molecular and mechanical, with emphasis placed largely on the development of lower order skills that are relatively easy to teach and measure."[13]

There is some evidence that suggests that this latter concern is already a pervasive problem nationally. Although elementary school students across the board are showing increased competence in basic skills, as indicated in Table 7.1, their secondary school counterparts are displaying a continuing lag in higher order skills in reading, language, and mathematics. According to reports from the National Assessment of Educational Progress, a congressionally mandated watchkeeper of scholastic achievement, although 17-year-olds retained their capacity to handle basic reading tasks successfully, the numbers of those who demonstrated complex inferential reading skills dropped over the nine-year period from 1971–1980.[14] A similar trend is evident in the Scholastic Aptitude Test (SAT) administered by the College Board which monitors fluctuations in percentages of those scoring at high (600–800), average (400–599) and low (200–399) levels on the test. Although SAT scores on the average have been rising recently, the College Board attributes these score gains to higher scores among minority group students, formerly scoring in the 200–399 range, who now score in the 400–599 range. However, the frequency of scores in the highest range during this same period has declined, indicating slippage in performance at the most complex, higher order levels.

Although it is not possible to show a direct causal connection between programmatic emphasis on a back-to-basics curriculum and later performance on the SAT, it is quite true that the emphasis on the basics may shut off access to other levels of learning.

In addition to the cautionary note offered by Eubanks and Levine, other substantial objections to the image of the school painted by the school effectiveness literature can be raised over the criterion used to measure effectiveness-performance on standardized achievement tests measuring students' knowledge of basic skills. This standard ignores the political context of schooling and the unequal outcomes for central city children as compared with their suburban counterparts, for girls as compared with boys, and for minority group children as compared with children from the "mainstream."

The Role of Schools in the Process of Social Stratification

Before considering how teachers and children construct school knowledge in the classroom, it is important to examine how predominant theories of social stratification and social mobility have outlined patterns of social outcomes. Social stratification, most simply, is the hierarchical ordering of occupations in terms of prestige and other status factors.

The investigation of social mobility or status attainment from one generation to the next has come to dominate sociology in recent years. In the field's two most prestigious journals, *The American Journal of Sociology* (AJS) and *The American Sociological Review* (ASR), studies of this type constitute the primary emphasis of reported research. According to Norbert Wiley,

> The modal article in the AJS and the ASR . . . was a path analysis of social mobility, charting the statistical influence from father's occupation through son's or daughter's education and other properties to the eventual occupation of the child.[15]

Generally, theoretical models in the social sciences are useful shorthand summaries of factors assumed to be critical in understanding a particular social process. In considering the place of schooling in the life course of the individual, sociologists have offered several competing models. Models of the status attainment process in social stratification have been important in at least three ways: They have

1. shaped commonsense views of the life course of individual educational and occupational attainment and achievement
2. influenced policy in the area of equality of educational opportunity issues
3. unfortunately, focused attention on problems such as "goodness of fit," "response error," and other issues peculiar to mathematical modeling and away from an understanding of the processes of interaction in the family, school, and work world which generate the factors examined by the models. Ironically, there has been little

effort among most sociologists to understand social interactional and social structural linkages.

There is no argument among competing theories of stratification about the impact of schooling upon occupational outcomes in adulthood. Rather, the major point of debate among social stratification analysts is the extent to which schooling serves as a direct *transmitter* of economic status as opposed to a *mediator* of future outcomes. Nonetheless, as others have pointed out, competing views of the status attainment process agree on the major components, namely social origins, socioeconomic status, and education. Briefly, the end result of the process, attained socioeconomic status, is said to be a function of background socioeconomic variables and factors independent of social origin.[16] The degree to which an individual's ultimate socioeconomic status is directly or indirectly transferred by the school across the generations is the essential point for argument, as noted above.

A simple model of the transmission of socioeconomic status is presented in Figure 7.1. This is a simplified representation in which "socioeconomic origin" summarizes parental occupational status, religion, race, and region. Likewise, "education" summarizes grades (academic achievement), years of schooling (educational attainment), and a host of teacher influences and practices which comprise the schooling experience. Finally, "socioeconomic status" summarizes the occupational position in the labor force and earnings, labor market structure, and marital and family structure in adulthood.[17] Thus, although the simple diagram would seem an almost trivial conception of determinants of the

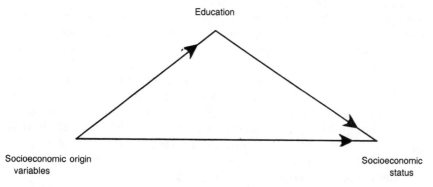

FIGURE 7.1   A Simple Model of Schooling and the Intergeneralization Transmission of Socioeconomic Status. (*Source:* William T. Bielby, "Models of Status Attainment", in *Research in Social Stratification and Mobility.* Vol. 1., 1981, Greenwich, Conn.: JAI Press, pp. 3–26.)

individual's occupational status in adulthood, the formulation turns out in fact to be quite rich. However, as mentioned earlier, although the model has proven useful in illustrating which factors are critical, it has not shown clearly how, interactively, these factors "determine" outcomes. The basic features of two variants of the status attainment process are discussed below.

The Transmission or Reproduction View

In this variation of the model, schools have little impact on the course of the individual's social mobility. Rather, schools are clearinghouses which provide an avenue to occupational outcomes essentially identical to those experienced in the family of origin. The purpose of schooling is narrowed to a credentialing function and schools are seen as reproductive of particular status cultures.[18]

Thus, children whose socioeconomic origins in the central city place them in economically disadvantaged straits in comparison with their suburban counterparts could expect to attend schools in which the emphasis is on low level cognitive skills. Since members of our society are in competition with each other for scarce positions in high status occupational roles such as corporate vice-president and surgeon, these positions must be "reserved" for those from privileged backgrounds whose fathers hold similar jobs and whose home and school milieus prepare them for elite positions.

The Mediation View

The mediation variant accords the school a more influential role in shaping socioeconomic status outcomes than the transmission or reproduction view. Schools actively sort, socialize, measure, and enhance the cognitive (and noncognitive) capacities of the individual. Both schools and students passing through them are more pliable than the reproductive view allows.

How do schools mediate the social background and developing social futures of children? The answer is complex. First, schools *do* respond to the measured ability (or IQ) of children; however, measured ability, though linked to social origins, is weakly related. Thus, there is room for slippage between children's social origins and their placement in accelerated or slow reading groups and in vocational or academic (college prep) programs.

Instead of viewing the schooling process as cementing a relationship between social origins and social outcomes, the mediation view allows for variance in outcomes. This variant of the status attainment model seems a more accurate one since "to a surprising degree, grades and tracking . . . [which in turn affect college plans and occupational aspirations] generate inequality in educational outcomes that are independent of *both* ability and social origins."[19]

In addition to the lack of attention to processes of social interaction, there are two problems that arise from both views of the role of schools in social outcomes. First, although the socioeconomic factor is certainly critical, there are other nonhierarchical components in the status attainment process. Race and gender are preeminent here. Second, the mechanical nature of family-work linkages forged by processes of allocation (grouping and tracking) have been emphasized although the fact is there is only an imperfect fit between background features, measured ability, and program placement.

The Mediation of Family Background in the School

Although family origins have an enormous impact on both academic achievement and educational attainment, recent research on teacher effectiveness has begun to reveal the limitations to family background as a source of influence upon students' classroom success. Briefly, the teacher effectiveness literature examines outcomes of classroom instruction as reflected in measured student achievement gains during the school year. This so-called "process-product" research can be seen as complementing the work on *school* effectiveness in that it illuminates the impact of *teacher* behaviors on student learning in the classroom. However, it suffers from the same limitations as the school effectiveness literature discussed above in that it tends to focus on the teaching and learning of basic skills and assesses student learning via performance on standardized achievement tests.

Research on teacher effectiveness, says Fenstermacher, puts forward a highly limited view of the educated person and the skilled classroom teacher: "What counts as effective is solely what has the effect of producing the outcomes considered desirable,"[20] that is, higher achievement in basic skills. In other words, the process-product research on teacher effectiveness lacks a "normative theory of education" because it ignores both the underlying value systems of teachers and the social, political, and economic settings in which they work. By concentrating on discrete teacher behaviors such as rates of drill, practice, and praise, as they affect reading and math scores, teacher effectiveness research has produced a very limited understanding of the social context of schooling and student learning.

Nonetheless, research, and particularly the Beginning Teacher Evaluation Study (BTES) in California, allows a fuller appreciation of the classroom teacher's role in the status allocation process and of the importance of classroom interaction than previous work on teacher "presage" variables had allowed. As seen in Figure 7.2, presage variables describe various teacher attitudes and values which are generally measured by paper and pencil tests rather than derived from observations of classroom process. In contrast, the teacher effectiveness studies have been conducted in classrooms and have attempted to link teacher-student behaviors (processes) with student achievement (product).

A consistent finding from the intensive study of a large number of elementary school classrooms by Jane Stallings, Jere Brophy, Bruce

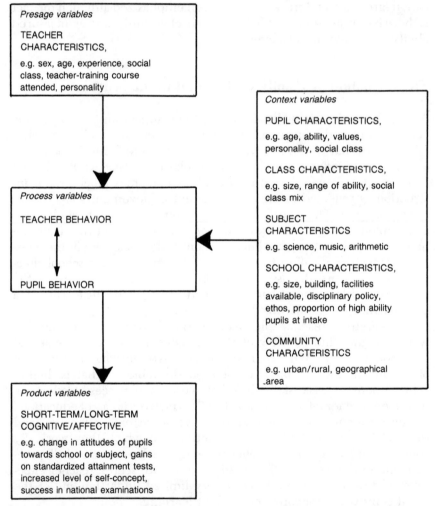

FIGURE 7.2   Teacher Effectiveness: The Basic Model for Research. (*Source:* Chris Kyriacou & Graham Newson, "Teacher Effectiveness: A consideration of research problems," *Educational Review,* Vol. 34, 1, 1982, p.4.)

Good, and others associated with the BTES is that academic achievement over the course of the school year is a function of both student aptitude (IQ) and the amount of "academic learning time" experienced by the student in the classroom: "The variance in student achievement not accounted for by background characteristics and aptitude is explained by the relative amount of time students spend actively engaged in learning tasks appropriate to instructional objectives." The BTES results clearly reveal that although the best predictor of a student's spring achievement scores is the student's fall achievement scores, the next best predictor is what the student's teacher does in the classroom.

To achieve a more comprehensive understanding of effective teaching, we believe that classroom interaction must be considered in the context of a status attainment perspective enriched by a well detailed picture of social interaction in a cultural context. By this we mean that classroom processes and outcomes must be placed in a framework that considers social, political, and economic outcomes as well as school learning (education). An adequate understanding of classroom interaction incorporates at least the following assumptions:

1. Schools are places where inequalities are created rather than just reproduced
2. Schools are part of a general social structure with a prevailing belief system that schools contradict as well as legitimate
3. Schools provide opportunity for mobility from one status group to another in a circumscribed manner that may only occur when there are large-scale social demands for change
4. In addition to economic factors imbedded in the social structure, other factors shape school outcomes. These include race, ethnicity, gender, individual histories, and, most importantly, culture.[21]

Not only does the concept of culture incorporate the shapes or forms of material and social organization of life, but it also involves how these shapes are "experienced, understood, and interpreted."[22] In order to examine school culture it is important to understand the social and material organization of the school, the form and content of the classroom curriculum, and the social relations in the classroom. Classroom social relations include both the teacher-student relationship and relationships among students, that is, the peer culture.

Of particular interest is the discourse that occurs throughout the classroom day not only in lessons but also in the midst of getting settled, lining up, straightening the room, and the like. We do not think it useful to distinguish too closely between a "hidden curriculum" which trains children to be better citizens, docile, passive learners or the reverse, and classroom instruction, the teaching-learning process. The distinction is blurred in classrooms to the extent that a teacher's directive to "sit down and get settled" is often embedded in an instructional activity. In other words, we doubt that participants themselves make fine distinctions between socialization and learning activities in the classroom. Moreover, this distinction has blinded observers in the classroom who see socialization as synonomous with "off task" time and social control. These observers have falsely concluded that socialization takes away from basic skills, instruction, and learning "on task" behaviors and the like. Rather, the view expressed here is that socialization expands (or circumscribes) learning by providing active (or passive) citizenship training and by explicating and clarifying (or obfuscating) classroom social relations.

To examine the role of elementary school classrooms in the status attainment process, we will turn next to a very recent series of observational studies. Most are finely grained ethnographic studies of classrooms in which the researcher-ethnographer has spent many hours observing over the course of the classroom day and sometimes extending beyond it into school playground activities and the home life of children. These lengthy observation schedules allow the researcher to frame an understanding of school culture from the participants' perspectives. Most of the studies considered here attempt to take the point of view of children who are considered to be as active in the construction of school relations as their teachers.

Home–School Discontinuities

The family assumes importance in the status attainment process because the home provides the first context for learning. Learning in the family is problematic when family emphases are critically different from the stress placed by the school on acquiring the "education code," a way of organizing and abstracting school knowledge summarized as various higher order cognitive skills including the capacity to abstract information and to recognize implicit meanings.

In discussing home-school discontinuities, we do not take the position that some family structures are inherently weak and predisposed to produce children "at risk" for success in school and beyond. Rather, the position here is that it is "the anticipated competencies, the nature of the personal attributes to be inculcated in children to prepare them for future adult economic and social participation, which influence parents and other childrearing agents to use particular childrearing techniques in raising their children."[23] Dissimilarities in childrearing emphases exist among different economic and minority group members and are attributable to structural conditions: children from different populations within our society simply are not all prepared for the same social and economic outcomes in adult life, and parents are among the first adults in the child's life to recognize this. In other words, structural constraints impose cultural dissimilarities upon individuals from an early age and are manifest in home-school discontinuities in "language, cognitive, motivational, and social competencies."[24]

In considering home-school differences, Ogbu distinguishes between "immigrant minorities" and "castelike minorities." The former group includes ethnic whites and nonwhite minorities who voluntarily settled in the U.S. and who generally do relatively well in school despite childrearing contexts in the home that differ from a white middle-class standard. On the other hand, castelike groups, including blacks and native Americans, Chicano and Puerto Rican Americans, and urban Appalachians, pressed by severe economic and social constraints deeply ingrained in their early experiences as immigrants to central cities, do less well in school. Ironically, members of groups in Third World countries (including the "Internal Colony" of rural and mountain Appalachia) perform well in schools organized according to an American standard despite childrearing inconsistent with white middle-class American procedures.[25] Thus, Ogbu argues, a cultural ecological approach must be framed for understanding the full set of home-school discontinuities pervasive in the experience of castelike minority group members. This approach emphasizes home-school disparities in the context of the constraints of political, economic, and social systems.

The Mediation of Personality

Children's experiences in the classroom are nested in the center of political, economic, and social worlds surrounding them in the manner presented in Figure 7.3. This holistic view considers both macrosocial structures and microsocial processes as concentric and mutually reinforcing. In this model, the classroom is seen as the site for the mediation of both personality and achievement.

Deep-seated personality characteristics manifest in feelings of self-esteem and other dimensions of identity play a leading role in orienting an individual toward achievement or failure in school and beyond. Low self-esteem, a sense of the futility of one's actions against overwhelming odds, develops in individuals whose experiences promote a sense of helplessness and failure. In the United States, self-esteem is associated with successful performance in the student role and orientation to occupations highly valued by society.

A recent ethnography carried out by Wilcox offers an analysis of the classroom teaching and socialization process that clarifies how children

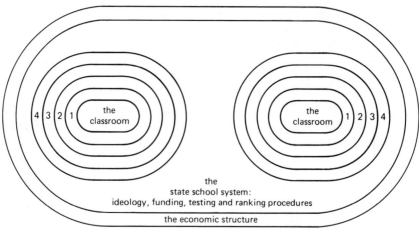

1 the school
2 the neighborhood: history, demographic makeup,
                      parents' relations with the school
3 the school district
4 the community: history, demographic makeup

FIGURE 7.3   Levels of the Sociocultural Context. (*Source:* Kathleen Wilcox, "Differential Socialization in the Classroom: Implications for Equal Opportunity," in *Doing the Ethnography of Schooling,* p. 276.)

are prepared for future work roles.[26] Wilcox argues that social class, sex, and race are particularly important in generating expectations of the teacher for classroom performance, and that teachers tend to label children in terms of those expectations and to carry out classroom interactions which effectively socialize or prepare children for a variable set of futures.

Using census data, Wilcox located two schools, one in a predominantly lower middle-class neighborhood and the other in an upper middle-class neighborhood of a major metropolitan area in California characterized as a "rapidly growing and dynamic region." Although the upper middle-class school employed an "open" classroom concept patterned after the British Infant School, its structure was tighter than that of the less affluent school. This finding was consistent with results of Wilcox's preliminary survey of 31 classrooms throughout the metropolitan area; however, it was inconsistent with the literature in political economy that suggests that working-class classrooms, organized to reproduce passive, uncritical workers, are more tightly organized.[27]

Although the upper middle-class setting was more rigidly structured, analyses of verbal directives used to control students' behavior revealed that children from higher status homes were consistently presented with appeals for internal control. For example, upon discovering two disputing children, the teacher said "I don't know what happened. You two will have to decide that by yourselves." Whereas these children were provided frequent opportunities to develop internal or self-generated rules for their behavior, less well-off children were consistently provided arbitrary standards for their behavior with such statements as "You get a cannot hamster out until you've finished your work." "No playing in the hall." "We don't hit or kick."

These findings, together with other results from the same study, illustrate the different futures mapped for children in the two classrooms. The social and economic assumptions portrayed in their classroom teachers' verbal directives are consistent with differential family backgrounds. The more affluent children were continually presented with opportunities to develop inner direction, a "can do" orientation, and a notion of future activity in college and professional careers; the less affluent children received a sense of the world as externally imposed and hierarchically organized, with personal roles limited to a present orientation to ongoing classroom events. These events, in contrast to the weighty academic tasks assigned children in the upper middle-class school, were frequently "freeform" and cooperatively accomplished. The more affluent children were acquiring a sense of purpose, seriousness, and goal directedness whereas the others were drifting, not receiving a clear message about the links between their current activities and their future roles.

A similar connection between elementary schooling and social class was found by Anyon who investigated reproductive patterns of work activity in five fifth-grade classrooms that varied in social class composition.[28] The classrooms were located in five different schools serving a large eastern metropolitan area. Anyon's field work included 10 three-hour observations in each classroom, interviews with 100 children and various school personnel, as well as analysis of the fifth grade curriculum in each school.

Consistent with the literature in political economics, Anyon found systematic differences among the three social classes, in school work, school knowledge, and student resistance. Working-class children experienced repetitive, rote work patterns through frequent participation in such activities as copying teachers' notes from the chalkboard, filling in blanks on work sheets, and responding to questions designed to "prove" that children had performed these and other similar seatwork lessons. Rather than a coherent, systematic body of knowledge, children in these classrooms were presented school knowledge as fragmented facts and behaviors. Teachers spoke of teaching "the basics," by which they meant discrete behaviors such as "how to spell out words and write sentences."[29] Moreover, in contrast to children in the more affluent schools, working-class children "could not explain . . . what corporations are, what inflation is, what an economy, a culture or civilization is, or what banks do." Several spoke of the United States as "the best place in the world almost in the same breath as they spoke of their own limited futures."

However, Anyon found working-class children to be less mystified than their affluent counterparts by the authority structure and ideological contradictions of the school. Resistance among students in the working-class context took one of three forms: passive withdrawal, feigning sleep or otherwise distancing themselves from the classroom interaction; group resistance (e.g., several class members tumbling from their chairs at the same time); and individual acts of protest (e.g., asking questions to waste time). The affluent students were more likely to either demand what they would like to do instead if they found a lesson boring or trite, or to withdraw whiningly into what Anyon terms "extreme individualism or narcissism" all the while complaining that they wished to accomplish the "stupid" lesson according to personal guidelines.

Anyon's perspective in this study is particularly illuminating because it casts light on the mediation of social background in the classroom by illustrating how children at least partially *resist* the culture of the school. Student resistance is particularly interesting in the case of girls. Girls are generally presented with contradictory messages about appropriate feminine behavior in terms of domesticity, nurturance, childrearing, and achieving self-esteem in United States society, that is, through success in the competitive world of work.

In a related analysis of classroom observations and interviews assembled during the course of the previously described research, Anyon examined responses to the following questions: "Will you get married when you grow up?" "Do you want to work when you grow up?" ("If so, what kind of work do you want to do?") "Do you think your husband will want you to work?"[30] Almost all the girls from both working-class and affluent classrooms said they wished to work as adults. However, all but one working-class girl was quite sure her future husband would not want her to work, whereas slightly more than half the middle-class girls expressed the same belief. Anyon concluded that virtually all the girls she interviewed were aware of the conflicts between their desire to work and the expectations held by their future spouses for their roles as nurturant wives and mothers.

In explaining girls' classroom demeanor, Anyon noted that several patterns of behavior expressed the contradictory components of accomodation and resistance to a feminine stereotype. First, although many girls complied with their teachers' insistence on neatness, obedience, and thoroughness in tasks, a number of girls in each of the classrooms attempted to excell academically and in school-related activities such as sports and musical instruments . . . which demand persistance, aggressiveness, a measure of independence, and effort over and above obedience and neatness.[31]

However, although excelling in a particular area, even the most capable girls were likely to devalue their own skills. Among upper middle-class girls, one bright (IQ = 145) and highly talented violinist claimed that although she was considering a career as a concert soloist, she was not sure she would persist in her plans because "men are number one" and "strong women wouldn't be pretty." For working-class girls, a dogged persistance in accomplishing tasks characterized behavior that was organized to resist both "present and future social discomfort" in their generally more disruptive classrooms and less secure lives outside school.

A second behavior pattern is what Anyon terms "the appropriation of femininity," a pattern that particularly marked the outward appearance of working-class girls. These girls were frequently observed wearing frilly dresses, adopting reticent behavior in class, and avoiding strenuous activity in organized team games on the playground. Exaggerated "feminine" behavior in the form of giggling, blushing, and whispering often attended their responses to teacher directives, which earned for them such labels as "silly little girls" from their teachers. One girl defined femininity as a source of pride. In the midst of other female classmates who were overtly sexual in their self presentation, this fifth grader told Anyon with great satisfaction of her intention to be a secretary as she patted the collar of her white sweater.

Among working-class girls, another form of self presentation was overt sexuality manifest in wearing nail polish, makeup, and fussy hair styles. These girls frequently flirted with boys and often challenged their teachers in order to gain attention from their peers.

More characteristic of upper middle-class girls was "tomboyishness" as a mode for resisting the feminine stereotype. One girl who refused to wear skirts and preferred work overalls as her classroom attire was later observed to wear a dress every day. The girl's teacher told Anyon that her mother, upset with her appearance, had been "working with her" to modify the girl's earlier "distasteful" clothing.

Boys are more likely than girls to be "behavior problems" in elementary school and their characteristic behaviors take the form of aggressive and disruptive activity in the classroom. Thus, Anyon argues that among girls, overtly resistant behavior may be an act of "organized nonconformity," behavior that deviates from both the norms of the school and traditionally defined forms of femininity. Most girls who defy school sanctions are likely to adopt strategies of distancing and alienation by absenteeism, backing off psychologically from classroom lessons, and the like. The important point of Anyon's analysis is that girls are active in the process of mediating their own development in the classroom, and that patterns of accommodation and resistance are readily identifiable by the classroom observer.

The third study to be considered here is a recent ethnography of an interracial middle school setting.[32] In analyzing gender role development in this setting, Schofield observed distinct differences between sex groups and between same sex groups of black and white children. Though both black and white girls valued physical attractiveness (as opposed to boys' emphasis on physical prowess), black girls imagined themselves as tough, an image that was also reflected in their white classmates' perceptions of them:

> DONNA (BLACK): The white girls are scared of the black girls.
> INTERVIEWER: Why do you think that is?
> DONNA: They just like to bully. They bully everybody.
> INTERVIEWER: Black girls do? Do they bully other black girls?
> DONNA: Those who let them. Most of the time white girls . . . can't defend themselves as well as a black girl can.

The image of toughness in black girls frequently lead to the perception among white girls that even the most playful actions had an aggressive intent. When asked how she knew white girls were scared of her, one black girl replied, "Cause they act like it. When we're just playing around with them, they get scared and run to the dean. I say, 'I was just . . . kidding.' They say, 'Oh, I thought you was for real!'"[33]

Because white girls were fearful of black girls, they were likely to avoid them, leading black girls to assume whites behave as they do because they were conceited or consider themselves too good to associate with blacks. Indeed, among black girls, Schofield observed considerable pressure applied to any who began to form a friendship with whites since these relationships were perceived as a rejection of blacks. In contrast, black boys were more likely to interact with white girls than with their black female classmates. Altogether, black girls were the least socially relevant group and were observed to receive the least amount of attention from both teachers and peers in school.

Schofield's work is extremely useful in clarifying the nature of the effect of peer culture upon social relations among preadolescent children. In this mixed-class school, race was more salient than social class, and gender more salient than race in mediating patterns of interaction among students. Moreover, the minimal amount of cross-race, cross-gender interaction that did occur was not at all conducive to the construction of equalitarian relationships. Cross-gender interaction reinforced traditional patterns of male-female relationships, with girls the passive recipients of boys' rather aggressive teasing. Cross-racial contact was generally stressful to all and perhaps most damaging overall to black girls whose self perceptions emphasized their out-group status as "tough," "bad," and poor academic performers.

Perhaps the most disturbing finding of all was the insistence among teaching and administrative staffs that race should be ignored as a factor although students maintained sharp racial boundaries throughout the school day and made distinctions based on race among themselves.

Most teachers held views, expressed to the interviewer, similar to those of Ms. Wire:

> INTERVIEWER: Do you think at a place like Wexler . . . [School] it is best to . . . deal openly with the fact that black and white kids may not be used to each other. . . . Or is it best to just treat them . . . like there is nothing special about the school?
> MS. WIRE: I don't know. I guess I sort of prefer the second approach. I don't know how I would handle the first approach . . . is probably what I am saying . . . I would get too bogged down in it.[34]

Thus, "most teachers did little or nothing to cultivate positive views of black and white identity in their students or to guide students as they begin to try to interact with out-group members."[35]

Teachers in this and in other interracial settings commonly assume that minimizing racial differences promotes harmonious intergroup relations. Perhaps more important, it keeps the lid on what they may perceive as a potentially explosive situation. A notable exception appears to be black teachers in the South who, in Clement's long-term study of a desegregated school, extended class discussions of black history, black biographies, and so on beyond the requirements of the curriculum to observe Black History Week for five days in the early spring. These teachers apparently value an emphasis on differences because they see this emphasis supporting the development of self-esteem among their black students.[36]

The previously reviewed studies taken together allow us to understand how the multiple effects of social class, gender, and race mediate the classroom and peer culture experiences of children. Although age has not been emphasized in the foregoing discussion, it is important to keep in mind that whereas social class, gender, and race affect the teacher-student relationship continuously throughout the student's elementary school years, these factors appear to assume special importance in peer relationships during late middle childhood and preadolescence.

The Mediation of Achievement

We place special emphasis on basic skills in literacy learning because, as we have seen, this is an area stressed increasingly in central city elementary school classrooms. Also, since grouping practices have been found in the status attainment literature to be related to such outcomes as postsecondary educational attainment and occupational achievement, we will pay special attention to the social organization of classroom learning in grouping for instruction.

Classroom language has been linked to teacher perceptions of student ability and ultimately to student placement and achievement by a number of researchers. There is little doubt that Dell Hymes, currently Dean of the Graduate School of Education at the University of Pennsylvania, is a chief architect of the linkage between education and linguistics. His statement regarding the linguistic nature of Native American communities captures the essential purpose for the investigation of classroom language use among culturally different children:

> The knowledge we need to have in order to understand the linguistic situation of Indian children goes beyond studying the formal characteristics of the varieties of language to studying patterns of language in their speech communities, i.e., customary community ways of answering questions, calling upon others, taking turns in conversation, speaking or remaining silent, giving instruction by verbal precept or observed example—all the ways in which etiquette of speaking and value of language may take distinctive shape. Many Indian children come to school speaking only English, yet encounter difficulty, *not because of language difference but because of difference in patterns for use of language.* . . . Children found 'shy' and nontalktive in class may be as talkative as any if observed in situations where the rights and duties of speaking are those of the community from which they come. In such a case one needs to know not language, but a community way of speaking.[37]

It is clear in Hymes' remarks that minority group children who encounter difficulty in the classroom do so because their customary "speech communities" utilize patterns of language use that vary from those which characterize instruction in the school.

"Becoming literate" refers to acquiring and demonstrating the ability to "read, write and spell 'correctly' "[38] and is virtually synonomous with success in the early elementary grades. By third grade, if not before, "attitude" coupled with demonstration of literacy determines not only promotion to the next grade but often becomes the major factor in program or reading group placement. Student "attitude" is reflected in such behaviors as attendance, completion of homework, posture, neatness of work, "fidgitiness," gaze, talkativeness, capacity to "cooperate," and so forth.

The importance of attitude is clear in Gilmore's description of the selection process for participation in the Academics Plus Program, an elite "basics" curriculum for students in the fourth, fifth, and sixth grades in a low income central city Philadelphia elementary school.

> The teachers of the students make recommendations to the teachers of the next year's Academics Plus classes. A student who may be doing poorly in class but exhibits positive attitudes and behavior may be chosen over an academically superior student who is a 'troublemaker.'[39]

Because teachers in the Academics Plus Program assign heavy workloads in the form of homework and other out-of-school responsibilities, "attitude" and the cooperation of students' parents are key components in the selection process. The significance of student attitude is not limited to selection for special programs; it pervades all matters of teacher judgment-making.

Although specific programs, such as the Academics Plus project in Philadelphia and the more general emphasis on the basics in other central city schools, have begun to reverse the trend of plummeting achievement test scores in large central cities, "rates of failure in learning to be literate continue to be disproportionately high among native English speakers from specific minority groups."[40]

An early assumption was that cultural mismatch or "interference" prevented castelike minority children (e.g., blacks, Native Americans, urban Appalachians) from learning literacy since their cultural traditions emphasized oral rather than written literacy. Also, linguistic variation in language use was assumed deterimental to learning the standard English form. English language variants included not only different phonological (sound system) and syntactic (word order) features, but also different sociolinguistic features.

As an example, Brice-Heath has documented sociolinguistic variation in literacy "training" experienced by black children from "Trackton"—a low income black community—in their homes and in their elementary school classrooms.[41] At home, these children "were not viewed as information givers in their interactions with adults" because their adult caretakers usually had other adult company with whom to converse, and children were not considered adultlike conversationalists. Although Brice-Heath observed considerable linguistic richness and variety in the home environments of black children, the children were rarely provided literacy "readiness" questions of the type that requested information known to both the questioner and the addressee. This kind of question predominates in the literacy learning tasks of the

elementary school. Teachers expect students to tie together information provided at one point in class with new information presented at
a later juncture. Accordingly, they phrase student-directed interroga-
tives to assess this classroom-specific form of student understanding.
Brice-Heath gives the following example of classroom questioning with
reference to the response anticipated by the teacher:

> TEACHER (*Pointing to a new sign to be used in arithmetic):* What
> was it we said earlier this sign is like?
> EXPECTED RESPONSE: The mouth of an alligator (an explanation
> used earlier in the day by the teacher).
> TRACKTON STUDENT'S RESPONSE: Dat thing up on the board. (The
> student looks at a bulletin board for social studies which has yarn
> linking various cities; the yarn forms a shape like the sign.)[42]

The student has not recalled and named the representation of an open-
mouthed alligator encountered earlier in the day in his reading book,
but instead, has named a valid though highly stylized object in the
room. "The comparison is valid, but the teacher's response ('Huh? Uh
. . . I guess that's okay') indicated she considered the answer neither as
useful nor as relevant as the one proposed in the lesson."[43]

Brice-Heath found similar home-school discontinuities in learning
classroom directives. Though their middle-class teachers relied on
statements such as "You forgot that again" to politely regulate student
behavior, children at home were rarely addressed in this manner.
Moreover, the usual response to an accusatory statement made by an
adult at home was to either bow the head or provide an entertaining,
"creative" and not necessarily truthful account.

Although it is now clear from the work of Hymes, Brice-Heath and
others that linguistic and sociolinguistic variation *does* exist between
the out-of-school and in-school experiences of certain minority group
children, what seems more important than this variation of and by itself
to the acquisition of literacy is *teachers' attitudes* toward linguistic and
sociolinguistic differences.[44]

To understand why high rates of failure persist among central city minority group children, it is necessary to examine the course of their experiences in classroom learning. Following are three studies of literacy learning in Philadelphia, Cincinnati and Washington, D.C., and Columbus.

Philadelphia: Role of the Home

In Philadelphia, a series of related studies were undertaken to examine
the acquisition of reading and language skills from several perspectives
including community involvement, parent-teacher relations, instructional techniques, and administrator (i.e., principal) effects. This pro-

ject, not coincidently, was undertaken by Dell Hymes shortly after his appointment as Dean at Penn, an event that co-occurred with state and local efforts to improve instruction in central city schools. Local improvement plans included a commitment to enhance the leadership of principals in central city elementary schools attended by large numbers of low income minority children, most of whom were black.

Three major assumptions guided the two-year study:

1. that most home-school issues and problems develop through a "lack of understanding, inadequate communication, and unclear explanations of parent and teacher roles and expectations"
2. that teachers will become "more effective in teaching literacy skills to children if they have adequate information about the children they teach and their families"
3. "that parents will be more effective in meeting their own expectations if they better understand the school's expectations."[45]

One series of studies in this project involved the Shortridge Elementary School located in a low income black neighborhood. It enrolled approximately 1,000 students who lived within a radius of five or six blocks from the school. Following an initial period of observation, the researcher conferred with teachers in the Academics Plus Program described earlier, carefully outlining the study's assumptions and requesting the teacher to provide a listing of ten families, five in which the child was perceived as having good support at home and five in which the child's parents were seen as giving poor home support. Teachers considered parents actively involved in their children's education only if they regularly performed the following supervisory and school support functions:

1. checking homework to see that it is correctly and neatly done
2. supervising and controlling television viewing
3. monitoring reading at home
4. sending children to school well-dressed, well-fed, and well-rested
5. attending school functions and parent-teacher conferences, especially those related to children's literacy development
6. sending children to school showing proper respect for the teacher.

The researcher made a series of home observations and conducted interviews with both the "much involved" and "mildly involved" parents. He discovered that *both* groups of parents had similar concerns:

1. not enough time to spend with children because of heavy work schedules, night shift work, overtime, and the like

2. how to control excessive television viewing
3. children's reluctance to discuss school matters
4. how to best assist children in meeting school expectations
5. how to get children interested in reading, especially those who have been "turned off" to reading.

In addition, all families felt that they were not consistently told by their children's teachers when children had been out of line in the classroom. As a result, the assumption that parents tolerated or condoned misbehavior went unchallenged. Parents felt that although teachers explicitly demanded respect from their students, they were unwilling to reciprocate. Parents also resented the school's expectations concerning dress and meals, believing these matters to be family concerns.

From the researcher's observations in homes and at school, he concluded that the more actively involved parents were younger and better educated, factors that tend to make people more flexible in their attitudes, in this case, toward home-school cooperation. They also tended to be more restrictive in their childrearing, imposing bedtime schedules, regulating television viewing, and allocating responsibility for checking homework to a particular parent, the mother.

Teachers believed that all but a few parents reinforced a positive view of school at home. When negative attitudes *did* appear, teachers ascribed student rebellion to "peer pressure and peer example"—the manner in which other students talked to teachers and other adults.

Cincinnati and Washington, D.C.: Effect of the Peer Group

The way language is used is determined largely by the social purpose of the interacting group. Language functions to regulate or control behavior, to inform, to express affect, and to clarify interpersonal relations. The peer group provides a classroom context that promotes conversational interaction which varies from that in teacher-directed groups, as studied in Cincinnati and Washington, D.C.

In a study of an urban Appalachian kindergarten classroom in Cincinnati, it was found that children in the context of pegboard-math problem solving tended to use language similiarly.[46] Children would generally spend the first few minutes actively informing themselves and their partners about the nature of the task at hand, the method of problem solving and so on, but would take "interpersonal breaks" during the task to discuss the weather, their recent exploits in the neighborhood, and the like. It was concluded that the nature of the task and the number of participants (two) generally kept these children focused on classwork even when unsupervised by the teacher; however, children were also inclined to require a conversational breather to relax, and at least briefly, depart from the academic chore at hand. In contrast, teacher-led reading groups composed of 9–10 children were uniformly characterized by language functioning either to control the behavior of participants or to elicit and provide information about the lesson at hand. Findings in this three-month study led to the following conclusion:

> Though girls were less likely to play out competitive themes and more likely to discuss everyday matters such as the weather or their classmates in their interpersonal conversation, they were as likely as boys to engage in conversation that similarly enabled building and maintaining friendly relations. In fact, the finding of no significant differences between boys and girls on *any* conversation measure is perhaps the most interesting finding of this research. The classroom observed in . . . this study was located in a traditional school and in a neighborhood composed of working-class and welfare (ADC) families who might be expected to inculcate traditional sex-role-related values in their children (Kohn, 1979). However, Appalachian folkways dominate this neighborhood which for approximately thirty years has been inhabited by immigrants from farmlands and coal mining towns of eastern Kentucky. Appalachian values of independence, equality, and autonomy are not sex-specific. Rather, both men and women in the culture are often expected to assume important responsibilities in adult life. Though women are often expected to be in charge of the family while men are accountable for family dealings outside the home, women's domestic responsibilities often extend beyond meal planning to include managing family financial responsibilities and holding a job outside the home. These cultural characteristics may outweigh social class norms in determining value systems held by members of this community.[47]

In a related study of a fourth grade classroom enrolling black children from low income households, Borders-Simmons and Lucas investigated language function and the degree of dialect use in various kinds of classroom activities.[48] The five videotaped events included a teacher-led full class discussion on the topic of health and personal hygiene; a teacher-directed small reading group lesson; a small group discussion of social studies not supervised by the teacher; an unsupervised reading group; and a peer tutoring session involving three children without their teacher's supervision.

This study's findings indicate that language use varies considerably across contexts with dialect features appearing most often in teacher-less events. When dialect features were examined more closely in connection with this finding, the researchers discovered that dialect use in teacherless groups was associated with "event management" by which they mean the process of moving the learning activity along, as in the following example from the unsupervised small reading group lesson:

(At this point in the lesson, C, the reading group captain, demands that six members of the group begin a discussion of the story of "The Little Red Hen." Note that utterances containing a dialect feature are marked with an asterisk.)

C: Allright, close your books. Close it.
I: (unintell.)
*C: (unintell.) ⌈ Alright, I'm ass y'all some questions
I: ⌊ Sure
C: What's the hen's name? (Hands are raised.)
I:
S: What is it? ⌈
C: ⌊ Danny
*C: Allright, I gotta go back to the book.
*L: You gotta to look for spelling word.
*I: No, he don't.
*S: I spelled (inintell.) He don't have to . . .
S: ⌈ unless . . . tell him to.
C: | Where did he . . . live?
L: ⌊ How you spell Red Hen, Red Hen?
L: You can't do that!
*D: In a old barn. In a old red barn.
I: (to S) You can't do that!
*L: You can't do that lookin in that book. You can't be lookin in that book.
S: I can find some short e words. That is . . .
*L: How is we gon . . . you
B: Go on Chris
*C: Hey ya'll I don't know if these words are right ya'll got down on y'all paper. How many chicks did he have? (Hands are raised.)
D: Ten
*B: He gotta ⌈ call your name   ⌉
L: ⌊ (unintell. protest) ⌋
C: (unintell.) chicks his chicks name I mean his name, Benita.
B: Peepee
S: (to Chris) (unintell.)
C: What did he eat, (hands are raised) Linda (laughter) Yeah.
L: Uhm, oats.
B: (waves her hand) Ooh-ooh-ooh (attempt to get turn)

L: Corn

I: Benita.

B: Who me?

*C: (unintell.) What, what what what try to eat the chicks

S: Huh?

*C: What try to eat his chicks? (Hands raised.) Irvin.

I: Hawk.

C: (What was (unintell.) ordeal) What, what was sharp on it, Benita.

D: What?

B: Claws.   (laughter)

C: ⌈ Claws. The claws (unintell.) ⌉

D: ⌊ ?   ⌋

C: Okydok. (Papers are handed in.)

*B: Here Chris, you gotta take down words

*L: (getting up) I know. I'm gonna go get some paper so he can give us some words to study. (Camera shifts focus.)

C: There you go.[49]

Although C does not always receive the response he is attempting to solicit from the other reading group members, dialect usage appears not to interfere with message comprehension in this unsupervised reading group discussion. Moreover, dialect features generally are absent from children's conversation in teacher-led groups. Unlike *students,* such as C who enacted the teacher role, the teacher was observed to center nearly all her remarks on initiating exchanges with students designed to elicit pertinent information or to control the interaction during the lesson. Children are more likely to provide responses to teacher bids, and their responses generally are functionally tied to teacher requests.

Among the central findings of this study is the fact that observed dialect features were *not* linked to message interference. In other words, communication was not distorted in any context by dialect usage, a finding at odds with the cultural mismatch position.

The two studies discussed above suggest that peer instructional groups mediate language in a way that differs from teacher-directed groups. Several aspects of these studies are particularly notable. First, language function varies, with peer groups more likely to use language to discuss interpersonal topics and teacher-led groups more likely to remain task-centered. Also, the topics of interpersonal conversation in girls' and boys' groups vary. Girls are more likely to discuss the weather, their clothing, and other topics likely to promote intimacy and solidarity, and boys are more likely to advertise their masculine prowess, fostering competitiveness and an interest in power roles. Finally, although dialect use is present in peer groups to a greater extent than in teacher-led groups, dialect features do not interfere with message comprehension, suggesting that teacher *judgments regarding dialect usage* rather than dialect usage per se is a factor in the mediation of achievement.

Columbus: Role of the Literary Instructional "Frame"

The importance of the social context or frame of the classroom group is strongly implied in the Cincinnati and Washington D.C. studies of peer group and teacher language use. However, the research of DeStefano et al. allows the further linkage to be made from classroom discourse in literacy instruction to classroom achievement.

The site of this study was a first-grade classroom in a central city magnet school. During the year of this research, middle to low income black and white "mainstream children" were bussed to a previously low income black and urban Appalachian (white) school. Although the teacher herself was from a mainstream cultural background, her previous teaching experience had been with children from the latter groups. To investigate the effects of literacy learning on the assessment of "readiness" by the classroom teacher, the researchers focused their observations on three children. One was from a mainstream background, another from the central city black culture, and a third from an Appalachian background. In all cases,

> Cultural membership was determined via family history and performance on sentence repetition tasks, revealing use of black English or an Appalachian dialect such as South Midland or a less marked form of American English.[50]

The researchers selected boys for study because elementary school-aged males generally have more difficulty learning literacy than females. The researchers immediately discovered restrictions on obtaining a subject for observation from the urban Appalachian culture:

> All males from the Appalachian culture who were in the first grade (five classrooms) in the school were repeaters, save two students who were daily taking behavior modifying medication. Therefore, it was necessary to select as a subject from the Appalachian culture a child who was repeating the first grade. The selected child's retention had been attributed to prolonged absence during the previous school year.[51]

The other two children selected for study had been in kindergarten during the previous year.

Children's literacy learning was examined at three intervals during the course of the school year. Initially, in the early days of the school year, observations were made to determine the nature of teacher-identified problems in literacy learning and general socialization which were closely bound. Observations were next made shortly before the winter holiday break, and, finally, at the outset of the last marking period in the school year.

There were changes in the social organization of the literacy learning frame over the course of the study. Most notably, during the first observation period in September, all children participated in a full class reading-readiness program. However, by November, at the time of the second series of observations, children had been divided into three reading groups in line with their teacher's perceptions of their reading abilities. The boy from the cultural mainstream was in the "high middle" reading group, a placement he held for the rest of the school year. The boy from an urban Appalachian background was placed in the "low middle" reading group where he remained. The boy from the low income black family received a permanent placement in the "low" group.

The teacher determined each child's placement according to informal ad hoc impressions of student "attitude" and readiness. For example, at the end of the year, she observed that the mainstream child, although "He did not really try very hard" and "wasn't applying himself" was nonetheless moving along in skill development at an acceptable rate. The researchers administered a criterion referenced test of skill progress and found that the largest percentage change in scores over the school year was for the child who had been placed (and had remained) in the lowest reading group. He also appeared to have a more abstract and insightful understanding of the concept of learning to read than either of the other two boys. In response to a question concerning the nature of reading, he replied, "We mark stuff," a straight-forward and accurate account of what actually occurred in lessons. He went on to explain that he himself, in learning to read, first "thought" and then "sounded the word out." Elaborating, he noted, "You have to know the sounds—so you could sound the word so you could know it." The other two boys made statements such as "You read to somebody" and "I'd teach him how to read" in response to similar queries about literacy learning.

It was difficult for the researchers to draw any comparative conclusion about the nature of the boys' discourse in reading group sessions because teacher discourse dominated instruction in the reading group. In an aside, DeStefano and her colleagues comment that the greatest opportunity for student talk in the reading group occurred during illicit whispered conversations. The researchers, however, do not discuss these interactions.

The teacher initiated 71.5 to 92% of all conversation exchanges in any of the reading activities observed in the classroom over the school year and student responses were limited to one-word utterances or, occasionally, to listing. Moreover, cultural backgrounds appear to have no observable effect on patterns of response in any of the reading groups. Generally, the teacher elicits and receives one-word responses to her queries. Fundamentally, two major rules guide this teacher's classroom policy: how students should behave in an orderly manner and how they should become literate.

The researchers concluded that students' interactive discourse indicated they have learned these rules but masked their relative success in becoming literate. In other words, all three children were observed to follow the rules for reading group performance by answering their teacher's questions with responses predetermined by the contents to fit the story under discussion. By the end of the year, none were "intruding" personal information into the reading group interaction. Instead, the following illustrates the typical reading group conversation (except that the student's response in this case is uncharacteristically lengthy).

> TEACHER: What is the problem about going to the zoo? Tom?
> TOM: They wudn't 'lowed t' go on the bus theirself.
> TEACHER: That's right.[52]

When the teacher bids for a response to demonstrate an understanding of the story, children are forthcoming with an appropriate answer for which they in turn receive the teacher's (in this case) positive sanction. In this manner achievement is mediated in the classroom in thousands of teacher-student interactions each day.

Conclusion

The previous case studies of teaching-learning processes in central city schools suggest that schools and classrooms mediate personality factors and student achievement. Of course, students bring their own individual sets of characteristics to bear in these processes and, as we have seen, gender and race, in addition to other family background features, notably the family's position in the socioeconomic status hierarchy, are powerful factors in classroom interactions.

We are particularly concerned about the personality development of black female central city school children who seem especially burdened by a complex web of race and gender stereotypes, peer expectations for their behavior, and resistance in many schools to a straightforward student policy that incorporates racial differences as a factor. It is as though many who work in desegregated school contexts hope that if differences are ignored, they will go away. Also of concern is the spotty achievement, in learning to be literate, of central city male children whose perceived "attitude," support at home, peer interactions, and linguistic performance in the classroom frequently generate negative appraisals of their literacy skills.

In order to examine processes of personality development and attainment of literacy skills in the classroom, you ideally should gain access to an elementary classroom where your observations could extend over the course of at least one full school year. This will be impossible for most students in college undergraduate and graduate programs of study. The point we are making is that the mediation of personality and achievement, as we have shown, is a highly complex process. To study it requires great sensitivity and skilled analytic ability on the part of the observer. In addition, such research demands the full cooperation and support of the school and especially of the teacher in whose classroom observations are conducted.

Thus, as a "next best" strategy, we suggest you make contact with a classroom teacher whom you know personally or whom you can reach through a school principal. Try to locate a classroom teacher who works with primary grade children in a central city elementary school and who has been in this role a number of years. If you have access to a teacher in a magnet or special program school who has taught at the same school or with the same group of children from a time predating the institutionalization of the new school policy, so much the better. You will be able to gain insight into the nature of program effects on teaching and learning from this individual.

In your informal interview with the teacher, make sure you touch upon the following points. First, ask the teacher to define "basic skills" in literacy and ask the teacher to discuss the priority he or she gives to basic skills instruction in the classroom. Other questions to pursue are What is the teacher's working definition of "effective instruction?" Has the teacher heard this term before? Has the school where the teacher is employed developed a policy to enhance effective teaching? What student characteristics does the teacher consider to be particularly important in personality development? Is "attitude" an important dimension of development? What student characteristics are particularly important to the achievement of literacy in the classroom? Keep in mind that the consequences in terms of personality development and achievement of gender, race, and other social background characteristics are often unconsciously ignored by teachers. Thus, you may wish to probe further by asking the teacher to paint a verbal "portrait" or biography of his or her most and least able students.

The responses you receive from the teacher can be illuminated by observing classroom interaction for yourself. If you *are* able to gain access to the teacher's classroom, be sure you make clear that your role is as a nonparticipant observer. It is helpful if the teacher establishes your presence in the classroom in this role or else children will seek you out as a conversational partner. Though conversing with children is a delightful experience, your objective is to pay close and careful attention to patterns of turn taking, language function, and so on. To monitor these and other aspects of classroom interaction with minimal distraction, you should, in addition, select an activity such as reading group work where the teacher interacts with a small number of children rather than with the entire class.

After you have interviewed a classroom teacher and perhaps have observed in the classroom, you will have an understanding of the teaching-learning process that is at the heart of the activity of schooling. You will *not* come away from the experience having unravelled the mysteries of classroom interactions and their effects upon children, but you *will* no doubt emerge with a healthy respect for the complexity of these processes.

Notes

1. Albert H. Rouse, Jr., *Status and Gains: Achievement Test Results,* April 1982, Cincinnati Public Schools, Cincinnati, Ohio.
2. *New York Times,* April 10, 1983.
3. Ronald R. Edmonds, "Programs of School Improvement: An Overview," in *Educational Leadership* 40, No. 3 (December 1982), p. 4.
4. Daniel P. Moynihan, *The Negro Family: The Case for National Action* (Washington, D.C.: U.S. Department of Labor, 1965).
5. Maureen McCormack Larking and William J. Kritek, "Milwaukee's Project RISE," in *Educational Leadership* 40, No. 3 (December 1982), pp. 16–17.
6. Ibid., p. 17.
7. James S. Coleman, *Equality of Educational Opportunity* (Washington, D.C.: U.S. Department of Health, Education, and Welfare, Office of Education, 1966).
8. Stewart C. Purkey and Marshall S. Smith, "Effective Schools—A Review," in *Elementary School Journal.*
9. Eugene E. Eubanks and Daniel U. Levine, "A First Look at Effective School Projects at Inner City Elementary Schools," paper presented at the annual meeting of the American Association of School Administrators, Atlantic City, 27 February 1983.
10. Ibid., p. 13.
11. Ibid., p. 46.
12. Ibid., p. 44.
13. Ibid., p. 14.
14. *New York Times* April 10, 1983.
17. Norbert Wiley, "Recent Journal Sociology: The Substitution of Method for Theory," in *Contemporary Sociology* 8, No. 6 (November 1979), p. 794.

18. Hugh Mehan, "The Functioning of Language in the Structuring of Schooling," a paper presented at the annual meeting of the American Sociological Association, San Francisco, 6 September 1982, p. 2.

19. Robert M. Hauser, Shu-Ling Tsai, and William H. Sewell, "A Model of Stratification with Response Error in Social and Psychological Variables," in *Sociology of Education* 56, No. 1 (January 1983).

20. Randall Collins, *The Credential Society* (New York: Academic Press, 1979).

21. William T. Bielby, "Models of Status Attainment," in D. J. Treiman and R. V. Robinson, eds., *Research in Social Stratification and Mobility*, Vol. 1 (Greenwich, C.T: JAI, 1981), p. 11.

22. Gary D. Fenstermacher, "A Philosophical Consideration of Recent Research in Teacher Effectiveness," in Lee S. Shulman, ed., *Review of Research in Education*, Vol. 6 (Itasca, Ill.: F. E. Peacock, 1978).

23. Paul Olson, "Rethinking Social Reproduction," in *Interchange*, 12, Nos. 2–3 (1981).

22. S. Hall and T. Jefferson, *Resistance Through Rituals: Youth Subcultures in Post-War Britain* (England: Hutchinson, 1975).

23. John U. Ogbu, "Socialization: A Cultural Ecological Approach," in Kathryn M. Borman, ed., *The Social Life of Children in a Changing Society* (Hillsdale, N.J.: Erlbaum, 1982), p. 261.

24. Ibid.

25. Ibid., p. 254.

26. Kathleen Wilcox "Differential Socialization in the Classroom: Implications for Equal Opportunity," in George Spindler, ed., *Doing The Ethnography of Schooling* (New York: Holt, 1982).

27. Samuel Bowles and Herbert Gintis, *Schooling in Capitalist America* (New York: Basic Books, 1977).

28. Jean Anyon, "Elementary Schooling and Distinctions of Social Class," in *Interchange*, 12, Nos. 2–3 (1981).

29. Ibid., p. 120.

30. Jean Anyon, "Interactions of Gender and Class: Accommodation and Resistance by Working Class and Affluent Females to Contradictory Sex-Role Ideologies," in L. Barton and S. Walker, eds., *Gender, Class and Education* (England: Falmer Press, 1982).

32. Ibid., p. 21.

33. Janet W. Schofield, "Complementary and Conflicting Identities: Images and Interaction in an Interracial School," in Steven Asher and John Gottman, eds., *The Development of Friendships: Description and Intervention* (Cambridge: Cambridge University Press, 1979).

34. Ibid., p. 39.

35. Ibid., p. 27.

36. Ibid.

37. Dorothy C. Clement, Margaret Eisenhart, and Joe R. Harding, "Teacher Socialization of Black/White Relations in a Southern Desegregated School: Pressures and Adaptations," paper presented at the annual meeting of the American Educational Research Association, Toronto, 27 March 1978.

38. Dell R. Hymes "Language in Education: Forward to Fundamentals," in Olga K. Garnica and Martha L. King, eds., *Language, Children and Society* (Oxford: Pergaman, 1979).

39. Johannah DeStefano, Harold B. Pepinsky, and Tobie S. Sanders, "Discourse Rules for Literacy Learning in a Classroom," in L.C. Williamson, ed., *Communicating in the Classroom* (New York: Academic Press, 1982).
40. Dell R. Hymes et al., *Ethnographic Monitoring of Children's Acquisition of Reading/Language Arts Skills In and Out of the Classroom*, Vols. 1, 2, and 3 (Bethesda: ERIC Document Reproduction Services, ED 208 096, 1982).
41. Johannah DeStefano, "Discourse Rules for Literacy Learning in a Classroom," p. 1.
42. Shirley Brice-Heath, "Questioning at Home and at School: A Comparative Study" in Spindler, *Ethnography of Schooling*.
43. Ibid., p. 118.
44. Ibid.
45. Ibid.
46. Dell R. Hymes et al., *Ethnographic Monitoring of Children's Acquisition*, p. 285.
47. Kathryn M. Borman, "Children's Situational Competence: Two Studies," in Garnica and King, *Language, Children, and Society*.
48. Ibid., p. 109.
49. Denise Borders-Simmons and Ceil Lucas, "Language Diversity and Classroom Discourse," paper presented at the annual meeting of the American Educational Research Association, New York, March 1982.
50. Ibid., pp. 23–25.
51. DeStefano et al., "Discourse Rules for Literacy Learning in Classroom," p. 1.
52. Ibid.

The Period of Adolescence and the Transition from School

The period of adolescence is perhaps the most popularized phase of human development. Although fun-loving and often mindless teenagers are frequently the objects of films and television sitcoms, the period of adolescence remains one of the least understood and elusive of all periods in the life cycle.

Among the many reasons for this lack of understanding, three seem especially important: the tremendous variation in individual development during the period of adolescence; the lack of a clear status for the adolescent in society; and the generally negative view of adolescents generated from research by social and behavioral scientists.

The Wide Range of Individual Development

Adolescence as a phase of development is considered to extend from the onset of puberty to the acquisition of legal statuses concerning school leaving, voting, and prosecution through the criminal court system. However, the onset of puberty varies by gender (generally about 11 for girls and 12 for boys). And within gender there is tremendous individual variation, with physical changes occurring much sooner or much later for many.

In addition to physical changes, the adolescent experiences tremendous cognitive change. Cognitive shifts affect mental operations of all kinds: political thinking, problem solving, and reasoning about interpersonal relationships, to name a few. According to Keating, the major changes during the period are characterized by five developmental capacities or characteristics: thinking about possibilities, thinking through hypotheses, thinking ahead, thinking about thoughts, and thinking beyond old limits.[1] Although Keating cautions that these cognitive activities are not "impossible" for children, they *do* occur less spontaneously in individuals before the adolescent period. The hallmark of all these abilities is the capacity to engage in abstract reasoning, to think about people, events, facts, and things that are not tied to concrete reality. And, of course, there is wide-range variability in the acquisition of these capacities not only in the age at which the adolescent achieves them but also in the domain (i.e., political reasoning, interpersonal reasoning, problem solving, etc.). Also, not all adolescents, or adults for that matter, become "fully fledged" abstract reasoners in all areas.

Thus, individual variation in growth and development in both physical capacities and cognitive skills is the hallmark of the adolescent period, making it extremely difficult to talk about a "typical teenager."

The Lack of a Clear Status

In our society, adulthood is incrementally achieved rather than set at a particular age for all statuses. Thus, both the adolescent and society are unclear about just how "adultlike" the adolescent really is even though the young person may be working full-time and/or living away from home in a dormitory or apartment.

In fact, many youths *do* occupy multiple and conflicting statuses during this period. For example, many are employed part time while going to school full time. Many may legally drive a car, but may have only limited access to a family vehicle. In other words, legal statuses with attendant adult privileges and responsibilities are conferred at different points and often incompletely during the period, thus creating status ambiguity for the adolescent. Is she or he an "adult" when a driver's license is obtained? When he or she has reached the lawful drinking age? When he or she may vote? Since adolescence is a period during which youth are in transition from a highly dependent status within the family to a relatively independent status in society, the rights, roles, and duties of the individual during this period are highly ambiguous.

Research's Negative View of Adolescents

The adolescent period has been characterized by social and behavioral scientists as a time of storm and stress in the individual's development and relationship with society leading to antisocial, nonconforming, and frequently destructive behavior. The major interdisciplinary journal reporting research on adolescents reflects this trend. During 1981, the majority of papers (22 of 39) published by the *Journal of Youth and Adolescence* were concerned with social problems confronting the adolescent. These research reports covered such topics as anorexia nervosa, delinquency, schizophrenia, cigarette smoking, sexual behavior, intoxication, and drug use. The remaining articles focused on life transitions (school to work, home leaving) and value-neutral topics such as aspects of psychosocial maturity and assertiveness. Only one research report examined a positive aspect of adolescent behavior: the development of altruism.

From the foregoing discussion, it is clear that the major theme characterizing the period of adolescence is *transition*, whether the topic is biological maturation, the attainment of legal statuses, or cognitive change. Because the general response to ambiguities inherent in adolescent transitions has been to characterize the adolescent as "rebellious," irresponsible, or troubled, we will provide a context for understanding the adolescent and the society in which he or she is maturing that will, hopefully, promote a more positive view.

The Expanding World of the Adolescent

Family and Peers

Cognitive development, as we have stated, affects reasoning in several areas including the realm of social and interpersonal relationships. Indeed, those very relationships in all likelihood "lead" the cognitive development previously described. Relationships are a sort of social laboratory in which the adolescent tests and refines hypotheses about the social world.

Social cognitive development in preadolescence and adolescence is broadly conceived as a set of attainments and internal developmental processes reflected in individual behaviors and attitudes. During this period in the life cycle, two dimensions of social development are of particular importance: (1) the child's changing orientations from family to peer groups and (2) large-scale alterations in interpersonal reasoning, self image, and occupational interest.

With disengagement from the family to increasing participation in activities with friends comes a change in the use of leisure time. In one study, researchers found that by the age of 15, only 31% of children from a variety of family backgrounds were more oriented to family than to other social groups. In contrast, among 10-year-olds in this cross-sectional study, 87% expressed greater orientation to the family than to any other group.[2]

Another study showed that alterations in orientation to reference groups of peers, parents, and adults outside the family were dependent upon both age and the issue at hand.[3] Younger (grade 5) children nominated parents as the most frequently sought source of information on social, moral, and informational items whereas older (grades 7, 9 and 12) children progressively sought advice from sources outside the family, particularly on social and informational matters. Sex differences were also apparent: girls of all ages sought the advice of peers on the basis of social comparison and intimacy, and boys consulted peers on the basis of superior information and experience. In conceptually related work, Williams found that patterns of identification with peers, parents, and adults outside the family were related to patterns of school achievement in 16 to 18-year-old males. Low achievers identified with their mothers and peers; high achievers identified with school personnel with whom they had friendly relations.[4]

The National Longitudinal Survey (NLS) is an ambitious project that explicitly attempts to respond to the fluctuating nature of development during adolescence which is seen by the survey as a period extending from age 14 to age 21. Since 1968, a series of surveys has been undertaken by NLS researchers who periodically investigate a new cohort of adolescents and continue to monitor the group for five years following the initial survey in order to chart change and continuity in attitudes, plans, and the like. Because the NLS data report findings on a representative national sample of individually interviewed youth, results can be generalized to the full population of 14 to 21-year-olds in the U.S.

One set of questions included in the most recent (1979) survey was directed to young people under age 18 and focused upon the role of "significant others," influential people in their lives whom they see as important in critical areas of decision-making. Significant others are considered in sociological and psychological research as "central to the development of the self concept, value formation, and the eventual fulfillment of adult roles."[5]

Most of the adolescents surveyed reported that parents were most influential in critical areas of decision-making, as shown in Table 8.1. Those mentioning a parent were most likely to nominate both father and mother; however, 29% mentioned only one parent and of that number almost 90% mentioned the mother as most influential. Peers ran a distant second to parents as most influential, and nonrelated adults, siblings, and other relatives were also mentioned but with less frequency. Despite repeated probing by the interviewer, a very few couldn't name anyone or named a person who did not easily fit one of the categories established from the data. The former group, the Isolates, constitute only 2.6% of all adolescents, and it should be em-

TABLE 8.1
Nominations of Significant Others by Adolescents Aged 14–17

Q: Who has influenced you *most* on how you feel about things like school, marriage, jobs, and having children?

Type of person	Percentage	Category of person	Percentage
No one	2.6	Isolates	2.6
A teacher	2.0	Nonrelated	5.9
An older friend	3.3	adults	
A guidance counselor	0.6		
Father or stepfather	9.2		
Mother or stepmother	19.8	Parents	69.6
Mother *and* father	40.6		
A brother	2.9	Siblings and	6.1
A sister	3.0	spouse	
Husband or wife	0.1		
A female friend about the same age as R	7.2	Nonrelated	12.2
A male friend about the same age as R	4.9	peers	
Another relative	2.9		
A co-worker	0.1	Other	3.7
Other	0.6		
Total percentage	100		100

Source: National Longitudinal Survey of Youth Labor Market Experience (1979).

phasized that 97.4% regard at least one person as influential in their lives.

Significant others are perceived as providing various levels of support in several areas of decision-making, namely occupational plans and family formation. A four point scale ranging from 1, strong disapproval, to 4, strong approval, was used in rating support for various kinds of jobs (i.e., carpenter, representing skilled labor; accountant, and electrical engineer, representing white collar professional and highly skilled technical work respectively) and plans to move far away, deciding not to have children and deciding to postpone having a family to pursue a career (asked of girls only). A score of 2.5 indicates approximately equivalent levels of support and disapproval for a particular decision while higher scores indicate stronger approval and lower scores stronger disapproval. As shown in Table 8.2, parents as well as other significant persons are perceived as less supportive of nontraditional choices for either sex. For example, for girls there is relatively greater parental disapproval for nontraditional jobs (carpenter, engineer, and the mili-

TABLE 8.2
Mean Support for Life Decisions, by Types of Significant Others and by Sex of Respondent for Adolescents Aged 14–17

Life decision	Unrelated adult	Parents	Unrelated peers	Sibling or spouse	Other	Total
You decided to become a carpenter.						
Female	2.46	2.64	2.47	2.53	2.38	2.60
Male	3.07	3.23	3.28	3.27	3.36	3.24
You decided to become an accountant.						
Female	3.19	3.49	3.29	3.34	3.43	3.43
Male	3.10	3.34	3.01	3.23	3.31	3.28
You decided to become an electrical engineer.						
Female	2.76	2.90	2.57	2.66	2.68	2.81
Male	3.37	3.50	3.46	3.45	3.51	3.49
You decided to join the armed forces.						
Female	2.17	2.31	1.95	2.13	2.04	2.23
Male	2.73	2.81	2.40	2.53	3.04	2.75
You decided not to go to college.						
Female	1.74	2.01	2.05	2.14	1.82	2.00
Male	1.99	2.01	2.43	2.23	2.03	2.07
You decided to move far away from where your parents live when you are 21.						
Female	2.60	2.27	2.57	2.49	2.11	2.34
Male	2.51	2.37	2.68	2.68	2.50	2.43
You decided never to have children.						
Female	2.11	2.31	2.18	2.31	2.29	2.27
Male	2.34	2.22	2.20	2.31	2.22	2.23
You decided to pursue a full-time career and delay having a family.						
(Females only)	2.86	3.07	2.87	3.02	2.98	3.02

Source: National Longitudinal Survey of Youth Labor Market Experience (1979).

tary). Surprisingly, parents are seen as relatively supportive of girls' plans to pursue a career at the expense of starting a family and are slightly more disapproving of boys' decision to never have children. There is little variation in perceived support by sex for the major decision to attend college. However, we agree with the NLS researchers who conclude:

> It is clear that adolescent girls are still being channeled into certain occupational areas (e.g., accounting) and out of others (e.g., carpentry and engineering). This is particularly the case for girls whose closest ties are with peers rather than with adults. To the extent that such channeling tends to restrict young women to poorly paid and overcrowded fields, counseling and training efforts should be directed at making the full range of occupations available and acceptable.[6]

As we have seen, the adolescent perceives parents as the most influential in major areas of his or her life; however, as young adults move toward roles and responsibilities in the larger society and away from the family, they spend increasing amounts of time with friends. In a review of patterns of leisure time among young adolescents, Rutter[7] notes that only 10 percent of the 14 and 15-year-olds he studied went out once a week with their parents in contrast to nearly all who spent time with friends or in "responsible, independent activities," such as babysitting and doing yard work, outside the home.

As a result of their increasing interaction with friends, shifts in the adolescents' social cognitive development occur in the areas of interpersonal reasoning (moral judgments) and affective role taking (the ability to infer feeling states of others). These cognitive developments reflect deep personality characteristics related to the consolidation of occupational interests and job-related attitudes.[8] The manner in which the adolescent internalizes these changes influences to a great extent the child's self-image or self-esteem. Although these shifts are internal to the child, they are moderated by social group influences as well as by the gender of the child and his or her self evaluation and problem solving skills.[9]

Leahy,[10] in a comprehensive study of the relationships among adolescent self-image, moral judgment, and parental practices found strong sex differences in the association of parental practices and self-image disparity (the difference between measured self-esteem and "felt" self-esteem). Leahy assumed that greater self-image disparity was linked to greater internalization of societal norms and external controls (a knowledge of societal law and order) which in turn was associated with more sophisticated moral reasoning. In the case of 15-year-old boys, all factors were judged to be influenced by parental practices. For same age girls, self-image disparity was unrelated to parental practices. Boys' self-image disparity was linked to fathers' control and supervision, father's ambivalence toward son's autonomy, and mother's maintenance of boundaries between son and "undesirable" others.

In other findings, greater self-image disparity, more positive ideal self-image and less positive real self-image were related to higher level moral judgment for both boys and girls. However, parental practices were differentially linked to moral development of boys and girls. The most sophisticated reasoning (i.e., most abstract) was related to boys' opportunity in the family to engage in the expression of conflicting opinions, alternative arguments in decision-making, personal feelings, and autonomy issues. For girls, there was no significant relationship between any parental childrearing practice and advanced reasoning, although lack of maternal intrusiveness showed some association with girls' higher order judgments.

On the basis of the findings we have reviewed, we can conclude that boys apparently may be more susceptible to parental influences whereas girls rely on other social groups to influence their development. There is evidence that girls, unlike boys, develop stronger support systems in close friendships with one or two friends.

Currently, there is a widespread perception among social and behavioral scientists that children's peer relations are important since they lead inevitably to (1) socialization into adult work and social roles, (2) reinforcement of evolving notions about sexuality and sexual behavior, and (3) provision of "adultlike" avenues for channeling agression in the case of boys and nurturance in the case of girls.[11, 12]

Two sets of peer activities seem especially important as interactional settings: play and games and "hanging out." Interaction in the course of organizing and playing competitive games has special importance in connection with anticipatory socialization into work and social roles. Children in preadolescence gain mastery of abstract conceptions such as power, roles, and strategies through participation in games.[13] These developments are critical to work roles, particularly in organizational settings where roles, rules, and the negotiation of power arrangements are critical. These developments also implicate social roles, particularly in power relations (dominance and submission) and altruism.[14]

Studies of peer interactions among 9 to 14-year-olds show that notions and behaviors related to work and leisure are refined within "bull sessions" occurring among networks of friends. For example, Fine observed that American middle and working class preadolescent boys assume the personae of major league baseball players in little league competition and practice with as much intensity as tribal youth take on the duties of their elders in mock hunting expeditions.[15] In contrast, young adolescent German girls at 14 are observed by peers, parents, and teachers to shun "energetic" play groups in order to spend leisure time in interaction with a single close friend.[16]

As opposed to play in games, interaction in the course of "hanging out" informally with friends, usually same sex peers, is less bound up with anticipatory learning of work and social roles and is more centrally focused upon issues of immediate importance to impression management.[17, 18] Sexuality and sexual attitudes and behaviors as well as the refinement of patterns of affective behavior are predominant themes in conversation of preadolescent and adolescent children's groups.

Among their friends, girls' activities are less rambunctious and physically demanding than boys' and take the form of play at games involving one-on-one competition, such as tetherball or racquetball.[19] Also, during preadolescence and early adolescence, girls are inclined to spend time with one or two others in exchanges promoting emotional and social support.[20] Unlike girls' more intensive associations, boys' groups are likely to be extensive, to involve friends and acquaintances, and to be more pragmatically organized, that is, structured to include enough (and often, more than enough) players for kickball games and the like. Girls' circles are created from more intimate contact with one or two close friends. Although not any more stable than boys' groups, they are characterized by a "more close knit, intimate grouping" likely to provide a nurturant, accepting climate for formulating a sense of identity, the primary developmental task of the adolescent period. Boys' groups, on the other hand, seem to be formed for purposes of building solidarity and practicing competitive behaviors. Boys' interactions, particularly in games and in team sports specifically, emphasize development of skills in strategizing and in managing others, both of which are related to successful adult performance in organizational settings.[21]

There is considerable debate over the consequences of previously described gender-related behavioral differences as determinants of adult outcomes. Lever has emphasized the negative consequences to girls who are usually not participants in competitive games organized in teams.[22, 23] Lever argues that, by virtue of their exclusion, girls are disadvantaged in gaining skills in negotiating competitive interactions, managing large numbers of co-participants, developing and articulating strategic maneuvers, and formulating legalistic frameworks for understanding human encounters. All these capacities are important in defining managerial responsibilities in adult life, particularly in the world of work. Others, notably Gilligan,[24] argue that such an interpretation misses the point; instead, girls, and later women, have alternate meaning-making social cognitive processes based upon a morality of interpersonal responsibilities and oriented more toward preserving and fostering relationships than toward winning. Our position supports both views. That is, we believe that activities such as games, sports, and talking with friends tend to "shape" young people uniquely (but not uniformly) by gender, giving young men a leading edge in corporate America. We also believe that these experiences coupled with biological differences foster more or less alternate cognitive perspectives and different orientations to social relationships.

In sum, although adolescence is a time of transition for all young people, development during adolescence is individual and unique. Though there are differences in development that are related to gender, all young people suffer from a problem over which they have little control: the host of ambiguities that stalk them through their teenage years and the subsequent negative response to these contradictions by their frequently hostile elders, perplexed by their diminished control over the young.

School

Going to school is the major activity of all people aged 7–15 years, regardless of social background. Better than 98% of this age group is enrolled in school. However, above compulsory attendance age there is variation in school enrollment, with Hispanic youth less likely to be in school than either black or white adolescents. In 1981, 91% of black and white 16 to 17-year-olds were enrolled in school; the figure for Hispanic youth was 83%. At ages 18–19, when many youth have left high school to attend college, approximately half of all black and white youth were enrolled in high school or college whereas only 38% of this age group among Hispanic youth remained in school.

The figures in Table 8.3 show patterns of high school enrollment for these racial and ethnic groups from 1970 to 1981. The figures are expressed as the total number (in thousands) of those in each group in attendance during each of the years shown. Two points should be noted concerning these figures. First, public high school enrollments far exceed private school figures, with less than 10% of the total group attending private schools. Second, by January 1981, enrollments for whites and blacks had leveled to approximately the same numbers as were enrolled in 1970. Over the same period, increasing numbers of Hispanic youth attended secondary schools, reflecting their increased presence in the general population.

Generally, despite the stereotype of alienated and disinterested youth, most students of high school age express favorable views about the schools they attend. According to NLS data, reported in Table 8.4,

TABLE 8.3
Public and Private High School Enrollment for Whites, Blacks, and Hispanics: October 1970 to October 1981 (Numbers in thousands. Civilian noninstitutional population)

Level and control of school	1981ᵃ	1981ᵇ	1980	1979	1978	1977	1976	1975	1974	1973	1972	1971	1970
White													
Total High School	12,062	11,862	12,056	12,583	12,897	13,152	13,214	13,224	13,073	13,091	12,959	12,998	12,723
Public	11,035	10,849	(NA)	11,549	11,741	11,980	12,093	12,112	11,966	11,967	11,876	11,937	11,599
Private	1,027	1,013	(NA)	1,033	1,156	1,172	1,121	1,112	1,107	1,124	1,083	1,061	1,124
Black													
Total High School	2,168	2,150	2,200	2,245	2,276	2,327	2,258	2,199	2,125	2,044	2,025	2,006	1,834
Public	2,102	2,085	(NA)	2,171	2,211	2,269	2,187	2,140	2,072	1,988	1,971	1,951	1,794
Private	65	65	(NA)	74	65	59	71	59	54	56	54	55	41
Hispanicᶜ													
Total High School	1,130	1,101	1,048	920	868	928	932	948	916	758	834	(NA)	(NA)
Public	1,056	1,029	(NA)	875	825	836	867	886	858	707	784	(NA)	(NA)
Private	74	72	(NA)	45	43	92	65	61	59	51	50	(NA)	(NA)
All Races													
Total High School	14,642	14,349	14,556	15,116	15,475	15,753	15,742	15,683	15,447	15,347	15,169	15,183	14,715
Public	13,523	13,249	(NA)	13,994	14,231	14,505	14,541	14,503	14,275	14,162	14,015	14,057	13,545
Private	1,119	1,100	(NA)	1,122	1,244	1,248	1,201	1,180	1,172	1,184	1,155	1,126	1,170

NA = Not available.
ᵃControlled to 1980 census base.
ᵇControlled to 1970 census base.
ᶜPersons of Hispanic origin may be of any race.

Source: U.S. Department of Commerce, Bureau of the Census, Current Population Report Series P-20, No. 373, February 1983.

this is true for adolescents of different racial backgrounds and among adolescents of different sex, region, and level of school.

Table 8.4 indicates that students in grades 7–12 surveyed by the NLS interviewers were for the most part either very satisfied or somewhat satisfied with the schools they attended. There were two exceptions to the positive views of school held by 75% of all the young people. Although they thought that teachers were generally helpful, and friends easy to make, those surveyed expressed the view that most of their classes were boring and that they could get away with just about anything at school. Perhaps the most interesting finding, in view of recent debate on the subject of teacher competence, is the large per-

TABLE 8.4
Attitudes toward School, by Sex
and Race for Adolescents Aged 14–21

Attitudes toward school[a]	Sex		Race			
	Female	Male	Black	Hispanic	White	Total
It's easy to make friends at this school.	92.8	95.6	90.0	90.5	95.4	94.3
Most of the teachers are willing to help with personal problems.	78.1	80.5	79.2	78.3	79.4	79.4
Most of my classes are boring.	52.7	52.5	46.8	50.5	53.8	52.5
I don't feel safe at this school.	13.6	9.2	16.9	16.9	9.8	11.3
Most of my teachers really know their subjects well.	89.6	92.2	88.1	87.2	91.9	91.0
You can get away with almost anything at this school.	24.8	24.9	15.5	21.3	27.0	24.8
My school work requires me to think to the best of my ability.	86.2	82.3	92.2	87.3	82.4	84.1
At this school, a person has the freedom to learn what interests him or her.	86.6	87.6	85.5	83.5	87.6	87.1
This school offers good job counseling.	78.5	79.2	75.4	79.9	79.4	78.9

[a]Percentage who felt the statement was somewhat or very true.
Source: National Longitudinal Survey of Youth Labor Market Experience (1979).

centage of youth across the board who consider their teachers to be extremely knowledgeable in subject matter areas.

Educational aspirations for the most part reflect adolescents' future occupational orientations. This is because those who do the hiring assume that different occupations require varying levels of formal post-secondary training and these assumptions are uniformly shared by members of society, including adolescents. Aspirations do not always mirror actual expectations either to attend or complete college once the individual has graduated from high school. Young people surveyed in the NLS research were asked if they had plans to attend college. Two-thirds responded that they wished to pursue postsecondary schooling. Aspirations were closely tied to parental educational attainment. That is, they were higher among those whose fathers had graduated from college and were strongest among those who fathers had completed graduate work. When aspirations were checked against actual expectations for college attendance, the proportion of those surveyed whose expectations equaled or exceeded their aspirations varied by sex, race, and parental income.

The variation by sex is slight for lower levels of education, with a

TABLE 8.5
Congruence of Educational Aspirations and Expectations, by Sex, Race, and Family Income for Adolescents Aged 14–21[a]

| Characteristic | Educational aspirations | | | |
	12	13–15	16	17 or more
Sex				
Female	88.2	74.4	67.5	65.9
Male	86.3	74.2	71.1	72.4
Race				
Black	89.2	75.1	66.8	62.2
Hispanic	80.7	76.7	63.1	67.8
White	87.4	74.1	70.1	70.7
Income				
$0 – $4,999	77.5	75.0	64.0	70.3
$5,000 – $9,999	84.3	69.6	59.8	59.2
$10,000 – $14,999	84.7	73.5	62.1	65.5
$15,000 – $19,999	91.0	78.9	67.7	61.1
$20,000 – $24,999	89.1	72.6	71.6	70.0
$25,000 – $29,999	92.7	75.4	70.3	67.5
$30,000 – $39,999	97.3	81.7	76.8	68.6
$40,000 or more	95.8	76.1	83.2	77.4
Total	87.2	74.3	69.2	69.4

[a]Proportion whose expectations equal or exceed their aspirations.
Source: National Longitudinal Survey of Youth Labor Market Experience (1979).

larger proportion (88.2%) of females assuming they will actually complete 12 years of high school and the first few years of postsecondary schooling. However, a slightly larger proportion of males see aspirations and expectations meshing with respect to the completion of four years of college and postgraduate education. In general, a greater proportion of white youth and those from wealthier families actually see themselves completing expected levels of schooling than minority youth from less affluent families.

These data raise important questions concerning equality of opportunity since many youngsters who aspire to higher education (and careers congruent with such training) do not anticipate realizing their hopes. Despite affirmative action policies and legalities, young women and young people from poor minority families continue to have truncated expectations for educational and occupational careers beyond high school.

We asked a random selection of 100 young people in grades 7–12 who were attending the School for Creative and Performing Arts in Cincinnati about their college attendance plans. A substantial number (64.8%) regardless of race, sex, or grade in school, expressed the desire to enter college the year after high school graduation. A smaller number (49.5%) actually thought they would attend. When we examined students' plans in light of their perception of parents' aspirations for their futures, two general patterns emerged. First, regardless of gender, age, or race, students perceived mothers as more likely than fathers to want the student to attend college after graduation from high school. With the exception of some of the younger students (particularly white females and black males), parents of children of either sex were likely *not* to want their children to become active as a performing artist immediately after their secondary schooling was complete. We may conclude that college has special value even for children (and their parents) who attend a school with a specialized program featuring training in careers not necessarily demanding formal education beyond the high school grades.

We believe that both parents and school personnel, particularly guidance counselors, are largely responsible for nurturing differential patterns of educational and career expectations. Parents are more likely to encourage their white male children to pursue professional careers and guidance counselors often reinforce these differential patterns of parental encouragement. Counselors, many of whom are white males, and females from middle class families are likely to feel more comfortable with clients whose backgrounds are similar to their own.[25] School policy regarding the counselor's role must reflect a concern for the student in terms of the student's best interest. Counseling should focus on developing educational and occupational plans congruent with the

TABLE 8.6

Primary Reason Why High School Dropouts, 14 to 21 Years Old, Left School, by Race and Sex (in percent)

Reason for Leaving School	Female				Male				Total
	Black	Hispanic	White	Total	Black	Hispanic	White	Total	
School Related	29	21	36	32	56	36	55	53	44
Poor performance	5	4	5	5	9	4	9	9	7
Disliked school	18	15	27	24	29	26	36	33	29
Expelled or suspended	5	1	2	2	18	6	9	10	7
School too dangerous	1	1	2	1	0	0	0	1	1
Economic	15	24	14	15	23	38	22	24	20
Desired to work	4	7	5	5	12	16	15	14	10
Financial difficulties	3	9	3	4	7	9	3	5	4
Home responsibilities	8	8	6	6	4	13	4	5	6
Personal	45	30	31	33	0	3	3	2	17
Pregnancy	41	15	14	19	0	0	0	0	9
Marriage	4	15	17	14	0	3	3	2	8
Other	11	25	19	20	21	23	20	21	19
Total Percent	100	100	100	100	100	100	100	100	100

Source: National Longitudinal Survey of Youth Labor Market Experience (1979).

TABLE 8.7.
Characteristics of Jobs Held by High School Graduates and High School Dropouts

Characteristics	Nonenrolled High School Graduates	High School Dropouts
Opportunities provided by job[a]		
Complexity		
To do a number of different things	74.6	57.3
To deal with people	83.4	72.9
To do a job from beginning to end	88.3	79.4
Personal Significance		
To develop close friendships in your job	81.2	74.8
To feel that the job itself is very significant or important in the broader scheme of things	76.8	67.7
Performance		
To know whether or not you are performing your job well or poorly	90.6	84.8
Autonomy		
For independent thought or action	73.4	65.3

Characteristics of job[b]

Environmental		
The job is dangerous	33.3	41.6
The physical surroundings are pleasant	78.6	74.8
You are exposed to unhealthy conditions	24.3	30.1
Your co-workers are friendly	96.4	95.5
Career-related		
The pay is good	73.8	68.5
The job security is good	82.8	74.8
Your supervisor is competent in doing the job	90.6	86.5
The chances for promotion are good	62.5	61.5
You are given a chance to do the things you do best	75.1	71.9
The skills you are learning would be valuable in getting a better job	76.1	64.4

[a] Proportion who felt the job gave a moderate amount, quite a lot or a maximum amount.
[b] Proportion who felt the statement was very or somewhat true.
Source: National Longitudinal Survey of Youth Labor Market Experience (1979).

express interests of the student. Moreover, it may be that families and schools have taken on too much responsibility for shaping children's lives. Other adults, particularly "delegates" from the world of work, should be encouraged to foster career ambitions and realistic plans to accomplish adolescents' educational and career aspirations. The Adopt-A-School programs described in Chapter 6 may be one way to facilitate the involvement of other nurturing adults in caring for the plans of youth during the transitional period of adolescence.

The Narrow World of the Dropout

There is one group of young people whose worlds are extremely narrow, who face considerably reduced labor market opportunities, and whose lives are truly in jeopardy: those who have been pushed out of school by events related both to the nature of schooling and to economic factors beyond the control of the youth and his or her family.

To understand the experience of those who leave school before completing a full 12 years, it is important to recognize the scope of the dropout situation. During 1979, of the nearly 33 million youth between the ages of 14 and 22, who were neither institutionalized nor in the military, 4 million were school leavers. Among those 18–22 years of age, 19% had left school before completing their senior year. Those most vulnerable are central city minority youth, especially youth of Hispanic origin. Among this group, 25% between the ages of 18 and 22 had left school in 1979. This figure contrasts with much lower rates for whites (10%) and blacks (16%).

Percentages of youth leaving before completion of high school have increased dramatically since at least the early 1970s. Moreover, these trends are not limited to a particular region of the country. According to a set of recent analyses, both the Midwest and West have seen sharply increasing dropout rates:

Enrollment data for Ohio show that the number of dropouts has increased 15% from the 1975–76 school year to the 1978–79 school year.[26]

In California, the attrition rate between the ninth and twelfth grades increased from 12% in 1967 to 22% 1976.[27]

National Census data confirm these trends: the percentage of high school dropouts among white males, 16–17 years of age, increased from 6.3% in October 1970 to 9.6% in October 1978.[28]

Among white females, there was a smaller increase, while for black males and females the proportion of high school dropouts decreased during the period.[29]

Thus, dropping out of high school is a phenomonon that affects youth from a variety of regional, racial, and ethnic backgrounds.

When NLS researchers questioned those who had quit school before graduation as to why they had left, they received a variety of responses consistent by sex. Young women were most likely to cite marriage and pregnancy to explain school leaving. Males (including almost 40% of young men of Hispanic origin) were most likely to leave for job-related or economic reasons including home responsibilities, good job offers, or financial difficulties. In other words, a set of related "push-pull" economic factors were likely to compel school leaving among young men. However, it should also be recalled that many young people express a sense of boredom with school and school-related reasons were especially pertinent to black and white youth of both sexes.

In a recent analysis of NLS data on school leaving, Rumberger examined several sets of factors underlying the decision to drop out of high school.[30] These included not only the immediate, primary reasons cited by the school leavers but also a number of underlying variables including

1. family background in terms of parental educational attainments, family structure (i.e., the number of parents present in the household), and financial difficulties (measured by parental unemployment)
2. psychological factors including self confidence, educational aspirations and abilities
3. patterns of behavior in school as indicated by rates of repeating grades and absenteeism
4. social problems including early marriage and pregnancy, criminal behavior, and patterns of alcohol use
5. local employment conditions and region[31, 32]

The results of Rumberger's analyses indicate the increased magnitude of factors 2–5 in affecting school leaving for those youth from low socioeconomic status (SES) backgrounds. Thus, "the probability that a young black woman from a lower social class background is a high school dropout increases by 40 percentage points if she had a child within 9 months of leaving school." Under similar circumstances, probability is less than 5 percentage points for young black women from a higher social background.[33] In other words, favorable economic factors in the family function to cushion the effects of negative patterns of behavior, psychological factors, social problems, and the like; conversely, unfavorable economic conditions amplify effects, making school leaving far more likely.

The results of Rumberger's analyses must be interpreted with caution. They should be viewed in connection with the picture of life in central cities that was outlined in Chapter 1. In other words, school leaving is not tied to poor family functioning or personal defects. Rather,

> because higher income families live in wealthier communities with better financed schools, their children are most likely to have more supportive and rewarding educational experiences. In contrast, children from poorer families may feel compelled to work and supplement their family's income as many Hispanic dropouts have indicated.[34]

Hispanic youth, as suggested in the preceeding statement, were *more* likely to drop out of school, citing family financial problems, when the employment picture was relatively positive and jobs were likely to be obtained. These youth apparently saw more to be gained, at least in the short run, from taking a full time job than from remaining in school.

The question arises as to what kinds of labor market opportunities exist for youth who drop out in contrast to young people who obtain full time work upon completion of high school. First of all, among youth ages 18–22 who do *not* attend school, the unemployment rate is almost three times as high among those who have dropped out as for those who have completed high school. Put another way, whereas *more than 25%* of those who leave before completion of their senior year are unemployed, *only 10%* who leave school after completion of grade 12 do not find work.[35]

When work *is* found, school leavers not only hold jobs that pay less than those in which high school graduates are employed but also hold jobs that provide fewer intrinsic rewards. These findings characterize groups of youth who held full time jobs and who were not enrolled in school at the time of the NLS study in 1979. Opportunities provided by their jobs are greater for high school graduates than for those who have quit school. Graduates are likely to hold jobs they see as having more complexity, holding greater personal significance, allowing more opportunity for performance feedback, and providing greater autonomy. In evaluating job characteristics, high school graduates are more likely to see their job environments and career opportunities in a more favorable light; however, they don't see chances for promotion as particularly good.

Earlier in this chapter, we pointed to the importance to adolescent development of the movement from dependence in the family to greater independence and autonomy outside the home. Employment is a major avenue to independence. Moreover, autonomy on the job fosters high self-esteem and an overall sense of competence. Independence in early job experiences is linked to high self-esteem quite apart from high regard for the self that may be generated in the contexts of either the family or school. Additionally, these effects appear to endure through the life cycle.[36] Thus, the question of dropping out of school takes on additional importance. Since school leaving, job quality (particularly with regard to autonomy), and personality (notably self-esteem) are intimately linked, we must be especially concerned about the development of the adolescent who leaves school prematurely.

Conclusion

We have attempted to create a view of individual development that is more favorable and at the same time more complex and varied than is usually offered in similar discussions. It is the society and not the adolescent who is predisposed to take a hostile, naysaying view of the young person and his or her relationship to the social world.

We are particularly concerned with the later life outcomes for early school leavers. Adolescents drop out of high school for a variety of personal, economic, and school-related reasons and *not* because they are rebellious, "lost," or incompetent to continue. Especially among Hispanic youth whose families both require and provide economic assistance (through family-based businesses), the world of work, at least initially, provides more opportunity than the process of schooling. Attention must be brought to bear on these issues.

In order to examine the extent of school leaving and employment opportunities for adolescents (especially 15 to 22-year-olds) in your community, you may wish to interview individuals who are likely to provide insight. Two community-based structures that should be readily accessible are your local Chamber of Commerce and Community Action Commission. The chamber is an organization that promotes business interests in the community. As with most bureaucratic organizations, it supports many activities and programs, several of which, particularly through the Private Industry Council, are concerned with youth. You may wish to locate the office or program that is chiefly concerned with education, youth, and work to arrange an interview with a chamber spokesperson. In your conversation, be sure to inquire about summer programs, programs for dropouts, and programs that address the topic of the school-to-work transition.

Community action groups in the 1980s are less likely than the chamber to have federal or local funding support for youth programs. The heyday of the community-based organization was the 1970s, although some activities linking youth to work may still exist in your locale. Since programs tend to be understaffed by unpaid volunteers, your contact with the Community Action Commission and other relevant neighborhood-based organizations may be limited to a telephone interview. However, we suggest you pursue contact with such groups in order to identify the full range of existing programs dealing with education, youth, and work. After you have completed your interviews, you should have a clear idea of the extent to which adolescents in your community have a supportive net of concerned adults outside the family and school to help them through the difficult transitions they face in maturing. Becoming fully fledged members of society is highly dependent upon completing the transition from school to work as smoothly as possible. This transition is especially problematic for central city youth.

The book began with a picture of central city life that while not thoroughly hopeless, contained many elements documenting the constrained opportunities and hopes of youth and their families. It is clear that many who live in central cities face lives with few possibilities for success in this society. In this chapter we have brought the volume to a close by examining the world of the adolescent, a world we see as potentially creating an expanding array of experiences that go hand in hand with the expansive nature of human development during the adolescent period. There is variation in development among youth. There is also variability in expectations for the life course. Particularly at risk are adolescents whose sex, race, ethnicity and socioeconomic background place them in less favorable circumstances than others. We believe these matters have important policy implications, some of which we have indicated throughout the discussion in this chapter.

Notes

1. Daniel P. Keating, "Thinking Processes in Adolescence," in Joseph Adelson, ed., *Handbook of Adolescent Psychology* (New York:Wiley, 1980), pp. 212–215.
2. C. E. Bowerman and J. W. Kinch, "Changes in Family and Peer Orientations of Children Between the Fourth and Tenth Grades," in *Social Forces* 27, No. 2 (1959).
3. J. W. Young and L. R. Ferguson, "Developmental Changes Through Adolescence in the Spontaneous Nomination of Reference Groups as a Function of Decision Content," in *Journal of Youth and Adolescence* 8, No. 2 (June 1979).

4. P. Williams, "Adolescent Identification and Academic Achievement: Reporting the Awareness of Similarity to Role Models," in *Journal of Youth and Adolescence* 9, No. 4 (August 1980).
5. Joan E. Crowley, "Influences on Youth's Life Decisions : The Role of Significant Others," in *Research on Youth Employment and Employability Development, Findings of the National Longitudinal Survey of Young Americans, 1979* (Washington, D.C.: U. S. Government Printing Office, May 1980), p. 344.
6. Ibid., p. 354.
7. Michael Rutter, *Changing Youth in a Changing Society* (Cambridge: Harvard University Press, 1980).
8. W. W. Cooley and P. R. Lohnes, "Predicting Development of Young Adults," *Interim Report No. 5, Cooperative Research Project No. 3051* (Palo Alto: Project Talent Office, 1968).
9. Kathryn M. Borman and Lawrence Kurdek, "Social Cognitive and Social Structural Linkages" (Cincinnati: Unpublished manuscript, 1983).
10. D. L. Leahy, "Parental Practices and the Development of Moral Judgment and Self-Image Disparity During Adolescence," in *Developmental Psychology* 17, No. 3 (1981).
11. Gary A. Fine, "Friends, Impression Management, and Preadolescent Behavior," in S. R. Asher and J. M. Gottman, eds., *The Development of Children's Friendships,* (Cambridge: Cambridge University Press, 1981).
12. Richard Savin-Williams, "Social Interaction of Adolescent Females in Natural Groups," in H. C. Foot, A. J. Chapman, and J. R. Smith, eds., *Friendship and Social Relations in Children* (Chichester: Wiley, 1980).
13. Janet Lever, "Sex Differences in the Complexity of Children's Play," in *American Sociological Review* 43 (August 1978).
14. Savin-Williams, "Social Interaction of Adolescent Females in Natural Groups."
15. Fine, "Friends, Impression Management, and Preadolescent Behavior."
16. G. Weise, "Fourteen-Year-Olds' Life Style Examined," in *The German Tribune*, No. 720, 1976, p. 12.
17. Fine, "Friends, Impression Management, and Preadolescent Behavior."
18. Chad Gordon, "Social Characteristics of Early Adolescence," in Jerome Kagan and Robert Coles, eds., *Twelve to Sixteen: Early Adolescence* (New York: Norton, 1971).
19. Kathryn M. Borman, David E. Barrett, and Padmini Sheoran, "Negotiating Playground Games," paper presented at the Annual Meeting, American Sociological Association, San Francisco, September 1982.
20. Savin-Williams, "Social Interaction of Adolescent Females in Natural Groups."
21. Lever, "Sex Differences in the Complexity of Children's Play."
22. Ibid.
23. Borman et al., "Negotiating Playground Games."
24. Carole Gilligan, *In a Different Voice: Psychological Theory and Woman's Development* (Cambridge: Harvard University Press, 1982).
25. Frederick Erickson and Jeffrey Shultz, *The Counselor as Gatekeeper* (New York: Academic, 1982).

26. S. C. Kaeser, *Dropouts in Ohio* (Cleveland: Citizens' Council for Ohio Schools, 1980).
27. C. Camp, *School Dropouts* (Sacramento: Assembly Office of Research, California Legislature, 1980).
28. W. V. Grant and L. J. Eiden, *Digest of Education Statistics, 1980* (Washington, D.C.: U. S. Government Printing Office, 1980).
29. Russell W. Rumberger, "Dropping out of High School: The Influence of Race, Sex and Family Background," in *American Educational Research Journal,* 20, No. 1 (Summer 1983), p. 200.
30. Ibid.
31. Ibid.
32. The reader should note the emphasis upon adolescent defects as opposed to weaknesses in the school program inherent in Rumberger's model to explain student dropout.
33. Rumberger, "Dropping out of High School," p. 209.
34. Ibid., pp. 210–211.
35. Ibid., p. 270.
36. Jeylan T. Mortimer and Michael D. Finch, "Autonomy as a source of self-esteem in adolescence," paper presented at the Annual Meeting, American Sociological Association, Detroit, August 1983.

Subject Index